Youth in Flames

**A Teenager's Resistance and Her Fight for
Survival in the Warsaw Ghetto**

Youth in Flames

A Teenager's Resistance and Her Fight for Survival in the Warsaw Ghetto

Aliza Vitis-Shomron

Tell the Story Publishing

Omaha, Nebraska

Youth in Flames
A Teenager's Resistance and Her Fight for Survival in the Warsaw Ghetto

Photos used on the cover and throughout the book are either from the personal collections of the author's family, or used with permission from the United States Holocaust Memorial Museum Archives as noted.

Tell the Story Publishing titles may be ordered from your favorite bookseller.
www.TelltheStoryPublishing.com

Tell the Story Publishing
c/o CMI
13518 L. Street
Omaha, NE 68137

ISBN: 978-1-936840-83-0 (Paperback)
ISBN: 978-1-936840-84-7 (Mobi)
ISBN: 978-1-936840-85-4 (EPUB)

Library of Congress Cataloging Number: 2015911235

Printed in the USA

10 9 8 7 6 5 4 3 2

The book is dedicated to the memory of my friends
in the youth movement in the Warsaw Ghetto,
to my husband Tzvi, and to my beloved children,
Chanan, Asa, and Iris, and grandchildren,
Roy, Tal, Adar, Petal, Yonatan,
Amalya, and Elinor. To you, my family,
I pass on this memoir for safekeeping.

Thank you, dear Tzvi, for your support,
And you, my sons and daughter,
and my friend Tzelina,
who have never disappointed me.

For more diary excerpts and photos, see our
gallery at www.WarsawGhettoBook.com

CONTENTS

Part III—Return to Life

FOREWORD

The book by Aliza Vitis-Shomron combines passages from her diary with a pool of memories and reflections, set down after many years and changes in her life.

One of the chapters in her book is entitled Between Two Worlds. The two sources that forged Aliza's inner world were her parents' home in Jewish Warsaw and the youth movement Hashomer Hatzair that she joined as a young girl in the Warsaw Ghetto. The significance of the concept *youth movement in the ghetto* is totally different from that with which we are familiar elsewhere.

Normally, a youth movement provides experiences imbued with the spirit of youth, appreciation of nature, and concern for problems of the society and the individual. Between the two wars, a Jewish youth movement was created, fostering dreams for the future as well as preparation for their actualization, in particular for life in the Land of Israel, in a kibbutz.

In the ghetto, where the Jews were imprisoned by the Nazis, living cut off from the world of nature, from contact with people outside its walls, without schools—and in homes where the adults were overburdened by great hardships, worry, and constant anxiety—there the Movement became a second home, a different reality.

The Movement was a home where one was allowed to think and speak about everything, to sing and laugh, to read books and forget the gloom permeating the parents' home at all times, and engulfing all the people in the ghetto. The Movement was a type of oasis of freedom, drawing upon its roots in the past and looking toward the future.

The friendships that sprang up in the Movement's underground center and in its small cells, the contact with the youth leaders, who projected self-confidence and possession of knowledge about everything, provided support and instilled optimism, unshakeable willpower, belief in human beings, and a different view of life, for which the young members yearned.

The framework for the younger group, set up in the ghetto, was abolished for security reasons a short time before the expulsion from the ghetto and the creation of the Jewish Fighting Organization, but the spiritual strength the Movement had instilled in the youngsters, and the contacts kept up in a different way, as described by Aliza, forged profound life-giving roots sustaining the few who survived.

Aliza gives a powerful and detailed description of the horrors of the great deportation from the ghetto in the summer of 1942, which sentenced to death 85 percent of the population of 350,000 in Warsaw at the time. The story of the family's struggle for survival and search for a way of saving themselves reflects presence of mind, courage, and rare coincidences. After escaping from the ghetto, Aliza remained for some time with some of her family on the "Aryan"—the Polish—side of the city, which was out of bounds for Jews, where they were not permitted to enter, and discovery by hostile eyes meant death. Then Aliza, together with her dear ones, ended up in a camp, a deathtrap for many, and again, miraculously, they survived.

Aliza Vitis-Shomron's journey, lasting several years, resembles walking through a minefield. However painful the experiences, the author succeeds in highlighting some positive aspects, the warmth of love and kindness; thus a ray of hope penetrates even the darkest pages, in manifestations of inner freedom and in the relationship among friends and relatives.

The author asserts that even now, as an elderly kibbutz member, "the beautiful and the evil" live side by side in her mind, and adds that "the hope that eventually there will be some kind of peace between the two nations living in this land, strengthens my belief that my grandchildren will live a good life, happier than my generation's and that of my children."

Professor Israel Gutman

Professor Israel Gutman, born in Warsaw, was wounded in the Warsaw Ghetto uprising and was deported to a series of concentration camps. He survived the death march from Auschwitz to Mauthausen. US forces liberated the camp in 1945, and he later immigrated to Palestine, later the State of Israel, where he lived on a kibbutz. Aliza met Professor Gutman in 1948 at a memorial ceremony for the Hashomer Hatzair. He later testified at the trial of Nazi Adolf Eichmann in 1961.

He was a professor of history at the Hebrew University of Jerusalem and headed the International Institute for Holocaust Research at Yad Vashem and served as Chief Historian. Among his published books are *Resistance: The Warsaw Ghetto Uprising* and *Anatomy of the Auschwitz Death Camp*. He died in Jerusalem at age ninety in 2013.

INTRODUCTION

I was born Liza Melamed. I wrote down the account of my experiences dozens of years before its publication in Hebrew. On arriving in this country [Palestine, later the State of Israel] in September 1945, I met Meir Ya'ari, the leader of the Hashomer Hatzair Movement. I told him my story, and he asked me to write down what happened to the Movement in the Warsaw Ghetto. We thought I was the only survivor.

I was sent to Kibbutz Beit Alfa to join a youth group [Hevrat Noar] there, and for two weeks, instead of having to work or study, I wrote down in Polish all I knew. I was very young (seventeen) and obviously did not have the whole picture. The information I could provide was quite limited, and since I had no documents, nor written or verbal sources to verify what I knew, I could only rely on my memory.

At the time, parts of the manuscript were published in the press or in various anthologies. I also brought with me some pages I had written while hiding in the *Aryan* [a term noted by the Nazis to separate Jews and others] part of Warsaw and the surroundings, and while in the Bergen-Belsen camp. From the ghetto I only brought one poem, "Things" by Wladyslaw

Szlengel, the ghetto poet. I had hidden the rest of my diaries in the yard of our house before leaving the ghetto, two days before the revolt broke out in April 1943.

Thus this book is partly composed of notes from an authentic diary; a larger part contains my memories, written in this country (Israel) at the age of seventeen, in Kibbutz Beit Alfa, and I also added another part later.

I hoped that my story and that of the Hashomer Hatzair Movement in the ghetto would be published and studied by our youth. I had promised myself to perpetuate the memory of those wonderful young people from the pioneer movements, and to preserve the story of their extraordinary efforts and determination under impossible conditions, their struggle against the enemy who destroyed our people, and the sacrifice of their young lives in order to save its honor.

Many years have passed and many books of testimonies and research have been published. After the years during which I sought to build a new life on the ruins of the old, I glanced at the manuscript and was shocked to see that its translation into Hebrew was out-of-date and inaccurate, and whole passages were missing. I knew I had to rewrite it; it was my duty. The violent conflict and the recurring wars in Israel and my anxiety about my sons delayed my task. I also found it difficult to delve once more into my past. I feared I would fall into the abyss and would not be able to rise again.

So it was only on the threshold of old age that I returned to the task. I corrected the dates and the information about the events with the help of historical sources. I added parts about my childhood and my family, and I wrote a later chapter linking past and present, but I took care to preserve the spirit of the manuscript and the way of thinking of that young girl, the teenager Liza Melamed.

Here is where I began to write my story.

On Kibbutz Beit Alfa, 1946

Nine months had passed since our liberation from Nazi enslavement.

I had spent five and a half years of my life in that war.

When the cruel, hateful events engulfed me, I was eleven. I was born in 1928. I could not understand all that was happening; I could not always make the necessary connections. But the events affected me deeply. They were engraved in my memory and their significance became clearer later. Today I am seventeen.

In August 1944, I was able to make contact with people who came to Bergen-Belsen from Auschwitz, and among them there was a woman from Warsaw. I shouted across the fence and asked her if she knew what had happened to the inmates of the Poniatow Camp. Surprisingly, she knew.

The bitter truth reinforced the dark predictions: The camp inmates were shot dead in Majdanek, in November 1943. My father, my Aunt Biela, and her husband were among them, and many more of those working in the factories of the German Töbens in the Warsaw Ghetto, who were taken to Majdanek when the revolt broke out and the final liquidation of the ghetto began.

I had been one of many Jewish girls "from a good family." I did not have to struggle for existence; my parents had taken care of that. During the last two years of the war, in the

Bergen-Belsen camp, I constantly dreamed about reaching Israel, to bear witness to the Hashomer Hatzair Movement's activities, and to tell the story of the heroism of my friends in the Warsaw Ghetto.

Now I was one of just a few that were left. I did not know whether any of my friends from the Movement in Warsaw had survived. Was I the only one?

I was liberated from Bergen-Belsen together with my mother and my younger sister on April 13, 1945. We had been separated from my father while still in Poland, and now we looked for his name on the lists of survivors—in vain.

There are things engraved in my memory with horrible clarity—dates, events in all their details. But there are people whose faces I remember, yet not always their names, and in particular not their surnames. I regret it; they may have relatives in this country.

When I left the ghetto to go to the Aryan side of the city, Rut (Ruth) Heiman, who had been the leader of my group in the Hashomer Hatzair Movement and later active in the Jewish Fighting Organization, said to me: "Lilit [that is what they called me in the Movement], if you survive, you must tell the world about the life and death of the Warsaw Ghetto, and about our Movement. Not all of us need die in the ghetto. Whoever can save himself, must do so. So go out, hide on the Polish Catholic side [Aryan] of the city. A group of girls from the younger units will go out and hide in a monastery. Maybe you'll survive."

I consider my writing down these memories as fulfilling her bidding in a small way. I wish young people in this country would read it. I have no common language with them. I feel

I am different, older. Maybe this account will open their eyes and they will begin to understand what happened in this terrible war to all European Jews and to the members of the youth movement, dedicated to their people and their Zionist hope and belief—to the end. Maybe they will also begin to understand those who survived, bearing within an abyss of grieving and mourning, even while dancing, playing, and seeming cheerful.

And who knows, maybe the wound will heal as time passes…and only painful memories will remain.

> Yesterday
> they suddenly called us
> to die.
> And I,
> maybe by mistake,
> went on living.
> And maybe
> By that hair's breadth
> My life continued.
> Many deemed it
> a miracle
> or maybe even a sign—
> And I ask
> Where are my friends?

The poem was written by Avri Beni, Auschwitz survivor and member of Kibbutz Givat Oz.

Part I : Between
Two Worlds

1 : Then and Now

It was during the autumn, the golden Polish fall of 1940. As usual, the streets of Warsaw were covered with rusty leaves. In the city parks, the merry chatter of the children, looking for ripe chestnuts fallen from the trees, had died down. School children began to prepare for their studies after the summer vacation.

But the autumn was different that year, in particular for us Jews. The golden fall was clouded. A strange unease hung in the air, the nights were suffused with dread, and fearful premonitions lurked in the morning, especially in the Jewish neighborhoods. Only one year had passed since that fall when the war broke out, and I felt as though the life "before"—"that good life we had before"—had never actually existed. It appeared to me as a pure sunlit memory of something never to return.

That summer I had my twelfth birthday and felt very grown up. Everything had changed. We didn't celebrate my birthday that year. Mother made it quite clear, in her usual tone of voice when she wanted to lecture me: "I hope you are by now old enough to understand certain things and to come down from your Olympian heights."

Before the war, sometimes Father used to surprise us by bringing a box of cakes, tied up with a thin string, from Kapulski's store in Marszalkowska Street. But now Jews were unable to get there. These areas belonged to a different Warsaw, the Polish, "Aryan" part. And Father did not want to humiliate himself by stepping off the pavement whenever a German soldier passed by. Yet for this birthday, Father brought a box of cakes for the occasion.

My birthday marked the day when I had to begin wearing a white band with a blue Star of David on my arm, like all adult Jews. *Yes, Mother*, I said to myself, *I understand far more than you imagine.*

I saw the anxiety on my parents' faces; they worried about making a living. Our family's workshop was idle, since most of the women working there were Polish—and Poles were not allowed to work for Jews. Every day we worried about Father. Since he had returned last winter from his arduous journey to the eastern Polish areas, annexed by Russia, he was living in constant fear of being kidnapped in the city streets.

All Jewish men, aged sixteen to sixty, were forced to work, but none signed up of their own free will. They were kidnapped, beaten, and humiliated. At night, German regular army soldiers and the brutal SS [*Schutzstaffel*, the Nazi paramilitary units under Adolf Hitler] drove around in cars and broke into houses, apparently to commit robberies or just out of hooliganism.

Stefa, our devoted Polish maid, also left us and returned to her family, living in a village.

[Editor's note: Shorter passages in italics, such as the next paragraph, are from Aliza's diaries and notes written during and immediately after the war. You will find them throughout this memoir. Although translated from Polish to Hebrew to English, the words are hers written during a time of duress and turmoil. We have chosen to keep the voice and tone because these words are living proof—not memory—documented for the world of this historic event in the eyes of a young girl and may be perhaps among the few actual diaries, along with the author, to survive.]

Before the war, how I loved to sit in the kitchen at dusk with Stefa and my younger sister, Mirka! The kitchen was tidy and clean after the day's work. In the large stove the cinders were still whispering merrily, little devils frolicking among them, sparks turning into knights and princes. Spirits filled the kitchen and we sat there, entranced, listening to Stefa's tales. I loved stories. That was my strong point: to make up fairy tales and write them down in my diary, or tell them to my sister.

All that was over. It was cold in the kitchen, as we had not been able to store up any coal for the winter of 1940. Only one year had passed since the outbreak of the war, and I think back again and again to that last summer in the little summer resort Shvider, to the south of Warsaw.

I could lie for hours on the lawn of the lovely villa we used to go to every year in the summer months. I used to love to go off on my own close to the forest, paying no attention to Aunt Biela's calls when she went looking for me. I continued to weave my wonderful stories, with me as the heroine, successful in all my exploits. Mother and Aunt Biela, her sister, admired me; no one scolded me for my shyness and clumsiness. In the end my sister was sent to look for me. And then they scolded me, and she was the one who cried.

All that ended all of a sudden, and with it ended the world of fairy tales.

It was at the end of August 1939. My parents, who continued to work in our family business, only used to come to us in the country for the weekends. Suddenly they appeared, with a horse and cart. "We must go home to Warsaw immediately. They say that the war is about to break out." The harsh, incomprehensible words hit us like a hard blow.

Within a week we were already in the midst of heavy bombing from the air. The Germans invaded Poland. It was a nightmare, lasting three weeks, during which almost all of Poland was overrun, and only the capital of Warsaw resisted heroically. Thousands of fires were burning in the encircled city, but it did not surrender.

For three weeks we lived in a cellar, lying on mattresses, in terrible fear of the *Stuka* planes, dive bombing with earsplitting screeching, and fully aware that when all that was over, the Germans would be inside Warsaw. After those three terrible weeks, during which a large part of the city was destroyed, and there was no water in the taps and no more food, the city surrendered.

I went to see the German victory parade in the city streets. I can still hear the deafening sound of their jackboots pounding the cobblestones as troops marched in unison. A faint echo lingered in the air. The inhabitants of the city stood by in silence. The Nazi occupation had begun.

Throughout 1940 we stayed in Warsaw, among its dusty ruins. Jewish children were no longer allowed to go to school. Before the war started, I was able to complete the fifth grade, and my sister was about to start the first grade. I went to a primary school for girls in Ptasia Street. All the girls were Jewish, as well as the staff. Only one teacher was Polish—the gym teacher, of course. This subject was not the strong point in Jewish education.

In the school there were long passages and hundreds of little girls ran to and fro, wearing black silk aprons and large white collars. In the morning all of us gathered in the large schoolyard and sang with devotion a prayer for the welfare of the Polish homeland, begging God—in Polish, of course—to defend it against all its enemies. Indeed, the Poles were great patriots and fought hard for their country's independence, which they regained only at the end of the First World War, through the famous Treaty of Versailles.

Poland's leader, Marshal Joseph Pilsudski, who led the Polish legions to victory against Russia, at that time torn apart by the Revolution, later became the all-powerful ruler, until his death in 1935. The whole country went into mourning, and so did the Jews. I remember his funeral. Like all the school children in Warsaw, we wore a black ribbon on our sleeves and stood for hours in the streets, grieving and weeping. The splendid procession passed, followed by thousands of people.

What will happen to us now that the "Father of the Nation" is dead? I did hear at home that he was an extreme nationalist and above all hated the communists, and clamped down on the socialist parties. On the other hand, during his rule, the constitution was laid down, granting freedom of observance to all religions and equal rights to all minorities, including Jews.

The way to school crossed Chlodna Street and Mirov Square. We lived in Ciepla Street 19, on the edge of the Jewish neighborhood. When the ghetto was closed in November that year, a wooden fence was built along the street, so that the odd numbers in this section were included in the ghetto. Only a year ago…

The end of the street suddenly opened out into the enormous Mirov Square, with the covered markets, Hale Mirovskie. In front of the huge building, the peasants spread out their buckets of cream, chunks of cheese and fresh eggs, straight from their farms. In the distance sat the big strong provincial men, selling barrels of sauerkraut and pickled cucumbers. Women in aprons sold a variety of pickled herrings—from the barrel straight into a piece of newspaper.

And is there a Jew who doesn't love pickled herrings with onion?! A Jewish folksong tells the story of a poor Jew who only earns enough money to buy a herring's tail…We had herrings on our table every day. And in the markets, the smell of freshly baked bread and kejsarky rolls [small buns] mingled with the smell of sauerkraut and juicy pork sausages. A feast for the eyes and the nose. Along the markets in the direction of the Saski Park there were stalls with meat and venison. I used to pass by quickly, glancing with aversion at the rows of hares, stripped of their skin, hanging on iron hooks. I thought: What a good thing it is that we Jews are forbidden to eat such non-kosher food!

The street led to the beautiful Saski Park, where I spent the most enjoyable hours of my childhood. We went there almost every day, with the nanny or with Aunt Biela. Mother had progressive ideas about how to bring up children, and she believed that we must have some fresh air every day and eat fruit and vegetables. She was very strict and her instructions had to be obeyed; and I am grateful to her for influencing me in that respect.

It was in the Saski Park that I got to know my friend Tzelina. Since then our lives have crossed again and again. In this park, beside the lake, stood a wooden palace, formerly the king's summer theater. There we used to turn into princesses and hold grand festivities. In winter the lake became a major skating rink.

Together we used to gather shiny chestnuts, falling from the trees in the autumn, and made necklaces out of them. We played hide-and-seek, hiding behind the Greek statues, decorating the park.

In the ghetto there were neither parks nor trees. It was so filthy and overcrowded that it became hard to breathe. We spent the nights in fear of ominous loud banging on the gates of the houses. The sound of heavy boots would resound on the stairs. Whose door would they break into this time?

We sat all curled up. Throughout the winter nights, we never undressed, we had to be ready. When they broke into the house, we immediately made sure that Father was well hidden. They only caught him once, and beat him with a rubber truncheon. I was secretly ashamed to admit that I was glad when they went on to the neighbors and did not stop at our door.

Grandfather Yaakov, Mother's father, stayed with us throughout that winter. He was given my parents' bedroom, so we all crowded into one large room. At night I listened to the ringing of the big clock on the wall and to the sounds coming from the courtyard. Grandfather walked about in his room, and I heard the banging of his stick on the floor.

Profound anxiety reigned everywhere, as new decrees against the Jews were published daily.

It was a very cold winter. All my fingers froze, though I wore gloves. I used to dip my fingers first into boiling water and then into cold water; nevertheless, they became covered with wounds.

We went along Tvarda Street to exchange books at the public library, in the direction of the Nozhik Synagogue, where Father used to pray on the Sabbath and during the Jewish High Holidays. I spent many happy days in its courtyard, in processions with little flags and red apples at Simchat Torah and with palm branches during Shavuot [the harvest feast].

Twarda Street was crowded and dirty like all the other ghetto streets. Little children in rags were sitting on the pavement, asking for help. Sometimes they sang and tried to dance on their skinny little legs. People used to pass by quickly, as though trying to flee from the bidding of their own conscience. Sometimes a compassionate hand would stretch out and give the child a coin or two. Suddenly a Jewish policeman would go up to the children and drive them away harshly, brandishing his rubber truncheon, chasing them into the house.

I cringed. I wanted to go up to him and shout at him to leave the poor children alone. Instead I just stared at him, like the other passersby. Some of them swore at him and walked on. I hated the arrogant Jewish policemen, even though I understood they were needed.

The *ordnungsdienst* [Jewish police] was composed of people from so-called good families. So I refused to understand how a Jew could behave brutally to another Jew. *Surely we are on the same side, facing the German enemy, so why do the Jewish policemen perform their duty with such enthusiasm? Is Man evil by nature?* I wondered.

Tzelina and I used to bring this up again and again while walking along the ghetto streets. We were trying to understand the new reality. All our concepts were in a turmoil. We felt we had been deceived. Literature, the poems of Slovatzki and Mickiewicz—all that belonged to another world, not to ours. And these feelings brought on a profound disillusionment and a painful new awareness. As though struck by a knife, I grasped that my childhood was over, never to return. Had it all been a dream, a lie?

2 : CHILDHOOD IN WARSAW

The history of my family is entwined with the stormy events of the twentieth century. If the wise men are right in saying that "man is only the sum total of his life's journey," then my life encompasses all that was beautiful and horrendous in that century and was deeply affected by it.

I was born in 1928 in Warsaw, the capital of Poland. It was that stormy period between the two world wars during which two totalitarian regimes emerged, arousing illusions of happiness, national vitality, and development, on opposite ends of a view of society: the communist Russian Revolution and the fascist Nazi regime in Germany. At the same time, there was an amazing flourishing of the Zionist idea of return to the ancient homeland, Israel.

My father, Shimek (Simcha) Melamed, came from a family of religious merchants, traditional, but not orthodox. Although his grandfather had headed the *yeshiva* [orthodox Jewish college] in the town of Kaminetz Podolski [now in the Ukraine], at a certain stage at the beginning of the century, Avraham-Mordecai Melamed moved to the capital of Congress-Poland [under self-rule, under the protection of Tzarist Russia].

His children discarded the ultra-orthodox clothing and wore European dress. Yet my grandfather wore a black capote [a long cloak with a hood] and a black skullcap. He married my grandmother, Rachel Hana, a wise woman, a Jewish mother who gathered around her eight children with their husbands and wives, whom I only remember vaguely. She wore the traditional wig. She had light-blue eyes, which she passed down to all her children and most of her grandchildren.

My father's family made their living from a small haberdashery store in the big market, Hale Mirowskie, and they also had a soda factory, with a store next to it, selling light drinks. In those days they used to fill up large containers with soda water and distribute them to stores. When father got married, he inherited the store and the factory and ran them. Since the factory was in the crowded Krochmalna Street, inhabited by the poor and always full of noise and commotion, Mother hated the business very much and wanted to sell it. In the course of time, Father gave in and together they set up a factory for producing woolen products, in particular, gloves.

All the eight children in my father's family went to Jewish state schools, so they had a general education, in addition to a religious one. Two of his brothers, David, the eldest, and Benyamin (Leon), had stores on Nalevki Street and lived with their families close by.

His five sisters—Mania, Bronia, Ester, Basia, and Sala— were married, and their husbands had haberdashery or textile stores in that same well-known street. They spoke both Yiddish and Polish at home, and Polish with their children. My aunt Ester (Estushia) and her husband were rich. Their beautiful house in Shvientojerska Street hosted all our large family during

Jewish holidays. Her eldest son, Geniek, studied medicine; their daughter, Helenka, studied law, but did not complete her studies. The house had many rooms, and the children of the extended family used to run about in them, playing hide-and-seek behind the heavy velvet curtains. It was great fun!

As was the custom in those days, in summer the family used to rent an apartment in one of the summer resorts in the area between Warsaw and Otvock and spend two months there. Those who had to continue working for a living in summer, stayed in the city.

The uncles had a large villa in Michalin. In the midst of the lawns and woods was a large wooden building with small apartments to rent. Next to the villa stood a synagogue and also the quarters of the Polish gardeners. Most of the visiting family members stayed in the villa, and they used to play cards, ball, or cricket and sunbathe and go for walks in the lovely neighborhood. Sometimes we traveled to Shvider, where there was a river with a large forest beside it. We, the children, had a happy time during the summer months while our parents suffered from the stifling, sweltering heat in the city.

I used to love the summer storms. The sun would suddenly disappear, the sky would turn dark, and it looked as though it would fall down on us. A gusty wind would whip up from somewhere, raising clouds of leaves and sand. Flashes of lightning severed the sky in quick succession, until the thunder came rumbling and crashing. Fear and trembling!

Once we got caught in such a storm, while on an outing with Uncle Leon, Aunt Irena, their sons, Adash and Meir, and their little daughter, Hanale. They had come to visit us, and we were happily wandering about, looking for blueberries and yellow mushrooms. Then the adults rested on a blanket, reading, talking, or playing cards. We, the children, went off on our own. Being the eldest, by now eleven, I naturally urged them to go and look farther and farther away.

Mirka was the first to warn me. "Let's go back," she pleaded. Already at that age my little sister was cautious. Mother used to say, "She has both feet on the ground."

But the approach of the storm aroused my adventurous spirit, and it was only when we heard the first clap of thunder that we became really frightened and started running back. I held little Hanale by the hand, but she was plump and her legs got entwined in the grass.

Suddenly there was a burst of torrential rain. We stayed under a tree, but Adash remembered that lightning may strike a tree and set it on fire, and whoever stands underneath dies. The children looked as if they were about to burst out crying. What was I going to do with them? We were at the mercy of the forces of heaven, in the middle of the forest, with darkness all around. Our parents were sure to be worried.

We had no choice. We had to go on running, with our wet clothes clinging to us. Then we saw our parents' frightened faces staring through the trees. Well, as usual, I got a good talking to from my mother. But there was more to come: When we got back to the apartment, Aunt Biela and Stefa took off our clothes and put us to bed with hot water bottles and served us boiling tea with lemon and sugar to make sure we wouldn't get a cold!

Uncle Leon was a wealthy merchant. His wife, Irena, was an active, clever person, a good saleswoman. They became rich within a few years. They had a large wholesale store and storerooms in Nalevki Street 19.

Uncle Leon and Aunt Irene decided to go into partnership with my parents: My parents would set up a workshop at home and knit gloves and woolen socks, and my aunt and uncle would provide us with the machines and raw materials and sell the finished products in their store. The workshop was set up in our apartment. For lack of room, the machines were placed in the homes of the Polish women who did the actual knitting.

One room was allotted to the knitted products, and the finishing was carried out there under my mother's watchful eye. She had a good relationship with the women workers. They greatly appreciated her honesty and her fairness toward them and her skillful management. This relationship later motivated the assistance that some of them gave us during the hardest period in our lives.

My father, Shimek, was clever with his hands. He knew how to deal with any problems with the machines. We did not see much of him during the week. We spent our days with the nanny and with Stefa, the Polish maid. But on Saturday, as soon as the large clock struck nine, hop, there we were, in our parents' bed!

That was the time when Father would tell us stories. Stefa served us strong tea with milk in bed, and the two of us—my sister, Mirka, four years younger, and I—were eager to hear the promised story.

"What is it today?" Father left us in suspense, but we knew he always told the same story of the goat and the seven kids. He made it either very frightening or funny, so that we never knew what was coming. And what would happen to the youngest kid, hiding in the grandfather clock, like the one standing in our dining room? Would it be saved in the end?

Father was a kind, affable person. He did not know how to refuse any request. People turned to him, and his younger sisters relied on his help. It happened quite often that he was away from home, helping others. Mother resented that he found more time for others, but less for his family.

To me she was the dominant person in the household, in our upbringing and in the management of the business, and in spite of the help she had, she bore the main burden. From time to time she gave vent to her frustration in a loud quarrelsome voice, but Father did not answer her. Mother did not spare me her sharp reprimands, tinged with a great deal of irony and criticism, since she saw me as "my father's daughter."

When she was angry with me, Father always defended me, creating a kind of silent understanding between us, even though I may have actually identified more with Mother's complaints. I loved my father and was sorry that in the course of time he intervened less and less in what happened at home. I was sad to see him distancing himself, leaving the decisions to Mother.

When I was accused of something (usually I deserved it), Mirka would immediately burst out crying, thus saving me from Mother's anger. It took Mother a long time to subdue her anger, but then she started to kiss me to make peace. My sister always identified with me, until the time when she could judge for herself.

In the Melamed family, I felt sure that things were carried out according to the rules and traditions. All the holidays were celebrated in the traditional Jewish way, but we did travel on the Sabbath and listened to the radio and enjoyed the cultural life around us—some of us more than others. My cousins' generation studied at the Jewish high school, and many of them went on to the university.

Had the large Melamed family survived, today they might have been considered Reform Jews [a sector that did not exist at that time]. From my father's side of the family, I absorbed Jewish folklore, traditions connected with the holidays and a vague Zionist longing, and from my mother's side, integration within Polish culture, literature, and language.

Mother did not know Yiddish, nor did we. Father did speak Yiddish, but not at home. The time came when I regretted not knowing that language because it made things difficult for me. People even criticized me for it, and once I was even showered with juicy curses by an old woman who called me, "You stupid *goya*," a Jewish girl who doesn't know the language of her own people. Mother did not like the Jewish environment in which we were growing up, and since she had an influence on the atmosphere at home, it was steeped in Polish rather than Jewish culture.

I am in the center, my sister Mirka is on the left, my cousin Adash-Avraham on the right, with Meir and Hanale Melamed.

One summer I had a crush on a Polish boy. I wanted him to pay attention to me so much that I bought a necklace with a cross and wore it around my neck. Mother and Stefa laughed at me, but I was serious about it. At the age of nine, I put the Jewish God to the test. I stood up in the kitchen and stunned Stefa by declaring, "God, if you exist, strike me dead here and now!"

Well, He didn't do it, that's a fact. Aunt Biela came running in when she heard Stefa's frightened cry and scolded me: "What are you trying to do, you silly girl, that's forbidden! No one knows for sure if He exists or not. We are forbidden to know, we can only believe, yes or no."

"But maybe Jesus is right and he is His chosen son? Why are Jews so obstinate about it? Why are we Jews?" I stood my ground. Aunt Biela, herself in favor of assimilation, was unable to give me an explanation that would satisfy me, and I was left to my doubts.

I remember a typical incident: Christmas approached, bringing the wonderful smells of fir trees sold in the city squares. I envied the Polish children, buying shiny decorations for the tree, and I begged Mother to buy me a little fir tree. She agreed.

We decorated the tree with glittering glass balls. Suddenly, just as we were enjoying it most, we heard the doorbell ring. The frightened Stefa rushed in, announcing, "Aunt Ester has come to visit us." In those days few houses had telephones. One couldn't arrange a meeting or a visit ahead of time. People came whenever it suited them.

Aunt Ester was a greatly respected traditional Jewish lady, and she did us an honor by visiting us. Father hastened to welcome her, and as he passed us, he saw what we were doing. "What's that? What is a fir tree doing in my house? Who dared to put it here? Take it away at once!"

His face was red with anger and shame, thinking what would happen if his sister saw this "sin" being perpetrated. We rushed the wretched tree to the darkest passage in the house to hide it from the honored aunt. I realized that what we had done was forbidden at home.

Today, I occasionally happen to participate in Christmas celebrations in Denmark, together with the family of my daughter, Iris, who lives there with her husband, Per, a Dane, who keeps traditions but is not religious. I enjoy giving and receiving presents under the decorated tree. I told the fir tree story to my daughter and laughed. How frightened and ashamed I had been at the time. Today I understand that keeping a particular custom does not affect our true feeling of belonging to the Jewish people; it is a matter of a much deeper sense of identification.

We used to celebrate all the Jewish festivals. Passover was a great occasion. On the day before, I used to go around the house with Father when he wiped all the windows with a feather to remove the last remains of leavened food. Mother took the special Passover dishes out of a suitcase.

Down in the courtyard, copper and iron dishes were made kosher in large tanks. The sounds of beating on pillows and down quilts came from all the apartments in this large apartment building. The smells of cooked fish and fried onion filled the air. The three courtyards, one behind the other, were surrounded by houses three or four stories high. To get from one courtyard to another, you had to go through the house separating them.

All the hundreds of people living in our apartment building were Jews, except the caretaker's family. The inhabitants were mostly poor, but there were also the educated and well-to-do who lived mainly in the front part of the building, in the large apartments. This building "breathed" the Jewish festivals, and it constituted a kind of autonomous entity, managing its own affairs, ranging from cultural evenings to collecting money for the poor people living there.

We were not allowed to go down to the courtyard to play with the "ordinary" children; we were considered "from good families." In those days, class distinction determined the way of life. People used to dress and behave as expected according to the class to which they belonged.

During the Feast of the Tabernacles/*Sukkot*, sukkahs were put together in the courtyard or on the balconies. At Purim, groups of children went around, dressed up, singing and acting the play about the wicked Haman and Queen Esther, in Yiddish and Polish. They knocked on the doors, were invited to come in, were offered Purim pastry and candies, and also received some Purim coins, according to each family's economic situation.

I asked my mother to let me join them. Already at a young age, I was strongly attracted to acting, but "what an idea!" was Mother's reaction, "It wouldn't do for you to go from one family to another, begging for charity."

Like all the little girls, Mirka and I wanted to be Queen Esther, but did not get the chance. Since we did not go to kindergarten—for reasons not clear to me to this day—we did not get to know the songs sung at festivals. Even though the school was Jewish, we did not learn any songs. In special lessons devoted to religious education, we studied Jewish history and customs, but not the Torah [the Old Testament].

I cannot say that I received a Jewish or a Zionist education. I had little knowledge about my people, and all I had absorbed was emotional in nature, through my experiences in the family circle during holidays and later through the Hashomer Hatzair Movement.

In Warsaw was a great deal of anti-Semitism, fostered officially by the government. For example, my cousin Gutek Grunwald came to Warsaw to study mechanical engineering at the Polytechnic. He came from the large industrial Polish city of Lodz, where two of my mother's sisters lived. He stayed with us for some time. He and other Jewish students remained standing during certain lectures at the Polytechnic, in protest against being told to sit at the back.

One day my cousin came home with a large wound on his forehead. He and his Jewish friends had been beaten by members of an extreme nationalist anti-Semitic organization— N.D. The Jews did hit back, but they were in the minority and had to run away.

At that time the *numerus clausus* policy was introduced at the universities, limiting the number of Jewish students. Those who entered higher education at the time belonged to the wealthy, assimilated families and had excelled in secondary school. They were perceived as a threat and in competition with the Polish intelligentsia.

Apart from Gutek's stories, I did not experience anti-Semitism directly then. Maybe I didn't have the experience, since we hardly ever walked around in the Polish areas. All our friends and acquaintances were Jewish. Over three hundred thousand Jews lived in Warsaw at the time. The Jewish neighborhoods supplied all our daily needs, so there was no need to "venture" into the Polish sections, except for the center of the city, where we used to walk. I'll tell about that later.

By the way, Gutek and his wife left at the beginning of the war with the big wave of immigration to the U.S.S.R., where they eventually ended up in Asian Russia and survived. They were the only members of mother's family who were still alive at the end of the war. Later they came to Israel. Their only daughter, Irit (Irka), lives with her two sons in the United States. Irit has no other family in the world apart from me and my sister, and in spite of the great distance separating us, we meet from time to time.

My mother, Raya Levant, came from a family that had experienced great tragedies and upheavals. Grandfather Yaakov came originally from Russia and grandmother Lizabeta (Liza-Leah) from the Ukraine, the town of Mohilev-Podolski.

At the beginning of the twentieth century, Poland was under the occupation of Tzarist Russia, and the family settled in the summer resort of Otvosk. Grandmother suffered from advanced tuberculosis (TB). She used to have a bloody cough. Otvosk had pinewoods and fresh air, so hospitals for TB patients were built there.

When the First World War broke out, grandfather took his family—his ailing wife and six children—and traveled in freight trains in the direction of Kirovgrad, to his rich brother, a grain merchant who lived in a large house.

Mother told us little about her childhood. We begged her to tell us more. Her stories made us tremble pleasantly with excitement and fear. They seemed so unreal to us, like a movie.

But she would not go into detail and put off telling us about her life again and again.

It was only as a grown-up that I could understand those stories by the way they were reflected in our lives, through Mother's sadness and depression, as an additional dimension of our later suffering. Only someone who has suffered in his or her own life can fully understand and feel empathy toward a person who is suffering.

"Mother," we would ask her, "how did you survive the pogroms? Tell us again where your father and older brothers were at the time." [Pogroms were violent riots to persecute and kill Jews.]

"What is there to tell? It was bad. That's all," she would reply.

"Tell us, Mummy, how old were you at the time?"

My father, Shimek (Simcha) Melamed, in 1921, when serving in the Polish army.

"I was only six when my mother died. I always remember her lying ill in bed. She did not bring me up. Father was left alone with four young children and two older boys. We lived in the house of our rich uncle. You are called after your grandmother, Liza-Leah," Mother said, smiling sadly.

"And when did you get caught in the pogrom?"

"The Bolshevik Revolution broke out in 1917. Mother was no longer alive. The Red Ukrainian revolutionaries smashed the prison gate, and I also saw people jumping out of the windows. And then the pogrom broke out. My older brothers were not at home, and Father had gone to his older sister, Bejle. We were alone, three little children: my brother, Sima, eleven years old; my sister Ida, nine; and I, the youngest, aged eight. We heard people shouting, and shots.

"Our Ukrainian neighbors came running and hid us in their pigsty. We sat there all night, trembling with fear. The Jews screamed throughout the night and begged for mercy. On the next day, it all calmed down. Father returned with Bejle, and then someone came and said that my eldest brother, Buria, was lying in the park, badly wounded. He was shot by thugs."

We asked more questions: "What did they do to him? Why? Did they kill him?"

"No, his wounds healed. Later he was crushed under a tractor, poor boy. He was so handsome, nineteen years old," Mother added. "My brother Solia was lost during the Revolution. We did not know where. Simply disappeared." In telling us, her eyes filled with tears.

"The opponents of the Revolution were called Whites. The Red Bolsheviks fought against them. Sometimes the Whites won, sometimes the Reds. We left uncle's house and traveled to the large city of Odessa. We hoped that the anti-Semites, their pogroms, would not harm us there. But there was nothing to eat there. That's enough, I've told you plenty," Mother would say, shaking her head impatiently.

Mother loved to sing. She had a wonderful voice. She also danced beautifully and taught us the dances popular at the time: the waltz, tango, foxtrot, and even tap dancing. But her cheerful mood would soon pass, replaced with a sad look, tinged with disappointment. A sense of what she had missed out on often came over her face. She was a talented artist at heart, but she had accepted the condition forced upon the Jews in this era.

She told us that her father looked handsome like a film star when he was young—tall, with a trimmed black beard. He had a sense of humor and a great deal of knowledge in many spheres, a real Russian intellectual. Only, he did not know how to earn money. That is why, when the fighting in Russia died down and he returned with his four children to liberated Poland and settled in the town of Otvosk, the girls soon had to give up their studies and learn a trade.

The two young girls, my mother and Ida, learned sewing in the elegant salon belonging to the aunts, my grandmother's sisters, in Lodz. But the aunts had a "brighter" future in mind for them: marriage. They began to sew their trousseaux well before the bridegrooms appeared on the scene.

Father and Mother met in Otvosk. Father fell in love with the beautiful girl with a lovely figure, intelligent and with a sharp tongue; but she had other plans. However, the aunts succeeded in persuading grandfather that it was the perfect match: a young man eight years older, well established, from

Father, Mother, and me,
in 1929.

Warsaw, from a Jewish family with deep roots. What could be better for an orphan?

Many years later, Mother confessed to me that she had not fallen in love with Father, even though she liked him. That may have been the reason for their frequent quarrels. She lived feeling she had not exploited her many talents, her intellectual capacity and emotional potential to love. A year later, her older sister, Ida, was quick to get married, since it was inappropriate that my mother, the younger one, got married first.

Before the war, I was often sent to Otvosk, to my cousin's home. Grandfather had a room crammed with bulky books, full of delightful illustrations, all in Russian, in Cyrillic writing I couldn't read. I was very curious and used to sit on the carpet and ask him about the princes and Tsars wrapped in their furs, about the battles between the Russians and the wild Tartars or the fierce-looking Cossacks; and grandfather, who had a great knowledge of history, enjoyed telling me stories, which sounded like old fairy tales to me. He was a teacher of Russian language, literature, and history. I must have inherited my love for these subjects from him.

In later years he became more concerned with religion. He used to pray and put on phylacteries [Tefilin]. Grandfather Yaakov looked impressive: He was tall, with a slightly red Russian nose, his white hair falling on his shoulders and a long white beard. His daughters were afraid of him. They said he behaved like a tyrant and would not tolerate any opposition, but to me he was gentle and patient.

The last time I saw him was when he came to us in Warsaw after the Germans had occupied the city. Mother was in a state of shock after the terrible bombing of Warsaw and lay in bed for three weeks. I did not understand why she stayed in bed, and it even made me angry. Grandfather tried to explain to me that her nerves were affected by the noise of the explosions. He empathized with his young daughter's emotional state and supported her. I thought that she was indulging herself while the whole world was collapsing around us. Grandfather stayed with us for several weeks and then returned to Aunt Ida.

We only heard two years later how he was killed. He and my aunt with her two daughters went into hiding during the great deportation from Otvosk. Grandfather was killed and the others were taken away in a freight train. Uncle Sima also disappeared during the Second World War, in Russia.

I remembered: "Uncle Sima is coming for Pessah. Girls, get ready for the party," Mother told us happily. He arrived, sunburned, straight from a ski vacation in the Carpathian Mountains in southern Poland. We immediately started to think up plans about how to enjoy ourselves together; it was clear that with Uncle Sima we always had a crazy time.

Mother and Sima were alike and loved each other very much. Uncle Sima was her only brother to survive the First World War. He was quite fond of us. "So where are we going, kittens?" he would ask smiling, his white teeth gleaming in his sunburned face, "to Lazienki, or the Luna park?"

The weather had already turned warmer, and we could leave behind our heavy winter coats and wear our checkered spring ones. The three of us crossed the yard: two little girls, one blond and the other dark haired, wearing linen hats, one pale blue and the other green, matching the colors of our coats, holding hands with our tall, handsome uncle, who was, in those days, a young, sought-after bachelor.

The children in the yard looked at us enviously, and we climbed proudly and merrily into the horse-drawn carriage waiting for us in front of the house. The coachman used to wrap his feet in a rug that smelled strongly of horses. The horse walked slowly over the cobbles, then the coachman spurred him on, and we set out at a gallop to the lovely parts of Warsaw.

Along Marszalkowska Street, Jerusalem Boulevard, turning into New World Street, passing through grand avenues lined by palaces of the Polish aristocracy, finally reaching the most beautiful park, Lazienki.

Peacocks were walking across the lawns and squirrels jumped about among the trees. No traditionally dressed Jews in a capote ever went there. Nor did other Jews frequent this park, fearing the worst from the bands of anti-Semitic ruffians.

But my uncle did not look Jewish, and with him we felt safe. By the lake there stood a beautiful tall palace built in the neoclassic style, one of the homes of the Polish kings.

Many years later, when I accompanied youth groups from Israel to Warsaw on their educational trips in the wake of the Holocaust, I took them to this park to show them that Warsaw is not only a remembrance site but also a city where people used to enjoy life and still do.

I told them about the stimulating cultural life that existed there, trying to resurrect the past, but the ghosts of my large family, deeply rooted in both the Polish and the rich Jewish culture once flourishing there, accompanied me all the way. Their ashes are scattered in Treblinka.

But their story is yet to be told.

The last meeting of the whole Melamed family took place before the outbreak of the war. Yaakov Levinson, the son of Aunt Mania, my grandmother's sister, successfully completed his lawyer's examinations and was about to marry Helena, also a lawyer. It was bound to be a large wedding, as expected of the son of a wealthy family, with a factory manufacturing tiles in Twarda Street in Warsaw. The wedding ceremony took place in the Nozyk Synagogue, and the celebration followed in a splendid hall.

It was spring 1939.

People were worried about the rumors of a possible war. The grown-ups around me discussed and weighed what would happen should Hitler carry out his threats against Poland. Thousands of German Jews of Polish origin had already been expelled across the border, pushed, destitute, into Poland. Thousands of opponents of the regime and many Jews were imprisoned in the Dachau Camp. Hitler, outrageously drunk with success, terrified the whole free world.

The Germans followed him in a hysterical euphoria. The first warning of what was about to happen was the Kristallnacht, when synagogues and thousands of books were burned and windows of Jewish businesses smashed by gangs of Nazi storm troopers on the rampage.

Hitler seized Austria in the famous Anschluss [the annexation of Austria into Nazi Germany in 1938] and terrorized the Jews there. He demanded and obtained the Sudeten district from Czechoslovakia. He formed an alliance with Mussolini, the fascist ruler of Italy. Now he demanded Danzig, Poland's large port and gateway to the Baltic Sea, which formed a passage separating Germany and East Prussia, an area lying between Poland and Lithuania.

I was almost eleven, I understood and sensed the atmosphere of uncertainty and anxiety about the future. But a wedding is a wedding. New dresses were ordered for all of us: for me and my sister dresses made of white taffeta, decorated with tiny artificial roses, with a silk light-blue belt, tied at the back in a special bow called *kokarda*. And for Mother, a black evening dress, decorated with glittering silvery dots, and a small jacket made of a glossy, silvery fabric.

We were all ready, dressed up, but Mother was not. Biela and Stefa were pulling hard to get her into the dress, but in vain; it was too tight. The zipper would not close!

"What are we going to do?" we asked in despair. We had an important part to play in the synagogue. We belonged to the group of bridesmaids who were to hold the train of the bride's dress. Mirka was crying, Mother was hysterical, Father clasped his hands in silence, and I gave annoying advice.

Finally, after undoing the seam and sewing it up again, Mother was inside the dress. Now she looked so beautiful, tall and slim. We were used to everyone turning around in the street to look at her, but this time I was full of admiration for her beauty. The anxious coachman was waiting outside with the carriage.

But what a terrible disappointment awaited us in the synagogue. It was empty! The ceremony had ended some time before we arrived, late. Disappointed, we went on to the banquet hall. When we entered, everyone cheered: "Raya! Raya!" Mother did look most impressive. At that wedding I danced with my teacher of religion, who was among the guests. He asked me to dance with him. The handsome teacher, with a little beard! Of course I made the most of it at school the next day; the girls were envious.

On the first of September the sirens sounded. The war had broken out. The Germans invaded Poland without any warning. My father was appointed the "commander" of the house. He was directly responsible for the team assigned to put out the incendiary bombs being dropped by the low flying *Stuka* planes mainly on the center of city and on the Jewish neighborhoods. Father ran about on the roofs and often prevented fires from breaking out.

One day that September a messenger arrived from Father's brother, Uncle Leon, asking Father to come at once—the stores of goods were on fire. Father was young, robust, and known for his strength. He ran immediately to the distant neighborhood, to Nalevki Street, and took charge of the firefighting.

Thanks to his presence of mind and efficiency, he saved his brother's stores of goods, which were his and his brother's family's source of livelihood. Maybe that was why Mother felt that the help given us by Uncle Leon in the hard years to come was due to us; it was not charity.

In the chaos caused by the constant explosions and fires, the voice of the commander of the city, Colonel Umjastovski, was heard on the radio. In a parched, emotional voice, he called on all the men in the surrounding city to leave it and go east, in the direction of the Russian border. He hoped that the retreating Polish army would be able to establish a new line of defense there.

But Starzynski, the mayor, called on them to remain in the city to defend it. The contradictory messages created confusion. In addition, rumors spread that the German soldiers were taking vengeance on Jewish soldiers. Within one day thousands of Jewish men got organized and decided to leave. My father, Uncle Sima, and his brother, Uncle David, also decided to go. Hurriedly they packed their backpacks with a few things and a little food and set out on foot among the thousands of vehicles fleeing the besieged city.

Father reached the city of Bialistok and remained there as a refugee. He sent us a message, asking us to get ready to join him. By then it was winter. At the beginning of the year 1940, the winter was particularly cold. I longed for my father and worried about him. I did not know where he was. We were alone, without any means of livelihood. Everything was closed; it was impossible to keep our workshop going.

One day someone knocked on our door. Bitter cold burst into the apartment together with the visitor. Mirka, standing next to me, did not recognize him. Father had a beard, looked haggard, and was wrapped in a fur coat and a heavy shawl. He embraced us, radiating happiness. He told us what he had gone through: walking in the snow, bypassing Russian and German guards and dishonest smugglers extorting money from him.

After resting just one day, Father began to talk us into leaving: "We must save ourselves and flee from the Germans. They are burning synagogues and killing people in the little towns in the eastern areas. And who knows what they'll do here. The Russians are letting the Jews in and are giving them work. They are not good people either, but we'll be able to survive the war there."

"What shall we live on? No house, no nothing. Wretched refugees?" Mother countered bluntly. "Besides, I know the Bolsheviks. They'll lock us up for being bourgeois; they'll separate us. The cold is terrible outside. How can we go with the little girls?" she said in plain logic.

Father gave in. He usually gave in to her arguments. He stayed at home with us, and we were again able to cope together, heartened by his presence and his strength. I felt happy and more secure.

Who was right in that controversy?

After the war we found out that, although the Jews had been expelled to Siberia and many died of cold and hunger, the great majority survived the war. And those who remained in the ghetto were all murdered, including my father.

3 : THE WARSAW GHETTO

I want to tell you about the Warsaw Ghetto.

Will I be able to describe it, the largest ghetto in Europe? The overcrowding, the feeling of humiliation, the raging typhoid epidemic, the filthy gray sidewalks and the houses crammed with masses of refugees from the country towns? Thousands of people wanting to survive, wandering around like mice trapped in a maze. The Warsaw Ghetto was a "Jewish State" under Nazi occupation—an accumulation of all possible contrasts.

Over 250,000 Jewish refugees who had been expelled from outlying towns and villages were forced into Warsaw to join 300,000 Warsaw Jews—creating over a half million people crammed into an area about 1.3 square miles (or over seven people per room).

Stores sold food smuggled into the ghetto, where one can buy anything—even eggs and milk. And outside lurked the *chapperim* [snatchers], girls and boys in rags with feverish eyes, lying in wait for people leaving the store, grabbing their food and at once plunging their teeth into it, through the wrapping paper. People would crowd around, kicking and shouting, but the "chapper" did not care, as long as there was food, no matter what it was.

The coffeehouses were full of smartly dressed women wearing elegant prewar hats. There were also *shmuglerim*, rich smugglers, the new ghetto aristocracy, and all kinds of people getting rich at others' expense. On the other hand, in front of the houses, on the sidewalks, human corpses lay covered by newspapers. The Pinkiert's burial society couldn't manage to load them all onto the carts.

In the Femina Theater in our street were performances in Yiddish and Polish: plays, sketches, and literary evenings. Actors, singers, and authors read and performed at literary parties in private apartments, after working hours. In many houses the house committee organized such evenings to help poor, starving families.

Our family was still relatively well off. Mother made soup for dinner every day; for breakfast and supper we all got two pieces of bread. Father and Mother were operating a knitting machine on their own. I also helped. When the stock of wool ran out, they found new material: "streich," thread from unstitched army blankets. It didn't matter. People always needed socks and gloves and were willing to pay.

My job was to turn a large machine that "scratches" the inside of the sock to make it warm and pleasant to the touch. The machine used to work on electricity, but there was no electricity in the ghetto. The machine was heavy and the work mechanical and boring. *I had no choice*, I told myself repeatedly. My parents expected me to help them. We had to run by ourselves what was left of the workshop; there were no workers, nor was there any room for them.

My friend Tzelina would come over occasionally and stay the night, or I would go to her home. A small carbide lamp stood on the dining room table. These lamps were an invention of the ghetto. The gas produced by carbide has a terrible smell, but at least there was a little light.

We would sit wrapped up in the corner, talking. Our parents were edgy, and all the people around us were nervous wrecks. They would shout instead of talking, or sink into the silence of despair. I also didn't see any point or hope in this kind of life. *Will this misery ever come to an end?* The Germans were winning on all fronts and the end of the war seemed so far away.

Halina, Tzelina's elder sister, was a real prophet of doom. She predicted a bitter end for all of us. To counteract despair, I immersed myself in reading. The ghetto libraries functioned as usual. I read Homer's *Iliad* and *Odyssey*, *The Magic Mountain* by Thomas Mann [considered one of the most influential books of German literature in the twentieth century, first published in 1924], books by Hemingway, Gorky, Tolstoy, and Dostoyevsky. I was growing up prematurely.

In the yard of Tzelina's house, Krochmaina Street 9, there was constant noise and turmoil because it was crowded with families of refugees. The Germans pushed masses of people into the Warsaw Ghetto. They had been expelled from the towns and villages in the area. Self-help organizations in the ghetto—Z.T.O.S. and CENTOS, public assistance organized by the Judenrat—could not cope with these waves of humanity, and the refugees were always the first to die of hunger or disease.

[Z.T.O.S. was the Jewish welfare association in the ghetto, helping the refugees and the needy. It set up a chain of soup kitchens and supported youth organizations and starving artists and intellectuals. CENTOS helped orphaned children. Both institutions were supported by funds provided by the American Joint Distribution Committee until December of 1941. The Judenrat was the Jewish City Council and was established by the Germans.]

The Germans decreed that every family must take in a family of refugees. Each apartment was to accommodate as many families as there were rooms. For the time being we were lucky. Our apartment remained in our hands.

The Shadow Children

The building we lived in was large and accommodated many families. It faced the wooden fence separating the ghetto from the Polish Aryan part of Warsaw, at No. 19, Ciepla Street. Through this fence, large-scale wholesale smuggling went on.

Two boys, Banek and Tadek Marisia, lived with their mother on the ground floor in the second courtyard. At the beginning of the war, their father went east with the men fleeing from Warsaw, and there was no trace of him. The elder boy, Banek, was fifteen, a clever and cynical fellow. He couldn't care less about authority. He used to mock the Jewish policemen and quarrel with the children in the yard. But that was all putting on a show.

I was in on his secret, and I knew that he smuggled in food and bribed the policemen. He took it upon himself to care for his mother and brother. Mrs. Marisia had been a clerk in a government office before the war. She was a gentle, intelligent woman, but totally incapable of coping with poverty and deprivation. She sank into a depression and only earned a few coins by cleaning the yard after the Polish concierge had gone home.

It was hard for us to see her sweeping the yard and opening the gate in the evenings. Her younger son, Tadek, did not look like a Jew, and although their mother forbade it, Banek used to send him to the other side of the wooden fence. I saw how he exchanged whispers with the Jewish policemen who walked along the fence, guarding it, and when the deal was "signed," Banek would lift a loose board, peer outside to see if the Polish policeman in the blue uniform had turned away, and then send out his eleven-year-old brother.

Bribing policemen was called in the ghetto jargon "a nickelodeon" [an old-fashioned jukebox]. Why? Because if you put a coin into a nickelodeon, it will play a tune. Little Tadek would return with his pockets bulging with potatoes or bread that he had stolen or scrounged on the Aryan side. He would wait for the whistling agreed on, and then would run to the fence at a crazy speed and slip back into the ghetto.

Sometimes a Polish policeman would catch him, empty his pockets, add a few slaps, and send him off to the ghetto entrance gate. There, things would become complicated. The agile but frightened child had to slip into the ghetto together with a group of Jewish workers returning from work at dusk. I used to see Banek standing at the gate, tense and silent, waiting for his brother. *Will he return alive?* Hundreds of children, boys and girls, used to provide for their families in this way.

Bands of adult smugglers used to walk about near our fence. I went up to Banek to see what was going on, but he pushed me into the door of the house. "Are you crazy? Don't get close. These smugglers are ruthless. If they catch you witnessing their transactions, you'll get it!"

But I did see whole sacks of goods being thrown in quickly—sugar, flour, anything. The ghetto wanted to survive. The creative Jewish brain invented thousands of tricks to deceive its tormentors.

One day I was about to go out through our gate into the street. Suddenly I was pushed aside by Banek as he was fleeing inside. He made a sign that I should keep quiet and slipped briskly into a nearby cellar. Two furious Jewish policemen burst in after him, shouting. One of them was holding Tadek, who was crying bitterly. The policeman hit the whining child, repeating constantly: "Come on, tell us, where is your brother? If you don't tell us, I'll hand you over to the Germans, you little worm!"

I stood there, stunned. "The little worm" looked at me pleadingly, and said: "Tell him he isn't my brother, I don't know him at all. I just wanted to go and see my friends from before the war."

I nodded and said to the policeman, "Sir, I have two cousins in the police force, maybe you know Lejzer Gold? He is a police officer and he won't like it when I tell him that you beat a little Jewish child."

"Shut up, you brat! Take the child. His brother is a dangerous smuggler. I'll catch him one day."

This is how I became involved, unintentionally, in Banek's smuggling business. His daring aroused my admiration, and when he asked me to, I agreed to stand guard when he was bribing policemen and smuggling his little brother out through the hole in the wooden wall. I didn't tell anyone about it, not even Tzelina.

He used to whistle to me, as agreed between us, and I came down from the third floor into the street, stood outside our gate under the little roof in front of a locked store, and watched with my heart beating loud as the little brother slipped out—or back in and threw down his little bag of food. Banek himself would slip out only if he had made a deal with a "good" policeman, and then I did not have to stand there. Banek used to sell his goods to the store owner, who sold butter and sausage meat, and, I think, also matches, soap, and haberdashery.

One day Tadek told me that Banek had not come back from the Aryan side for three days, and he was afraid that something had happened to him. The child was frightened, and his blue eyes were full of hope that I would save his brother. *What could I do?* I became terribly afraid.

I went into the street and asked the policeman if he knew anything about the boy who had gone over the fence there. He looked at me and said, shaking his head, "That's how they disappear. They catch them on the Aryan side every day— gangs of gentile informers or policemen. Sometimes they only give them a beating and let them go; sometimes they shoot them. Wait a bit longer, maybe he'll slip away."

But Banek never came back.

Nothing had helped him, neither his fluent Polish nor his "good" looks [meaning Aryan features—blue eyes, blond hair] or his intelligence. He simply never came back. I secretly mourned his almost-certain death. Later we moved into the large ghetto [the so-called small ghetto was emptied after the deportation to the death camps and those remaining were moved to what became known as the large ghetto), and I never heard anything more about his family.

Banek was one of the thousands of children who tried to live in that jungle and survive.

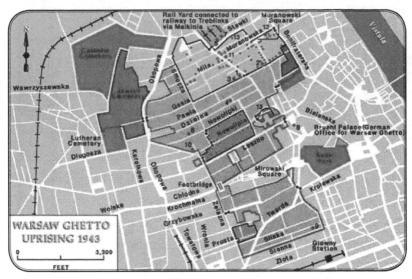

A map of the Warsaw Ghetto.

Thrown Out of Our Home

For many weeks we heard rumors that the Germans intended to reduce the size of the ghetto, but no one knew which streets would be taken over. One morning, I think it was at the end of September 1941, notices were posted on the walls of buildings, announcing that parts of what was called the small ghetto would be transferred to the Polish side, and thousands of Jews would be ousted from their homes, among them those living in Ciepla Street 19, in our building.

Aunt Biela came back and told the neighbors in the yard. Immediately, people started to come down from all the floors into the yard. The rumor spread like wildfire. Father and Mother sat stunned, and my sister, Mirka, started to cry and hug Mother. *Where shall we go?*

Until then we had been lucky. Throughout the whole year since the forceful formation of the ghetto, we had remained in our own home and did not even have to take in refugees. We were living in relative comfort, in spite of the decree of the Judenrat, stating that families, ousted from the small towns, must be crowded into existing apartments, eight people to a room. Now we would be pushed in with strangers, squeezed like sardines. And what would happen to all the knitting machines, still left from our workshop, with which we made our living. Where could we put them?

"There's no time to lament," Father said. "We share our fate with the other Jews. The sooner we start looking for an apartment, the more likely we are to find a good one."

At first Mother went into hysterics and clasped her hands, but her practical sense won out. She came to her senses and at once started to plan whom to turn to. To Father's family in the big ghetto? To acquaintances? To the housing department of the Judenrat?

And I? I ran to Krochmaina Street to my friend Tzelina to tell her what was going to happen. Luckily, that street was not to be vacated; even before the war it was very crowded, inhabited by the poor. Now we would be living far from each other, and there was no transport inside the ghetto, only rickshaws attached to tricycles. But a ride in a rickshaw was expensive. And what about the nights we used to spend together in the bedroom in her apartment, in endless heart-to-heart talks?

On the following day Father found a room with a kitchen in Nowoliple Street 42, in the large ghetto. Aunt Biela, who had been staying with us until then, found a place for herself next to the Czyste Hospital where she was working as a nurse. We began to consider what to take with us and what to leave behind. There was not even enough time to sell our lovely

Rickshaws and horse-drawn wagons carrying passengers in the ghetto.

furniture such as the sideboards made of carved mahogany in the dining room, my parents' beautiful bedroom—all the property amassed in the course of many years.

The furniture was too heavy to transport, and, besides, there were no trucks in the ghetto. We had to abandon our furniture to looters. Father hired a cart, and he and the coachman hitched themselves up into it instead of a horse, and I pushed from the back. We had to cover a huge distance, many kilometers. We went back and forth several times in the course of two days.

Father was a strong, well-built man, but the journey to Russia a year before had depleted his strength. His face was drawn, but he pulled on and on.

Later I came across the poem "Things" by the ghetto poet Wladyslaw Szlengel, in which he describes the long journey of the Jews of the Warsaw Ghetto on to their final destination, Treblinka. At that time we did not know what was in store.

I copied this wonderful poem on leaving the ghetto and smuggled it across to the Aryan side. I have it with me. Here is a shortened version of the poem, in free translation by the translator of this book, based on my translation from Polish into Hebrew:

From Hozra, Wspolna and Marshalkovska streets
Carts are streaming…Jewish carts …
Furniture, tables, stools,
Trunks, bundles,
Suits, pictures,
Glasses, plates, kettles,
All of them going from Hozra to Sliska
A bottle of vodka in the pocket
A piece of sausage
In carts, rickshaws and wagons
The wretched crowd is moving…
From Sliska to Nizka
On and on they go.
Furniture, tables, stools
Trunks, bundles
But no carpets now
No sign of silver dishes
They remained in Sliska
All those little knickknacks.
And then they left Nizka
On their way to the rickety sheds.
No more furniture and stools
No more pots or bundles
No more carts. Now on foot
The wretched crowd is trudging.

On our way, in Zelaznej Street, not far from the gate of the ghetto, the cart almost turned over. Suddenly German policemen with shining boots appeared. They pushed my father over too and struck him with a rubber truncheon. I started to scream. The coachman ran away but, miraculously, the cart regained its balance. The policemen went back to the gate, laughing.

Father shouted at me, "Stop screaming!" but I was shaking all over.

The street was full of carts and people carrying loads on their backs. We continued dragging our cart. Suddenly a commotion broke out in Leszno Street. We stopped. In the crowd I saw a thin fellow, dressed in rags, stuffing into his mouth something wrapped in a newspaper, biting into it repeatedly, paying no notice to a woman trying to pull the packet away from him.

The woman shouted, "Catch him, quick, the scum has stolen my bread!" The bystanders nodded and did not move. Such scenes occurred frequently. One more miserable "chapper," risking his life in despair.

In Leszno Street, which had been a wide, elegant street in the good old days before the war, were stores selling the best of everything. There one could buy food smuggled in from the Aryan side—sausages, horsemeat, cheeses, and canned food. But who could afford it?

In the scuffle, Father had suffered a heavy blow on his shoulder. I saw that it hurt him, and I pushed the cart with all my strength. I was wondering what all that furniture was for. *What is it worth?* The apartment is tiny, and there will not be any room for it. Maybe we had better use it to keep the fire going. *Why do people cling to these things?* At that time I did not know the meaning of Szlengel's poem, written a year later, when all that was left was in a backpack.

With great effort we reached our apartment. Mother was already waiting for us there. Everything was put in place within two days. Yes. The beds stood along the walls, the table and chairs in the middle, and armchairs, chairs, crates, and even Mother's chest were hanging on the walls.

In the kitchen we piled up several knitting machines and the large machine for the inside of the socks, the one I worked on. The main thing was that we all had a bed and did not have to live together with other people. And how funny this room looked! We had to be careful when we stood up. What would happen if the sideboard suddenly fell off the wall? Never mind. It's packed, but we are alive and well and we'll hold out. Maybe the war will be over in a few months.

We put out the stinking carbide lamp. The night was dark. There was a curfew outside. What will happen tonight? Will the Germans knock on the gates, looking for victims? It was only then that I pressed my head into the pillow and wept silently.

The Youth in the Ghetto

Yesterday, suddenly, my mother's cousin appeared. I hardly recognized her. What had happened to this girl of twenty? Her eyes had a glassy look, her face was gray, there was blood on her hands and shoulders.

"God, what's happened to you, Irka?"

Mother took her into the kitchen, I ran after them. She rolled up her blouse and I saw red stripes on her back. "Irka, tell me what happened!" Mother shouted.

Irka did not answer and went on showing the bruises on her body; in the end she began speaking in a dejected voice. "They kidnapped me this morning in the street. I fought with the policemen, but they pushed me into a closed truck. There were already some young women inside. We drove almost an hour, until we arrived at a German military barracks. We went pale. My blood froze in terrible fear. But we did not exchange a single word between us. They took us to the dining hall, ordered us to take off our coats, to clean windows and wash floors. Then they came and told us to undress completely. It was terribly cold and we were naked. And that's how we had to scrub the floor. Then they began to take us out one by one to another place…me too." She broke down and only her hoarse sobbing was heard in the room.

We sat in silence. We did not know what to say. Mother hugged her trembling shoulders. A sadistic wild beast is tearing us to pieces, murdering body and soul, poisoning our spirit.

In spite of the kidnappings, the decrees, and the robberies at night, life went on. Time passed, and in our hearts, those of the youth, questions cropped up, perturbing, harrying thoughts. I walked about in the streets of the ghetto with Tzelina. A slow drizzle fell. The sky was gray and overcast. Sometimes we stayed at her home, sometimes at mine. We could not find any respite.

We sat on the windowsill, looking longingly into the distance, beyond the roofs of the houses, to the east. Surely salvation would come from there. We still believed we would survive the war. Never for a moment did we think that Hitler would win.

We felt great pain. The pain sparked a revolt. It is hard to describe the depth of that insult and rebellion, how we felt, at the age of thirteen, on the threshold of adolescence. The questions erupted with great agitation, full of hatred: *Why on earth do we deserve this?* We were alone. We looked with loathing at the young people, pouring day after day to the "promenade" in Leszno Street. We went to see what drew them there. It was a section of the street leading from the Femina Theater, at the corner of Solna Street, to the corner of Tlomackie Street, opposite the Great Synagogue. A relatively quiet area.

Walking along the garden of the Anglican Church (closed, of course) enabled one to see a lawn and trees. Masses of youngsters, aged eleven to twenty, swarmed in the street. Girls, wearing makeup and their hair in sham curls, looking like young prostitutes, with groups of boys following them. The young ones hid behind the older ones. They were wary, because in these gangs "might was right."

Most of the boys were poor, but there were also quite a few from well-to-do families. All of them were afraid of Martin, a terrible, violent fellow. He held sway over the ghetto youth. When he appeared on the promenade, at once there was action. Martin's face was pockmarked, his eyes were clever and cunning, and he would merely hint what was to be done. He was accompanied by servile boys and giggling girls.

We used to look in another direction, because several times they had attacked us, threatening us with drawn pocketknives and grabbing whatever they liked. They mostly got into skirmishes with members of the Zionist Youth Movement who stuck together and were not afraid of fistfights. In the ghetto it was accepted that the end justifies the means. He who is stronger is the winner. They used to steal, popping up suddenly in the dark lanes [the whole ghetto was dark, because of the blackout, and later there was no electricity]. It was the girls who feared them most because there were rumors of rapes.

The schools and clubs were closed, and there was no place for games or sports. Only study groups, costing money, were operating in private houses. The people suffered from poverty and hunger. The parents were on edge, tense and anxious about making a living. The youth ran away into the streets, and there they learned that might is right.

The moral rot seeping down from above, from the corrupt Judenrat and the Jewish police, from those who collaborated with the Gestapo, called the "Thirteenth Police," spread its tentacles to the youth and the children. [The Thirteenth Police was a so-called police unit, commanded by Avraham Gencewich, who had connections with the Germans. In the ghetto, people were afraid of this unit and believed they were Gestapo agents and informers.]

Fortunately, my parents put me down for a "complet"—that is what the underground study groups were called. Teachers, who had taught in secondary schools and Jewish schools before the war, got organized and established proper frameworks for study, following the old official curricula.

Tzelina and I went to the complet of a secondary school. I have forgotten its prewar name. My sister also joined study groups, operating within a network of public kitchens. [The public kitchens operated with the assistance of the Joint, a foundation to help Jewish refugees, funded by contributions from American Jews until 1941. These funds were transferred illegally through neutral countries. Members of the pioneer youth movements participated in the serving of soup, under the aegis of the social self-help organization, which organized activities such as study groups and various youth activities.]

She managed to learn how to read and write. Mother insisted that we go on studying, whatever the conditions, and so remain within an organized group. She always considered our education important. She was ready to put her own needs last, for the sake of the well-being of her little girls.

When we lived in Ciepla Street, there was enough room in the apartment to host my complet twice a week. In our apartment we had Polish literature and language lessons with Miss Weinbrot, and history lessons with Professor Danski. Maybe he was not a real professor, but that is what secondary school teachers were called.

He was a special type of teacher, and I owe him my love of history, my curiosity for the humanities, and the amazing fact that I remember to this day most of the material that I learned at that time: the history of Greece and Rome and the Middle Ages—the seventh- to ninth-grade subject matter.

He limped, used a walking stick, and did not find it easy to climb up to our apartment on the third floor. The payment was minimal, so it was evident that these teachers were working with a deep sense of a mission.

Professor Danski believed that there was some logic underlying all events, so he repeated constantly that Hitler's and Mussolini's fascist regimes would inevitably disappear. They were a temporary phenomenon that had its reasons, he said, for nothing occurs in history without a reason. It is an eruption, like that of a volcano, of the domination of brute, bestial force, recurring after a flowering of civilization and of the human spirit. It will pass, but may return in other times and places. So we must hold out spiritually and physically, for humanity will seek to regain its balance and sanity will prevail.

I think his words influenced us and led us to the encounter with the Hashomer Hatzair Movement, which opened for us a window to young people who believed in national aspirations and led to a life of integrity in the sea of corruption and despair.

"Frankenstein" on the Bridge

I was sitting with Tzelina on the concrete barrier on the corner of Ogrodowa and Zelaznej eating cake. We loved napoleon cakes [kremschnitt] and gradually collected small change to buy a cake and share it. Although neither of us actually suffered from hunger, we longed for something sweet, some kind of candy. We sat there, concentrating with all our senses on the wonderful taste and smell of the cake. We gathered up every crumb with great care—and that was the end of the feast.

That day our feast was especially sweet and well deserved.

We had just returned from the small ghetto where Tzelina lived. We had been to our French lesson at the apartment of Bella, also a student in our complet. I used to love the French lessons, even though the teacher was strict and did not let us speak Polish or translate words into Polish. She taught "French in French" and would say, "Make an effort until you understand."

At first I hated her for it, but soon, having no choice, I began to understand French. Today I am grateful to her because after a year and a half of her lessons I picked up the language and could use it after the war, when I was in Belgium.

We had eaten the cake after an unpleasant and frightening experience. We were still shaken. In order to get from the small ghetto to the large one, we had to cross a huge wooden bridge over Chlodna Street. That street remained in Polish Warsaw, since it was a vital traffic artery. The streetcar, turning into Zelaznej Street and crossing the ghetto in Leszno Street, passed through it. The bridge was always crowded. Masses of people crossed it every day, and it was also fraught with great danger.

Sometimes soldiers of the SS jumped onto it, closed the entrance and exit, and began to search people and kidnap them for forced labor. Those crossing the dangerous bridge were terrified, but there was no choice.

Lately, a German, who was branded "Frankenstein," used to go up onto the bridge. When he got up there, he suddenly opened fire with a gun in all directions. [Frankenstein refers to the book by Mary Shelley, based on an ancient gothic legend.]

When we came to the bridge, we looked around to see if there were any Germans there. We went up quickly, elbowing our way through the crowd. The passersby were nervous and walked as fast as they could. Suddenly shots erupted from somewhere. I didn't understand which side they came from. I continued to run down the steps at top speed. I caught a glimpse of the men shooting. They were standing in the street below, shooting onto the bridge, amusing themselves.

The crowd, in a panic, rushed down, trampling on the weaker people. My heart beat wildly. I lost Tzelina and was straining not to be trampled by the people fleeing. Suddenly I bumped into a child crying. For a second I hesitated. *Would I make it?* I got hold of the child, hugged him, and pushed the running people aside: "Jews, be careful! Don't trample on us!"

The shooting continued and within a few minutes the bridge was deserted. I took the little child to the gate of the nearest house and sat down on the pavement. The child stopped crying and looked at me attentively, in amazement. At that moment I saw a woman running about frantically. It was his mother. I handed the child over to her, and she grabbed him from me and ran on. I remained sitting, waiting for Tzelina. Suddenly the woman came back and blessed me in fluent Yiddish. I was ashamed of not understanding the language, but her intention was clear.

A few minutes later, the bridge filled up again with masses of people, walking in both directions. Suddenly the image of an ants' nest came to my mind. Someone stepped on it, and the ants began to flee in all directions, but soon returned to their work and their usual behavior. So do we. They trample on us, beat us, torment us, and it doesn't take long and we are back doing our own thing.

Maybe that is the secret of the Jewish people's survival throughout the generations. They burned down synagogues, and new ones were built. They expelled us from the town, so we went to another one. They killed, raped, tortured us during pogroms, crusades, the inquisition, and now comes the horrendous rule of the Nazis.

And we shall survive. Some will remain lying on the bridge, shot dead. The others will go on their way. Tenacity, belief in God's protection of His Chosen People—the survival instinct or the will of God?

The bridge that joined the small ghetto to the large one,
above Chlodna Street in Warsaw.

So I sat by the bridge. The people continued to stream past me endlessly between the two ghettos, until Tzelina found me.

Life Becomes Meaningful

Dina Feinmesser signaled to Tzelina and me that we should stay on at her home at the end of the lesson. Dina's mother had been our homeroom teacher before the war, in the fifth grade. Now she made a living for her family by giving private lessons, because Dina's father was an invalid and had lost his job. He had worked in an office, and, of course, there was no work for him in the ghetto. He spent hours sitting in his wheelchair, pale and silent.

Her eyes shining, Dina told us that she had joined the Hashomer Hatzair Movement, and she was given the task of enlisting new members. She invited us to a meeting, which was to take place in the public kitchens, in Nowoliple Street 24, and she told us not to tell our parents.

It was on the fifteenth of February 1941.

I didn't think twice about it. I was eager to meet the youngsters. I used to see them on the promenade, walking along in tightly knit groups. I wondered what was the secret behind their cheerful mood in such hard times.

When we entered the hall, Dina immediately jumped up to welcome us. Like all the others, she was wearing a gray shirt with a blue tie and introduced us to an older girl, maybe eighteen. She smiled pleasantly at us as two dimples brightened up her face, "My name is Rut, and I invite you to sit down next to the girls in my group."

"That's our group leader, Rut Heiman. Like all the other leaders, she is a member of the Tel-Amal troop," Dina whispered to us excitedly.

We sat down in the visitors' rows. There were dozens of boys and girls there. They quickly got into line for the inspection. I watched them with curiosity. I had never been at a scout meeting; my parents were strongly opposed to it. I did not tell them anything about coming here because I felt old enough to decide for myself.

After the lineup, which was impressive, the members of the Movement sat down and began to sing, accompanied by an accordion. They sang with great enthusiasm in a language strange to me—Hebrew. Then slides from the Land of Israel were shown: pioneers, working on the land, from Kibbutz Mishmar Haemek, children in shorts and strange hats, accompanied by nurses wearing babushkas, all of them with fair hair. *Is that what Jews look like?*

The youth leader spoke at length about the "new Jews," about our nation reborn, Jews working on the land, without any pressure from non-Jews and landowners. They are building their own settlements and also guarding them against their hostile neighbors. In the end, dozens of voices shouted the words, "Fear not! Be strong!" expressing firm belief and commitment. For me and for Tzelina, it was a miracle!

We left elated by the experience and the revelation. Is it possible that the real solution to the Jewish people's suffering will be found in the Land of Our Fathers? I had not yet absorbed it fully, but I felt a great change coming over me, as though my eyes had opened to something I had not been aware of. My heart was filled with hope.

We ran home through streets, by now deserted. Soon the curfew would start.

In the Hashomer Hatzair Movement

Our lives changed completely, especially our inner lives. All our energy, time, and interest were invested in expanding our group. Many girls dropped out. Some came to find a way and an aim in life, others out of interest and for fun, but most of them left. Their parents were against their participation in illegal activity because all youth movement activities were illegal in those days.

The more determined ones remained, until there was a well-integrated group of nine girls, guided by Ruth Heiman. The change was also accompanied by a change of name. We received Hebrew names: I was called Lilit, Tzelina became Miriam. Our troop comprised four groups of girls and three of boys.

We became bound by strong, emotional ties. Our group sprang from our revolt against the existing situation. In the course of time, this revolt sought a path and a solution, and a whole ideology began to take shape. We used to meet three times a week in the homes of the members of the group. It was difficult because the apartments were crowded. We used to sit down on the floor in a corner of the room and hold our meeting. We always began with a song. Then Rut would bring up a topic for discussion, a passage from a poem, or some other text.

We talked about the evolvement of various regimes, about the beginnings of capitalism, and the wrongs inflicted on the workers. Sometimes we heard a political lecture; sometimes we learned about revolutions and their causes. We became more aware of what was going on in Soviet Russia, until we understood the concept of socialism.

We spoke about a better future and believed with all our hearts that it would come, and surely we would participate in the building of our Jewish homeland, where social justice would reign. We could see before our eyes the Jews persecuted for hundreds of years and the Jews persecuted in the ghetto— all the injustice the Germans and anti-Semitism were inflicting on us. We sought a solution, as though it depended on us.

Sometimes, when doubt set in, we said to ourselves: maybe it would be better for the Jews to merge into the Christian environment, to become completely assimilated, to give up our uniqueness, our faith, which led to ostracism and caused us such terrible suffering. Let the term *Jew* disappear from the face of the earth. There will only be Polish, French, and German people— nations devoid of religious designation. But then other doubts came to mind: How can we forgo our identity, our struggle for recognition? Shall we choose the path of least resistance and renounce all those Jewish martyrs? That is impossible!

The solution is different: to survive this dreadful war. Then all the Jews left will leave the Diaspora and immigrate to Israel to establish a socialist regime there, respecting the rights of everyone, to create a "new Jew." A worker, free of hate, with equal rights, together with the Arabs living there.

How wonderful it was to feel part of a Movement, intending to lead the nation toward a better future. We were immersed in ideology and felt we were in the vanguard of a nation's reawakening. We were frontline soldiers of a fight for the future of us all. We had extricated ourselves from the swamp of the Diaspora, from the petit bourgeois life most of us had led. We were through with our previous kind of life. Our aim was to save a maximum number of Jews in the ghetto and to help as best we could.

And we did help.

Members of the pioneer youth movements in the ghetto worked in *punkten* [assistance facilities] for refugees and hungry people, and in the public kitchens. We produced many underground newspapers, among them *El-Al*, *Against the Current*, and *Yutchnia*, which provided political news from the front, according to information obtained from the one and only radio available to the Hashomer Hatzair underground [the possession of radios was strictly forbidden, and they all had to be handed over at the beginning of the war]. The radio was kept in a hiding place.

The newspapers were edited and published with great talent and devotion by Shmuel Breslav, one of the older members and leaders of the local branch, who also belonged to the

Movement's leadership in Poland. He was a handsome man, an intellectual, noble-minded and highly active.

We used to get the papers, pass them around by hand, and bring them back to the leaders. I was afraid to show them to my parents because they were greatly opposed to my participation in underground activities. I think the members of the leadership of the Hashomer Hatzair in Poland at the time were Shmuel Breslav, Mira Fuchrer, Tusia Altman, Miriam Heinsdorf, Mordechai Anielewicz, and Yosef Kaplan. We heard secretly that there was a plan to create "groups of five," who would train in the use of weapons—until the time comes. These groups were organized by Shlomo Vinogron.

In 1941 the Hashomer Hatzair Movement operated with tremendous energy. The activities of the Movement were carried out in groups of boys or girls of the same age. A number of groups of the same age made up "a troop," and several troops formed a "nest," a branch of the Movement. Every group and every troop had a name, which was a symbolic expression of the members' aspirations, in the spirit of the times. Some of the troops comprising older members adopted names of the Movement's kibbutzim in the Land of Israel.

We, the young ones from the troops "In Flames" and "On Guard," depended mostly on rumors. We respected and admired the older members of the underground and tried to emulate them. For instance, we heard that some of the older members, who looked Aryan, used to go to the smaller towns on missions from the Movement—among them Tusia Altman, Astrid from the "Merchavia" troop, and members of other movements—"Dror," "Gordonia," and "Akiba."

Those missions were dangerous. They were supplied with false Aryan documents and had to evade the Polish police and the many informers swarming at railway stations. Getting by without the mandatory travel permits, they would reach small Polish towns in order to encourage the members of the Movement, to bring the Movement's newspapers, and to establish a pioneer underground in the towns of the "General Guvernament," that is in Central Poland, occupied by the Germans. They even managed to get to the "Zaglembie" towns in areas annexed by the Third Reich.

At the Lag Ba'omer Festival in 1941, a special meeting of the branch was held to commemorate the Spanish Civil War, and on that occasion our troop "In Flames" was received into the Movement. The troop, consolidated thanks to the hard work of the leaders of the "Tel-Amal" and "Banir" troops, was created while the flames of war were raging and numbered dozens of members aged thirteen to fifteen. The names of the groups in the troop all symbolized fire: Our group was called "Avukot" (Beacons); the names of the other groups were "Zikim" (Sparks), "Lehavot" (Flames), "Shvivim" (Flickers), "Hasneh" (Burning Bush), and "Lamarom" (Rising).

I was excited before that meeting, where all the troops would appear with their leaders, and where the head of the branch, Mordechai Anielewicz, was going to speak.

I remember his words well. They are engraved in my heart, because they showed us the way to confront the desperately hard present. I often recalled those words when I was in Bergen-Belsen; they strengthened me and gave me back my sanity.

He said something like this: "We are in the midst of scum and degradation, and we must fight this filth as a pioneer youth movement. Let us not forget that the hardest struggle is that within us. I mean: We must not get used to the conditions in the ghetto, forced on us by the enemy. He who adapts to them ceases to distinguish between good and evil. He becomes enslaved, body and soul, to the humiliating conditions of life. Whatever happens to you, always remember: Don't yield to this reality. Rebel against it!"

Already at that time, in 1941, two years before the uprising in the ghetto, he began to prepare the youth to think about resistance and how to preserve their human dignity. These were the words of a leader and strategist.

And one of the youth leaders also greeted the troops in warm, unforgettable words: "In these dark and menacing times, young people, our new comrades, are joining us. We'll not welcome them as we used to, by raising the national and the Movement's flags, and with the sound of trumpets of the scout band. At a time when poverty and hunger surround us, and vile creatures in uniform suppress all our thoughts and conscience, let us welcome them with love."

Another meeting of the branch was held that year. It was in October 1941, after the German invasion of the U.S.S.R. That meeting was particularly festive and took place in the Judaica Library next to the Great Synagogue in Tlomackie Street. Many visitors were invited, among them Irena Adamovicz, a Polish friend of the Movement, representing the Polish Scout Movement, and Emanuel Ringelblum, the historian and organizer of "Oneg Shabat," an organization comprising hundreds of volunteers that had made it its aim to document every event in the ghetto and collect every publication, every piece of paper of historical value.

[Irena Adamowicz and her friends from the Polish Scout Movement provided a great deal of assistance to the underground pioneer movements. She was a pious Catholic. She was in close contact with the Polish underground and was later recognized by Israel as a Righteous Gentile.

Emanuel Ringelblum died in the Holocaust, but the archives were saved. They were concealed in iron milk cans and hidden in the ghetto. After the war they were found under the ruins of the ghetto, and they serve as a most important testimony about what happened there and a valuable source for historical research.]

I stood in a row with the members of my group, with Rut, our beloved leader, in front of us. Rut was very excited. She and her friends from the "Tel-Amal" troop were to swear the solemn oath of the older members in front of their leader, Mordechai Anielewicz, member of the "In the Frontline" troop, and head of the central leadership. All the troops prepared a rich artistic program.

I participated in a choir, conducted by Zeev. Aviva prepared sketches with her drama group. I remember that they acted the sketch Bonche Shweik by Y. L. Peretz, which tells the story of a humble Jew who performed many good deeds, but asked nothing for himself. In our wonderful youthful naïveté, all we wanted to do was to give, to help the weak and needy. My hand, holding Miriam's, was damp with excitement. How happy I felt that day that I belonged to a community of people of such caliber, with such high moral values.

Unfortunately, the subsequent events battered us cruelly. That was the last meeting before we finally went underground. Dismal days were awaiting us. Just as Mordechai had foretold.

The Typhus Epidemic

Throughout 1941 a typhus epidemic engulfed the ghetto. The Germans tried to confine it by closing infected houses and disinfecting all the lodgers and their apartments. Under those crowded conditions, it was impossible to preserve cleanliness and rules of sanitation. Piles of dirty snow absorbed the garbage. Children hung around them, looking for frozen potato peelings. In the shelters for refugees the conditions were unbearable. The epidemic affected almost every family in the ghetto. Corpses were taken out of every house day after day. The ghetto hospitals were full to overflowing.

The fleas carrying the disease multiplied endlessly and passed from one person to another through contact in the crowded quarters. I remember Kremlitzka Street, a narrow but important street, connecting Leszno and the small ghetto with the area of Zamenhof and Nalevki Streets, where crowds of people pushed and were pushed around to get through the street as quickly as possible. The middle of the street was taken up by horse-drawn ambulances, rickshaws pulled by bicycles, and handcarts.

Beggars were standing or lying along the walls, their faces were frightening. The children had swollen limbs and eyes narrowed to slits peering out of sunken faces, and gangrene on their naked legs. Some of them had yellow faces and skin like that of old people. They stretched out their hands or lay silent in their despair. Little children gathered together and hugged each other to protect themselves from the cold. The people passed by without looking at them, trying not to care—or maybe they really did not care anymore. Maybe the Germans had destroyed our capacity for compassion and caring for others. Would everyone just care about those closest to them?

That winter my nine-year-old sister suffered from severe pain in her stomach. The doctor came. His unequivocal diagnosis was a serious inflammation of the appendix, and she must be operated on immediately. The child was taken to hospital in great hurry. The operation was successful, but the pain did not stop.

A week later they had to open up her abdomen again, and then they discovered a serious infection—the result of the bad sanitary conditions and lack of appropriate medication. Mirka's life was in danger.

Aunt Biela and her husband, Dr. Ignac Shpak, used their contacts and saw to it that she received special treatment, but she remained a long time in hospital and stayed in bed at home for two more months. Throughout that time the typhus epidemic was at its height, and we were afraid she would catch the disease in the hospital. For a long time she walked with her back bent because of the painful scar.

At that time I made friends with Aliza, a member of my group. The situation at her home was desperate. She did not tell me about it for a long time, but one day she said, "I have nothing to give my two little brothers to eat, only soup from the public kitchen. They cry all the time." With tears in her eyes, she told me about her mother and father who were both ill, and there was no one to help her.

I immediately went home with her to Gensia Street. We climbed a filthy staircase to the second floor. The apartment was freezing cold, but clean. Aliza let me peep into her parents' bedroom. I had known them before. When the war started, they came from Plotzak. Her father had been a carpenter, but there was no work for him in the ghetto. He was an outgoing, likeable person with a sense of humor. Her mother was a housewife. Aliza was the eldest, a responsible girl, her dark eyes tinged with sadness.

"They both have typhus," she whispered.

"What?" I couldn't believe it. "Both of them? And you...are alone with them? Who looks after them?" I was shocked. This fourteen-year-old girl was bearing a burden far too great for her. "Why aren't they in hospital?"

"There was no room, we have no family here. Lilit, you must help me," she pleaded.

But how? I thought about it and decided to ask the help of my aunt who was a nurse. She promised to speak to her superiors, but every bed that became available after someone died was immediately taken. Another day passed. Throughout that day I sat with Aliza at her home. I moistened her father's lips, gave her mother water to drink, and made sure that the little ones did not come close to their parents.

Typhus is highly contagious. If Mother had known that instead of going to my lessons I was looking after typhus patients, she would not have let me come home. I had been exposed to that terrible disease and would have endangered my own family. But I did not think much about it; I acted out of an urge to help my friend. I was worried.

We decided to tell the girls of our group about Aliza's parents. Our troop had a meeting place in a small square in Mylna Street. One could always find friends there in the evening.

I told Rut and the girls what was happening. The girls were in a dilemma. Rut did not want to be the one to decide. "Whoever can help will do so," she said. She, on her part, would look for a way to get them into a hospital. Dina told me she would come, but the other girls disappointed me. We preach mutual help. But when it comes to the test, each one just cares for herself and her family. I was too naïve to realize that sometimes there is no point in futile self-sacrifice that cannot change dire reality.

I heard that, during that disease, there is a critical day, and if a person survives it, he will remain alive. Aliza's father did not overcome the crisis. He died after two days of great suffering. Her mother was hospitalized, thanks to the help of friends from the Movement. Rut had fulfilled her promise. We all followed her state of health closely and collected food for Aliza and the two children, but nothing helped. Her mother also died. Aliza became the head of the family.

Social self-help, an organization with great influence in the ghetto, found places for the two children in an orphanage. The orphanages were filling up constantly. That winter, thousands of people died daily in the ghetto. Skeletons, covered by paper, were lying in the streets. The Pinkiert burial society did not manage to collect them from the homes.

Meetings at the Cemetery

In spring 1941 our group, "Beacons," used to meet in the Jewish cemetery in Okopova Street. What a terrible paradox!

My grandfather and grandmother, Father's parents, were both buried in that old cemetery. In fact, it was the only place in the ghetto where one could find a little greenery. Tall trees cast their shadows over splendid graves of rabbis, writers, and public figures of the last century. Their names and the deeds they performed during their long lives were carved in gold letters on the gravestones and evoked a solemn and exalted aura.

We sat on the gravestones, yet did not sense the ambience of death because the world around us had turned into a huge graveyard. It was the only place in the ghetto where we could hear the birds sing. Wildflowers pushed their way up joyfully between the long-neglected graves. Here I again felt free, and the zest for life burst with intensity from my young body.

Death did not frighten me. I thought, how lucky were these people who had died a natural death after living out their lives to the fullest. Their loved ones accompanied them, most probably weeping bitterly. *Shall I be able to live out my life, or will I vanish like a passing shadow, as a leaf floating down in the fall?*

Not far from us, in the northern part of the cemetery, workers were constantly digging mass graves, into which the naked corpses of men, women, and children were thrown, picked up from the streets. No one accompanied them. They lay in endless rows. My curiosity drew me there. I saw how they poured lime over them and then covered them with another layer of bodies, until the huge grave was filled.

Who will remember them? Who will know their names? Who will avenge their deaths?

These were people—children born and destined to live a long life, respected old men and women, youngsters who had not yet experienced love. They had names, addresses, different color eyes, freckles on the nose, bald heads. They had families, a history, opinions, and feelings. Now they are a silent mass, and no one will know their real names.

The people of Israel!

Sitting on the gravestones, we were able to express our sorrow, our disappointments, the despair each time seizing one of us. Then we joined in supporting each other, doing our best to help.

We spoke about the future. We read poems by Julian Tuvim, Yitzhak Katznelson, the ghetto poet, and Heinrich Heine—poems about the bitter reality, but also about beauty, love, and lofty ideals.

Among us was a beautiful girl called Alma. She had two blond braids, a smooth skin, and looked like a peasant girl, like one of those described by Wolfgang Goethe, the great German poet. She excelled in reading poetry, particularly the protest poems by Tuvim, the Polish poet of Jewish origin, about "Crazy Zoshka," "the little Jew," wandering about from yard to yard, poems telling, in an untranslatable language, in popular jargon and with tremendous power, about the wrongs perpetrated against the poor, the exploitation of workers, the humiliation of women, the degradation of the Jews.

We loved him, we identified with him. We also read poems by Bialik. Alma read beautifully his poem "The City of Slaughter," which expressed the poet's wrath and lament at the pogrom at the beginning of the century in the town of Kishinev, where "the slayer slew, the blossom burst, and it was sunny weather!" The poem "Upon the

Slaughter," with the wonderful lines, quoted here, was written as though for us:

> Heavenly spheres, beg mercy for me!
> If truly G-d dwells in your orbit and round,
> And in your space is His pathway that I have
> not found,
> Then you pray for me!...
> Who cries Revenge! Revenge!—accursed be he!
> Fit vengeance for the spilt blood of a child
> The devil has not yet compiled...

The oppression, which started with pogroms, had become genocide.

"The Grocery"

Our group continued to meet once a week. We still walked in the street in groups, sometimes we even sang. The relations within our group, "Beacons," were very intimate: we were nine girls, attached to each other with heart and souls, and together with us, our much admired leader, Rut. We used to meet in the afternoon in Mylna Street. Miriam was my best friend, but we were all quite devoted to each other, also Aliza, Judit, Bella, Erella, Dina, and Naomi.

As winter approached, we brought our warm clothes to one of the girls' homes to share them. We could not bear one of us having no shoes or coat to wear, nor to ignore signs of hunger in any one of us. Most of us came from middle-class families and somehow managed, but several of the families of our group lived in poverty.

Miriam's parents had a bakery, and they lived well. My parents still had a stock of wool left from before the war, and they were able to produce on their own some woolen or wool-like socks. But we knew that the situation of Dina's family was hard, and at Aliza's home the situation was desperate.

Although we did not talk about it, we came up with the idea of a "grocery" [the name we gave in Hebrew to our collection of food and clothes for needy members]. We would take half of our meals from home and bring it to our daily meeting place where one of us would distribute the food to the girls in need. We did it quietly and tactfully. Eating together in the evening became quite natural.

The "grocery" method aroused harsh opposition from our parents, and I had a lot of problems at home on account of it. We used to get two pieces of bread at every meal. I knew that Mother would not let me take bread from home, so I used to hide one piece of bread deftly under the seat of my chair.

Once Miriam drew me to our regular meeting place in the square. "Have you brought it?" she asked.

"I didn't manage it, Mother caught me," I admitted. "And you?"

"Yes, I have two pieces of bread with sausage. What did your mother say?"

"I got into serious trouble! It was very unpleasant. I put my piece of bread under my seat during the meal while I was eating the other one."

"Your mother sees everything. She saw it, didn't she?"

"You know her, what a sharp tongue she has and how quickly she gets angry. Maybe she was right. She said that she and Father go to great trouble to get food for us, and they can't provide for anyone else, apart from our family. And she added that if we want to survive life in the ghetto and the war, we must only care for ourselves and leave pitying others for better days. I was embarrassed and shamefaced. Father joined in, he only asked, 'Who is it for?'"

"Did you tell the truth?" Miriam asked.

"Yes. I said that the girls in my group are as dear to me as my own family and I know that some of them go hungry. That's why we organized to share and help each other and every evening we bring—those who can—some food collected by one of us, and share out the grocery to those of us in need."

"Oh, your father can understand that."

"Yes, but they were offended because I said that the girls are close to me like my own family. 'What nonsense,' Mother said. 'One changes friends, but your family is always there to provide support and to depend on. You are naïve, my child.'"

"And you won't go on taking food for our grocery?" Miriam asked sadly.

"I will, I will," I promised.

Members of the Movement

Every evening my parents were worried about me, because I always used to come back a short time before the start of the curfew. Nothing was more important to me than my group and the Movement. I was convinced that what we were doing was right and important. Our parents would have to get used to the fact that their children had grown up a great deal and had become independent. We, the members of the Movement, the *Shomrim* [young guards], growing up during the war, were evidently different from other children, growing up before the war. What they had experienced in the course of several years, we had experienced in just one and a half years.

I remember the stories that Rut, our leader, told us about the sessions at the summer camps, wonderful outings in nature, learning scouting, about the hostel in Rymarska Street No. 12, about rows with the "Beitar" youth [a conservative right-wing Jewish youth group]. She showed us photos of a different kind of life, from another planet. How we longed for that wonderful life of the prewar youth movements, how we wanted to be idealists like they were. We felt we were different, as though the Germans had killed some kind of innocence within us, and we would never be able to regain peace of mind and trust people. Our worldview was forged by our personal experiences; therefore, our opinions were uncompromising, and we were serious about everything.

It was really a beautiful period in our lives, even a happy one. I felt involved in actions for the sake of noble goals. Each one of us had an opportunity to become active and exploit our talents. Rut urged us to read, think, and fulfill our potential.

Rut Heiman had come to Warsaw with her parents from Lodz when the war started. Her father was a secondary school teacher and managed to get a job in the ghetto, teaching in one of the underground secondary schools. Rut had joined the Movement before the war and belonged to the "Tel-Amal" troop. Members of that troop had participated in a youth leaders' seminar in May 1940, and many of them were our leaders. Those wonderful people! All of them died. I will also tell their story.

I can see Rut before me now: dark, her eyes black and her lips a little thick, but her smile pleasant and welcoming. We loved and admired her, as only teenagers can. Rut was also assertive and knew, with empathy and understanding, how to detect the weak points in each one of us.

In one of my many talks with her, she said, "Lilit, you've completely immersed yourself in the Movement's activities and you are doing a lot. It's fine, but don't forget to reflect about things, to fully grasp what you hear, to examine critically. The turmoil makes one forget the essential…"

"Rut," I reacted in surprise, "what is essential, if not working for something, devoting oneself wholeheartedly to something one believes in?"

"I find it difficult to tell you what is essential. I am also still searching; but I think it's good to look inward, also to listen to the criticism of those around you, to reflect about things. In this way you will be inwardly in harmony with your actions."

I did not fully understand what she meant, I even felt a little offended. Only later, when I was left alone, without the support of Rut and Mira, did I grasp it.

We also admired Mira Fuchrer. I can see her now, with an aura of secrecy around her. We knew she was the friend of Mordechai Anielewicz, the head of the Movement. There was even gossip that they lived together in Leszno Street. They both belonged to the troop called "In the Frontline."

We heard that, when the war started, most of the older members left Warsaw and went east. They wandered about in groups and sought a way to cross frontiers to freedom and immigrate to the Land of Israel. Some of them were caught by the Germans, but most of them ended up in Vilna, the city that had become the capital of independent Lithuania.

Thus the Movement in Warsaw was left without its leaders, which is why Tosia Altman, Mira, and Mordechai returned.

Later, Aryeh Vilner and Shmuel Breslav also came back. Hundreds of members of the Movement gathered in Vilna. What happened to them after the Germans had occupied it?

Mira was small. She had short brown hair, full lips, and her voice was always hoarse. Her high cheekbones gave her a severe and somewhat Asian look, and her smile was charming. She loved to laugh! She used to sit among us and listen. In the end, when she spoke, her words sounded clear. In winter she used to wear a short sheepskin coat, high boots (that was the fashion), and a blue beret.

She radiated authority and total devotion to the Movement. That is how I imagined the people of Narodnaya Volya, Russian revolutionaries from wealthy families in the nineteenth century, about whom we heard stories at the meetings of the Movement.

We listened to Mira with great interest. What she said was logical, and her analysis and assessment of the general and political situation seemed to me to be correct and concisely expressed. Later, in the intervals between the *aktzien,* I met her in the apartment of the Movement's den, disguised in preparation for going out of the ghetto on a mission to the Aryan side. [*Aktzien* were the times the Nazis stormed the ghetto and killed, raped, and deported inhabitants.] We laughed at the way she looked, with her belongings rolled up. How she loved to laugh.

Mordechai urged us to learn Hebrew. He knew Hebrew well, and I sometimes heard him speak Hebrew to Shmuel Breslav. At that time learning Hebrew called for a great deal of faith in the future. Mordechai had a special status: He was both head of our den and of the top leadership of all the Polish cities.

I can see him now, and I shall never forget him: tall and graceful, but looking strong, his back straight, a wild lock of light brown hair falling to the right of his forehead, his eyes gray, his chin determined, and his lips thin. I mostly remember him looking serious, but when he smiled, he was attractive. He was handsome and did not look typically Jewish.

I did not see him often, but we took his political-ideological articles in the Movement's newspapers quite seriously. He was the leader of the "Tel-Amal" troop, and they were our leaders.

Tadek [Tuvia Sheingut] was also our leader. I remember him coming in his working clothes (he worked as a locksmith) and lecturing about astronomy. After a hard day's work, he would travel with us to distant worlds. We loved him. To us he looked like one of the idealistic Russian revolutionaries of the previous century. He was brave, which became clear later when he acted on behalf of the Jewish Fighting Organization on the Aryan side, in creating ties with the Polish underground. Endangering himself greatly, he prepared apartments to hide

Mira Fuchrer, the friend of Mordechai Anielewicz (photo taken before the war).

in when the opportunity arose and tried to procure weapons for the fighters.

Aviva, lively, energetic, and with great vitality, organized a drama club, apart from leading groups. Yardena was serious, introverted, but affectionate and had understanding for our pranks. Shoshana Vartman was a good-looking and intelligent girl. Slim with clear light-blue eyes and golden curls framing her fine face.

When Mira stopped leading our troop because she was busy in other ways, Shoshana took her place. I remember her as a supportive, trustworthy person. During the *aktzien*, the two girls, Aviva and Shoshana, left the ghetto, trying to find their way to the partisans. They were caught and sent to Treblinka.

All of them were active in the Jewish Fighting Organization.

Two sketches, drawn by the author from memory in 1951 of Mordechai Anielewicz (right), head of the resistance movement, and Rut Heiman (left), the author's troop leader.

Distributing Letters

All Jewish men had to work, but many evaded it. The men reported for work on receiving the order from the Judenrat, or were caught in the street and sent to forced labor camps. They would return after a few months, exhausted, hungry, and sick. The wealthier ones were able to avoid this ordeal by paying money.

We, the "scouts," boys and girls aged fourteen to sixteen, were enlisted for various kinds of voluntary work. Among other jobs, we had to distribute letters sent by the people in forced labor camps. The Jewish police made this exchange possible, and surely benefited from it. The people reporting for work came mostly from among the many refugees who came to the ghetto or were thrown into it from the towns and villages in the vicinity. They lived in centers [called *punkt*], former public institutions, turned into halls; the conditions there were unbearable. I can never forget the scenes I saw when I came to these places to distribute the letters to the people staying there.

Healthy and sick people, whole families, were crowded together on mattresses. The few belongings they had brought with them were lying beside them on the floor. Most of them were swollen with hunger, hardly able to lift their heads. A spark of joy flickered across the woman's face when I handed her a letter from her son. She put out an emaciated hand and asked me to read the letter to her. She did not have the strength to lift herself up, and she cried silently.

I asked her where she came from. Instead of replying, suddenly her eyes lit up. She drew me to her with a sudden movement and said, "You are a good girl. Take my children with you. You have good clothes, you are sure to have some food too. Take them." She continued in Yiddish, "Here are my children, Moishele and Leah."

I looked around, but I did not see any children. "Where are they?" I asked, not understanding at all.

"They are in the street, begging. Take them to your home, give them food, they are dying, they are dying." The woman began to weep and fell back on the mattress.

I had goose bumps all over me. Ariela, who was with me, came up to see what was happening. She pulled me away from there. I was trembling.

Where are the children? Is she seeing things? Are they really in the street, or are they already dead? I did not have the strength to cope with this situation. It was apparently too much for me, at my age. I walked along the street with Ariela and wept. On that day I could not continue with my task. I went home.

The Concert

In winter we were going to celebrate the anniversary of the creation of our troop. It was a great occasion, so we prepared for it a long time. One of the families placed a room at our disposal for one night. We spread out mattresses and rugs on the floor, and after a long soul-searching session late into the night, all the girls in our group stayed the night together in that room.

Loud peals of laughter came from the room as we gave each other amusing presents. We ate sweets that we had been collecting diligently over a long time. We enjoyed ourselves like little children, and we really did forget the ghetto and all the horrors around us. We behaved naturally: teenage girls, who had grown up prematurely.

On the next day we had an elaborate program. After doing some morning exercises and eating breakfast together, we went for a walk. It was Sabbath and the streets were quiet. A great deal of snow covered everything and sparkled in the winter sun. The sky was blue and the air pure and cold. Fresh snow covered the piles of trash and dirt. No one removed it, but the road was clear. Only here and there, corpses were lying, covered by newspapers, but we did not want to look at them.

We had tickets to a concert of the ghetto philharmonic orchestra, to be held at the Femina Theater. It was my first concert. I do not remember the name of the work they played; that was not important. I sat there, arm in arm with Miriam, weeping. I was so moved. She pressed my hand, showing me she felt the same.

At the end of the concert, suddenly, the sounds of "Kol Nidrei" by Bloch. Loud weeping resounded in the hall. The audience moved restlessly. And in spite of all the sorrow, I felt that there was a great deal of beauty and vitality in the world. I felt that I wanted to live; I would use all my strength to survive—*überleben*—to get through the bad times. To survive at all cost.

An important event occurred in the troop: a literary trial about the book by Paniat Istrati on the revolt of the Haiduks, about the uprising of a people oppressed by a more powerful one during the Ottoman occupation in Romania. The subject was topical, and we all became engrossed in it. We held a small-scale trial with a prosecution and defense, and we philosophized about it three whole days.

On that occasion I got to know Yaakov better. He belonged to the "Burning Bush" troop. He was a harsh, forceful prosecutor;

he accused the strong nation of shameful use of its power. All the rage accumulated within him against the Germans, the police, and the Judenrat was apparently unleashed through this trial. I liked him, and from then on we used to meet sometimes and go for walks together.

After the incident of my stealing the bread, I had another one with my parents connected to my "craze about the Movement." I tried to explain to them how important it was that in the ghetto of all places there should be pioneer youth movements and that our future as a people—if we survive—is in an independent Jewish state in Palestine.

"Look what the Diaspora has brought upon us! A Jew is perceived as a worthless creature, no enlightened country defends us or protests vigorously against what is happening here! No one cares," I said.

Father agreed with the spirit of my assertions, but contended that the members of Hashomer Hatzair were communists, and communists lie. They pretend to love others, but they rob people of their property. Neither of us was able to persuade the other with the arguments we put forward.

Another important event took place in our troop: an exhibition. Each group prepared exhibits describing values we believed in. Since I was active in the cultural committee, in preparing the decorations and in the choir, I was tremendously busy. At that time my parents found a better apartment nearby—two rooms in Nowolipki Street—on a street parallel to ours. We again packed everything and dragged it there, this time without any help.

The festive opening of the exhibition was held on the day we moved to the other apartment. We were all to come wearing white shirts. And my parents had given me the task of guarding the pile of things in the yard while they were gradually dragging them up to the second floor. I did not dare tell them I had to go off. I was hoping the pile would be cleared in time.

I waited. Five more minutes. *I'll be late—never mind! But not to take part in the choir? What's going to happen? How can I leave the things in the yard while my parents are upstairs? It's irresponsible. Why on earth are they so slow? How can I explain to them that I must go? I can't disappoint my friends, I've committed myself.* In the end I did not have the courage and I ran off. I left our property unguarded.

For years Mother reminded me of my transgression. Looking back, I can see she was right, but at that time it was the only thing I could do.

Warnings before Disaster Struck

The winter of 1942 was hard. Famine increased and so did the deaths in its wake. We stayed in bed for hours, trying in vain to keep warm. The evenings were dark, there was no lighting. News came of German victories both in the east and in the west. News of mass deportations of Jews from the smaller towns preyed on our minds.

A Jew in rags, called Rubinstein, was running around in the streets of the ghetto pretending to be crazy (or he may have really gone mad), and in humorous rhymes prophesied that evil would strike the ghetto elite. People crowded around him and listened, enjoying the show.

He shouted, *"Alle gleich, alle gleich,"* meaning all are equal (in death before God). He mocked "the important people" of the Judenrat, the great burial society Pinkiert, and asserted that only three people would survive the war: Cherniakov [the head of the Judenrat], Pinkiert, and he himself. Rubinstein's prophecy about evil was fulfilled, but none of the three survived.

It was dangerous to pass by the gates of the ghetto. Sometimes shots were heard from there. Soldiers fired into the crowds. That was the time when news first came from the Vilna ghetto. Messengers were sent to Warsaw to tell what was happening there.

I can remember well that gray November evening in the hostel at the branch in Nalevki Street 23. A wooden partition separated the branch center, located in one half of the apartment, from the hostel of the kibbutz *Ma'apilim* [the term denoting illegal immigrants to Palestine]. It had a dining room and also a little room where the meetings of the central command were held. The newspapers were also edited there and maybe the radio was there too.

The "Gal-on" group, which had come into the hostel, was new, its members lived together as a commune, in the guise of a *punkt* for refugees, run by the welfare authority. Many of the members of the Movement lived in poverty and hunger. Gradually they overcame their shyness and came to the kitchen of the center, where they received a thin but warm soup. But the center was decorated with drawings and the branch library was also there.

One day we were summoned to a meeting of the troop at the center to meet a messenger who had arrived from the Vilna ghetto. We all sat on the floor facing a young woman of about twenty-two, whose hair was already sprinkled with gray. In the twilight she looked beautiful and impressive, yet her eyes were devoid of emotion as she spoke.

"It was a ghastly night. We members of Hashomer Hatzair were hiding together in one apartment. We listened to the noises in the street. German trucks stopped, and we heard shouting, firing, heartbreaking weeping. That's how they emptied street after street. Where did they take them? To a forest in the vicinity, Ponar—apparently a scene of mass murder.

"Thousands of Jews have already been taken there. There are witnesses who escaped from the trench and said that they make men, women, and children stand in rows beside the trench and they shoot them. We are living in constant fear. I came here to tell you and warn you. We have reliable information about the liquidation of ghettos throughout eastern Poland, in the Ukraine, and in Lithuania.

"We've decided to defend ourselves. The youth remaining in the ghetto have decided not to go like sheep to the slaughter. Half of us will stay in the ghetto, and the rest will try to find a way to reach the partisans. Abba Kovner has written a proclamation calling on Jews to fight back, calling for armed resistance against the Nazis: We shall not go like sheep to the slaughter! We've decided that when our end comes, we shall not die without defending ourselves. And if we have no more weapons, we'll spit in their faces; at least we'll show them our contempt, before we die. But our deeds shall not be forgotten."

She spoke fluently, but sometimes her voice broke down and an oppressive silence fell. We were in shock. It was hard to believe. *Can they be murdering women and children?*

We walked back together. Darkness fell and Kremlitzka Street was crowded with people hurrying home before the curfew. Many had a phosphorescent pin stuck in their clothes to provide a little light and help them make their way through the crowd.

I was thinking: *Is that what awaits us?* They can't kill innocent people just like that. The world will hear about it and cry out against it. The Jews in America and in Palestine won't let it happen. *Is that really so?* Time will tell and history will hold accountable.

The House in Mila Street

At that time I gave up my studies at the complet and together with Miriam we went to learn with Tzameret Vahenheuser of the "Burning Bush" troop, after Rut, our leader, had asked us if we were willing to study with Tzameret and so help her financially. She and her mother were in a difficult situation. Rut told us great things about Tzameret: She was well educated and intelligent; before the war she had studied at the university with the Movement's support. She had led the troop "In the Frontline," to which Mordechai, Mira, Shmuel, and other important members belonged.

The Movement was generally opposed to higher education in the Diaspora and demanded that members who had completed secondary school join the training courses and immigrate to the Land of Israel, fulfilling their commitment to Zionism. In her case an exception had been made because of her failing health, but also on account of her intelligence, so she did not leave together with her friends. Now she was suffering from hunger.

Miriam and I agreed immediately. How could we object? Our parents also agreed, so one winter day in 1942, I came to the house in Mila Street. On entering the yard, I was immediately overwhelmed by a horrible smell. The yard was flooded with sewage, flowing straight down from the windows and freezing on the ground. In the middle was a mountain of trash and filth that had never been removed and was, of course, frozen.

I stood there, unable to believe my eyes. I looked up at the three-story building, similar to many others around there. Many windows had no windowpanes and were stuffed with rags. I entered the house with great hesitation. It was unbelievable; many stairs were missing. Every second or third step had been removed. Here and there the banisters were also missing. The wooden stairs had been torn out and burned to provide a little warmth. I could hardly drag myself up to the first floor.

Another surprise awaited me there: The door was not locked at all; there was nothing to steal. I knocked, but no one answered. The room was freezing cold and the air was stifling, smelling of frozen fetid beet. It was empty, without any furniture. Along the wall were two straw mattresses with two thin children with swollen faces and limbs lying on them, hugging each other to get a little warmer. I had seen many like them in the streets. *God, what are you doing to these children?*

I bent down to them, weeping. The older child was about eight, his face was swollen with hunger, and only his eyes, like narrow slits, showed he was reacting. I was afraid to ask them about their parents. From that day on, whenever we came to Tzameret, we brought them some food. This time with my mother's consent.

Starving, dying children on a Warsaw Ghetto street.

In the other, larger room, Tzameret lived with her mother. It was clean and poverty was not so blatant. Tzameret was small and thin. Through her black-rimmed glasses her dark eyes had a penetrating look, which made her resemble a bird. I stood motionless, still overwhelmed by my impression of the house and the children. She understood immediately and gently invited me to sit down. I waited for Miriam to help me out of my confusion.

Miriam came late. She was pale. I knew my friend well and how sensitive she was. She will not want to come here again.

But Tzameret could read our thoughts. She said, "You are trying to come to terms with what you have seen, aren't you? It's terrible to see children who were left alone. Their father died of typhus and now their mother is lying ill in hospital. It's hard to see and hard to live like that. Sometimes one wants to lie down and never wake up again—to surrender to the will of the Germans. That's what they want. That in the end we die without being killed by them. That's why they created the ghetto. Not to let us live on, but to see to it that we die like dogs from fear, hunger, and disease. Are we going to fulfill their expectations? We are human beings and as such we have a choice, each one of us. You may not learn a lot of mathematics or French from me, but I'll teach you how to choose and to remain human beings under the conditions in this house."

Her words stunned me. They were new to me, daring and defiant. I mumbled that I had to think about what she had said. I wanted to go out with Miriam and talk it over with her, but Miriam was captivated by the charisma of this tiny woman. She was ready to stay.

So we went on learning from her how to preserve our human dignity even in a filthy dunghill. Tzameret presented us with problems and asked us to reflect on them deeply and seek solutions. She knew well what goes on in the souls of adolescents. Sometimes I felt exposed to her penetrating look, revealing my thoughts and feelings.

Tzameret was pessimistic and realistic. She asserted that the Jews of Warsaw would come to the same bitter end as the Jews of the other Polish towns. We smiled in disbelief. Although rumors and bad news came in constantly, and there were even witnesses and survivors from Chelmno and Belzetz who spoke about gas chambers, the mind could not grasp it and the soul refused to believe it.

I sometimes wonder at the lucidity and logic of her thinking, in spite of the miserable conditions under which she lived. We studied with her until the deportation—the big *aktzia*. We did not know that her predictions would come true so soon.

Tzameret was writing a diary. The leadership decided to find a hiding place for her on the Aryan side; the members hoped that this would enable her to survive the war and tell the world what we had suffered. But fate dealt with her as cruelly as with all the others. She was caught on the Polish side through informers, arrested, and executed.

My wise teacher. I shall always remember you.

The Last Meeting of the Troop

On the eighteenth of April, suddenly there was slaughter in the ghetto. Thunderous knocking on the gate of the building, and shouts of *Aufmachen!* [open] woke us up with a start. We were seized with fear.

We dressed quickly, to be prepared for anything. A few minutes passed—maybe just seconds—during which the whole building with all the hundreds of residents froze in paralyzing dread. I knew that the next moment the gate would break under the pressure of our persecutors, and they would burst in, yelling wildly.

My little sister, Mirka, was shaking all over, but I, surprisingly, felt completely in control. The Germans crossed our yard, screaming and firing, and entered the third yard. From there we heard voices pleading and loud shouting, as though they were dragging people out by force. Then there was silence. And soon the house was again humming like a beehive. Stamping of feet resounded on the staircase. What had happened?

It turned out the German soldiers had broken into the home of the Neuman family and dragged out the father. Next morning they found his body in front of the house. This time the Germans went straight to his apartment, with a list of names. Among those killed there were apparently some of the rich people of the ghetto—among them the owners of bakeries and others who were assisting the underground and supporting various illegal activities.

That night the Germans dragged dozens of people in their night clothing from their homes, killed them, and left their bodies in the street. Even though there was no connection among those killed, it was a clear message and a warning.

Next day was the Sabbath. Our group was to have a meeting at ten o'clock, as usual. It was a spring day and the sun's rays looked strange. There was blood and fear in the streets. The sun darted over the sea of garbage piled up in the yards, penetrated into the miserable lodgings, and smiled at the tired people. No one smiled back.

After that pogrom, the order was given to destroy any material connected to the Movement, even the records of the groups. We were forbidden to meet in the streets of the ghetto or even to walk along in small groups. Our group was forbidden to meet in the small square in Mylna Street, and we regretted it greatly. We did not meet Mordechai Anielewicz again.

The time had come to part.

The members of the troop and I did not know about the decision to disperse the troops. We were called to the cellar. Dim candlelight flickered in the cellar, and members of the troop took turns in guarding the area around the house in

Gensia Street. We sat crowded on the dirty floor. We, the girls of the "Beacons" group, hugged each other anxiously. A sense of danger and stifled fear of the unknown choked me.

My friends Judit, Miriam, Aliza, and Alma looked dejected. Who knows what is happening and what is going to happen. It did not occur to anyone to sing, as we always used to do at our meetings. It was suffocating in the cellar, in the ghetto, within us—everywhere.

We sat silently for a while, and then we heard Mira's quiet, hoarse voice: "Now we may experience moments of crisis in our lives and we have to part and disperse the troop."

The silence was as heavy as a steamroller. Mira's voice rose and fell, "We must prepare for a painful parting. The situation requires it. Remember, our goal is always, until the last minute—if it comes—to remain *Shomrim,* to preserve our dignity as human beings. We must not degenerate into moral filth. We shall not scorn the ideals that have been instilled in us. We shall preserve courageously our aspirations as free human beings. We shall not fail, nor debase ourselves in the face of our enemy who seeks our death. We may not see each other again. Remember!"

Here her voice rose with razor-sharp determination: "It is not so hard to behave as a human being when you can count on others, when you have friends around you to support you. Your real test will come when you remain alone, all alone, to face the German enemy. Remember the words of the song, sung by our brothers far away in the Land of Israel, during the riots: 'All of us enlisted to the end of our days, only death will release us from the ranks.'"

No one dared to break the silence after this severe blow. We tried to grasp what had been said. We had not yet experienced painful partings during our young lives. They still lay ahead. The critical hour came in two months. Tzameret's gloomy predictions were about to come true.

We dispersed slowly, each one going her own way. But for some reason, at the corner of Zamenhof Street, we met once more, several girls from our group, in order to talk over together what we had heard and what we were to do. We refused to part. The deep friendship of the girls of our group, our growing up together, had created a bond that could not be severed. We wept quietly.

Part II

The Struggle for
Life and Honor

4 | THE GREAT
    DEPORTATION

Excerpts from My Diary

7th July 1942–12th September 1942

Czerniakov, the head of the Judenrat, has committed suicide:
He poisoned himself. The ghetto is in turmoil. They say he
did not want to sign orders presented to him by the Gestapo.
The ghetto is permeated by anxiety, but has also breathed a sigh
of relief. Everyone hated him. Pity we Jews did not get rid of him
ourselves. People are standing in front of the notices, cursing him
and all the collaborators, all the traitors. But there is premonition
within: Why did he kill himself, what was the terrible thing
demanded of him? People argue, but no one dares to voice
the self-evident conjecture. And maybe this hated person was
actually to be pitied and respected? People start talking about it.

In all the streets of the ghetto they've put up large notices
in German. A proclamation on behalf of the German Reich
states that all inhabitants of the Jewish quarter in the city of
Warsaw are to be transferred eastward, to work camps. The
Aussiedlung will be carried out according to plan: six thousand
people every day. Every person is permitted to take 5–10

kilograms [nearly 20 pounds] of belongings and valuables. The responsibility for the execution of the decree is delegated to the Judenrat and the Jewish police, by order of the SS. Exempt will be the people employed by the authorities—the police, Judenrat, and hospital employees, as well as all those working in "shops" for the Germans.

I stood in the crowd and read the notice again and again. I didn't get the full meaning. People were arguing as though they had gone crazy, trying to understand how many will be expelled. All the inhabitants of the ghetto are out in the streets, asking each other, trying to grasp the significance of the orders.

And it did happen.

In the evening I ran to the Hashomer Hatzair branch in Nalevki Street 23. Many members were coming and going. And then the orders arrived from the leadership: The branch in Nalevki Street will be the information center. Liaisons will be chosen from each troop, whose task will be to keep constantly in contact with the branch. Arie Gzybowski, our man in the Jewish police, will provide early information about the streets and houses from which the people will be expelled. Members of the movements will be warned. And the main thing is to escape expulsion, to hide, not to get caught!

People were walking around at their wits' end, as though they had gone mad. They wandered about in the streets, searching for a way out. In the meantime, the managers of the "shops," the workshops working for the Germans, were issuing new work cards. These *Ausweise* become a matter of life and death. Whoever had "protection"—acquaintances close to the "shop" managers—had a chance to buy such a document for money and jewels.

At home everyone was running about. They were consulting each other, including me. Father went out to look for acquaintances, industrialists from the wool branch like him, in order to obtain entry into one of the "shops" under German patronage issuing the documents. He came back with good news. We were to transfer three machines to a building in Smochia Street. Mr. Grunstock promised him that a Polish acquaintance would organize it all. He had contacts with Germans dealing with the provision of uniforms for the German army. Apparently, for the moment we'd be able to get a temporary work card to protect us. We decided to go and stay the night there, in the hope that it would be safer.

This step was preceded by a heated argument. In our Novolipie apartment, we didn't get to know the neighbors and had no hiding place. Father wanted to move to the "shop," lock the apartment, and take only the things we needed most.

Mother said that there was no knowing the Germans' intentions, maybe after a few thousand refugees had been expelled, the rest will stay. Surely it's impossible to transfer 350,000 people to camps in the east. The expulsion must at some stage come to an end. And in the meantime they'd rob the apartment and we'd have nothing left.

On that same day we slept at the shop, they descended on our street and began to pull people out of their apartments by force. In the evening I returned to the apartment with my father, and we found only a few of our neighbors. The building looked as though there had been a pogrom. The neighbors told us that they had given the Jewish policemen money and jewels, and in return they were allowed to stay at home. The others were pushed onto carts and taken to assembly points.

During the first days they took the refugees from the *punkten* and prisons, and also poor people lying about in the streets, and patients in hospitals. Only those in hiding remained in the houses. The Germans published a declaration that all those who come on their own to the *Umschlagplatz*, the assembly point at the railway station, would get three kilograms of bread and one kilogram of jam. Quite a lot of people gave in, they had no strength left.

On the next day we put together clothes, some bed linen, and kitchen utensils and stuffed them into backpacks. Then we put on our winter coats and moved to the "shop." Mother wanted to lock the apartment, but her hand shook and she did not manage to get the key into the lock.

"Help me, Liza," she said. I did. Mirka's face was red from weeping. Just like in the poem by Szlengel: from street to street we wander, but each time with fewer belongings.

> ...Then from the sheds to Ostrovska Street
> Through the Street of the Jews
> Without bundles or chattels
> Furniture or stools,
> No carpets, no teapots,
> No plates, no vases
> Holding one suitcase
> A warm shawl...that's all,
> A bottle of water
> A bag on the shoulder
> Herds trampling on belongings
> Walking through the streets at night.
> No need for anything now
> Straight on and on in fives
> Striding through the streets.

I am writing on the few pages I brought with me in my backpack from the apartment. [The original pages were written in Polish and translated into Hebrew and later into English for this book.] We haven't gone back there since we left it. We are afraid to leave the "shop."

Father installed three knitting machines, to pretend we were working for the Germans. The manager is trying to get us some work, but everyone is too preoccupied. All the people are worrying about their families, scattered in the two ghettos, trying to get some news. The main thing is that our parents have an *Ausweis* recognized by the police and the Germans. We have no idea where Aunt Bjela and her husband are, and also Father's brothers and sisters. I am lucky that the "shop" is very near to the Hashomer branch.

The commotion there was great. I looked for Rut and suggested to her that she should work in our "shop" after speaking about it to Father. She prefers to stay with her family in Leszno Street. And what is going on at the branch? They are sending a number of emissaries to the Aryan side. I hear names like Tosia Altman, Vyga, Astrid, Tuvia Scheingut (Tadek); they are to go off. In fact, Tosia has long since left; my leader is also gone. He went even before the *aktzia* to Czenstochowa and Bendzin to an area annexed to the Reich, called Zaglembie.

At last I've found Dov from my own troop. We went together to Merdek (Mordechai Grobas) and asked to become liaisons. "We want to help, do whatever is needed."

"Kids, for the time being, go on coming here twice a day—if you can—but be careful of searches. Most of us have no *Ausweis*. If they catch us, we'll have to fight back, but we still have no weapons. So run away, okay? Keep in touch with members of your troop, try to find them and enlist them."

"But where are they taking those that are expelled?" I asked.

"Until now no one knows; surely not to other cities. Maybe to camps…" He seemed restless, waved to us, and went off quickly.

"Dov, where shall we find other members of the troop?"

At that moment, Alma, David, and Shoshana appeared, happy to see us. We decided we would survive together, come there every day, keep in contact with Merdek and the other leaders, and look for more and more members.

Distribution of Leaflets

On one of those days when I don't remember if I ate or slept at all, I got to know, during a hurried visit to the branch, that I was to participate in an important activity. At six o'clock in the evening, after working hours, I reported to the attic of one of the houses, trembling all over with excitement. I told my parents that I was going to the branch and promised to return soon. Mother's stare of disbelief followed me. She knew it wasn't true, but by now she had lost control over me.

We gathered there, about ten boys and girls, most of us from the younger troops. No one knew why we had come. I whispered with Lilit from the "Sarid" troop, a year older than I. When Merdek arrived, I calmed down. I loved and admired him.

He brought many pages, printed on a typewriter. The leaflets were signed by the Jewish Fighting Organization (Z.O.B.). They warned the Jews to avoid being sent away at all cost by escaping, by jumping from the railway coaches—for the destination is death, not a camp to live in. "The Nazi beasts want to exterminate all European Jews. That is the bitter truth. Do not give in! Fight them in any way you can!"

At last the voice of the underground was heard. At last the youth wants to rebel, to fight them. I felt happy that I had the chance to distribute this leaflet, but Merdek warned us: "You must go in pairs, push the paper under apartment doors or into mailboxes, and run. People may react negatively and accuse you of provocation and of wicked impudence. Run off at once!"

We were aware of the greatness of the hour. I went with Lilit to Gensia Street, the side with odd numbers. Crowds of people were running around at the time, in search of a hiding place for the following days.

We mounted the stairs quickly. We knocked on the doors; people opened them, took the leaflet, and read it. Some shouted at us and berated us, others responded more kindly: "You good children, why are you adding to our worries and causing unnecessary panic?"

We managed to go through several houses, when we noticed at a distance, coming from the direction of Zamenhof Street, German cars followed by trucks. Within minutes, after a turmoil, the street was empty: *Blockada*. The *aktzia*—grabbing Jews for expulsion, had begun. [With a blockage, the Germans and their helpers encircled the street in order to hunt for people there.]

We ran with the fleeing crowd, holding the packet tight. We mustn't fall down! We mustn't fail! Faster, faster! But where to? We were far away from any hiding place, from our families. *Is that it? That's where they'll catch me? And it will be the end of me.* That's what went through my mind as I heard the whistling of the Jewish police and the shooting of the Ukrainians behind me, those despicable collaborators.

My heart beat loudly. The house we dashed into was apparently a children's hostel or orphanage. The children began to descend the stairs, accompanied by their educators and nurses, in order to gather in rows, frightened to death. Some were crying, some holding each other by the hand. The staircase was bare. There was nowhere to hide. Other people were walking about in the corridors, looking for somewhere to hide.

A woman was shouting hysterically that she had left her little children alone at home, in another street. Someone said that today was a terrible day because they took lots of people from the little ghetto and destroyed fake workshops, those without authentic licenses.

What can we do? Lilit pulled me toward a large wooden crate at the end of the corridor. "We've got to save the leaflets, and they mustn't catch us with them! They'll kill us on the spot."

I refused to get rid of them. The shouting in the street approached. They may enter the gate any minute. It turns out that the crate was full of clothes ready to go to the laundry. Like mad, we threw the clothes out, got inside and covered ourselves up with rags. How long did we stay inside? I'll never know; the stench and lack of air apparently caused us to faint.

It was good to be in a stupor, but a thought flashed through my mind: *Mother doesn't know anything. And she'll never know how she lost me. Goodbye, my family, forgive me for going away—I had to.*

Suddenly there was complete silence. We touched each other and began to peep outside. It was quiet. The director spoke to the freezing children standing on the stairs, "Children, God helped us. Let us thank him for saving us; they passed us by."

We went out without delay and continued to distribute the leaflets along the street that was slowly waking up. When I returned to my parents, it was already dusk. I opened the door quietly. When they saw me, my sister clung to me.

"Liza, we thought you'd never come back. Where were you?"

I stood still. I saw that Mother was very angry. Suddenly she said: "You can go back to where you were, you don't need us." She got up, took hold of my arm and pulled me out onto the steps. "You have no feelings. You have to learn a lesson!"

I sat on the stairs, sorry for them. Had they known what I had experienced, they wouldn't have thrown me out like that. But I didn't sit there for long. Behind the door I heard voices, quarreling. Suddenly Father appeared, my kind, compassionate father, and embraced me hard. I sensed how sorry he was as I buried my head in his shoulder and wept. And we entered, hugging each other.

During the day we remained in the "shop" without doing anything there. It's a mock "shop." We know that our days here are numbered, but during the first few days it has given us a sense of safety.

One morning when we came "to work," we found several people there. It turned out that the German police had been there on the previous night and had taken away the manager of the "shop" and his family and all those sleeping there. The

Germans threw away the *Ausweise* with contempt; they became worthless with a wave of the hand. We decided to get out then and there. But what was going to happen to the machines protecting us?

Father was in despair. Even though the "shop" was worthless, he wanted to stay there. Without the machines it was impossible to be accepted into another "shop." Mother went to the policeman and tried to bribe him. Apparently she gave him a gold ring. He turned around at once and Mother motioned to us to go inside. We succeeded in entering the building, taking out one machine and carrying it into the house across the street.

Luckily the house was already empty, up for grabs. All the tenants had been expelled or had dispersed. My parents went back and transferred the second machine, but they were unable to take out the third one. Far away I saw two Jewish policemen approaching, and I made desperate signs to my parents to disappear. They were lucky. We left the machines there and only went back in the evening and dragged them to our new hiding place under cover of darkness.

The new place was just a courtyard of a house in Nalevky Street. The house was full to overflowing with people. After a little persuasion, we entered an apartment on the second floor. It turned out that my cousin Lazar, who happened to pass by, knew a family there and told them they must take us in.

My feelings toward him were ambivalent. I couldn't forgive him for continuing to serve in the police, even though he told us that he did not participate in those "hunts" and only accompanied those who were expelled. That's quite enough. He asserted that he did it to save the family, my aunt Ester Lechtus and her husband, his wife, Helenka, and their two sons, Benek and Genek. And he did manage to arrange for them to stay with the brushmakers in Swientojersa Street. That's a good "shop," and the *Ausweise*, issued by its German boss, Töbens, are acknowledged by the SS. He also told us that he ran around to find other family members in order to rescue them from the kidnapping. But all the same, I despised him.

[The brushmakers' shop was a separate area of two streets in the reduced ghetto. It belonged to Walter Kasper Töbens, a German industrialist, who set up workshops working for the German army by exploiting the slave labor of the ghetto Jews. For their work he provided them with documents protecting them from deportation. In the end heavy fighting took place during the uprising. The workshops were liquidated together with their workers.]

My other cousin, Mietek, was also a policeman, but he took off his uniform and joined his family. This surely shows courage and self-sacrifice; at least he saved his conscience.

We agreed with the other lodgers, crammed in with us in that apartment, to shut off one of the rooms by moving the large closet, so as to hide the door leading to it. We entered this room through a hole in the back of the closet, leading to the hidden room. It had some water and a few mattresses spread on the floor. Luckily, we prepared all this in time, for immediately afterward there was shouting, whistling, and shooting in the street.

"Blockade, blockade!" people shouted in the street and on the stairs. Fear seized everyone, mortal fear. They all dispersed in search of a hiding place. The house was steeped in silence, the doors were left wide open to suggest that the building was empty. The house with its hundreds of occupants breathed heavily, full of dread, but without a sound. One by one we immediately rushed into the closet and into the hidden room behind it.

Silence, tense silence. No one moved. Mirka was hugging Mother. She stared at the door, like all of us. My ears strained to bursting to detect the slightest noise. My heart beat wildly. Where was Father, I wish he would hold me. We could hear shouting and screaming in German: *Alle raus!* [All out!] "Come down, all of you come down! Whoever is found hiding will be shot at once."

Crying and pleading, and loud stomping of boots on the stairs. The door of the apartment opened, sounds of people breaking in, shouting in Ukrainian and Lithuanian, cursing. They knocked on the walls, moved beds, kicked the table. We all turned inwardly in tense silence. Father was praying, his lips moving voicelessly, others were joining him. I was praying in my heart, pleading to be able to live a little longer.

The hobnailed boots left the apartment.

Emotionally exhausted. We came out to see the results of the pogrom perpetrated all over the house. They took away all the lodgers they could lay their hands on, without checking their documents. The survivors scrambled like mice out of their holes. Another day had passed.

And what will happen tomorrow?

We had no news from Mother's family, from Otvock, and we were worried. Mother found a way to contact Janka Wisniewska, a Polish woman who worked in our workshop before the war, and asked her to travel there and let Aunt Ida and grandfather know that, in spite of the expulsions, we were all right and not to worry. It was a lie. We are alive today, in the evening we may be on our way out, who knows where.

From the first day, the gates of the ghetto were locked and Polish people were forbidden to enter. Yet somehow here and there some food got in, but it was terribly expensive. A kilo of bread that cost twelve zloty a week ago had gone up to eighty. But who could think about hunger? We were living in a feverish state; the mind is empty of all else but for the instinctive urge not to get caught, to find a place for the night. We were in the midst of a huge hunt for people. They say that the expulsion was conducted by groups of SS who had come from Lublin. We were running around in a closed cage, until in the end there wouldn't be anywhere to hide. But I wanted to be with my family, we must stay together.

[The deportation was carried out by the Germans within the framework of the Reinhart Operation commanded by Herman Hafle, with the help of auxiliary forces, including Lithuanians, Latvians, and Ukrainians. The *aktzien* were commanded by Brandt and Mande of the Gestapo.]

We moved again to another "shop." The documents they issued were green. With the help of this *Ausweis* it was still possible to convince the Jewish policemen and even to return from the assembly point, but the Germans annuled these permits day after day. People were confused and ready to give anything just to enter a good German firm, such as Schultz or Töbens.

At the Branch

I just returned from the branch. My head felt like a stone. Members of the Movement walked around there anxiously. I found Dov. Two days ago he distributed leaflets and pasted notices on walls together with Miriam and her group.

"People came out of their apartments and shouted at us to scram. They called us provocateurs! Why do they give in so quickly, and just run away? We must rebel!" He spoke with vehemence. We met one of the adults and asked him what was happening.

"It's not good, no. The leadership had decided to send Shimon Heller and Shoshana and Aviva of the "Tel-Amal" troop who both look "good," to Czenstochowa, to Mordechai. They arranged forged documents for them, and the Polish policeman at the ghetto gate was bribed. They were supposed to be Poles who had gotten stuck in the ghetto before the expulsion and wanted to get home. But someone suspected them and all three were taken to the *Umschlagplatz*—the square where Jews were gathered for deportation on the trains.

Shimon succeeded in escaping and at once ran to alert Arie Gzybowski, our man in the police, to free the girls before the train came, but they were late. The human transport in the freight carriage had already left in the direction of the east.

I also heard about the fate of my friends from the troop. Someone had seen them take Judit, who belonged to my group and my complet. They've most likely also caught Shulamit, Zeevik, and Dina. And clever Adina.

I was brokenhearted. I sat down in the corner with Dov. I had no contact with Miriam. There was no telephone. We could only walk in the streets for two hours, at the end of the work and before curfew. People walked around with their belongings, looking for a hiding place for the next day in private houses vacated during the blockade.

Where is Aliza?

At the beginning of August, I again participated in the distribution of leaflets, and this time it all went smoothly. When I did not get any news from Aliza, I decided to run and see why she had not turned up at the branch. Aliza lived with her uncle and aunt, after her parents had died. Her little brothers have probably already been taken from the orphanage and expelled.

This time I told Father that I was going to Orla Street. I would be wary and careful. He could not stop me. I insisted, since I was a member of the underground and had all kinds of errands. He had to learn to live with it, but I would be cautious. I had taken upon myself to keep in touch with the members of my troop.

At six o'clock in the evening I started to run and push through the crowds along Gensia and Zamenhof Streets. Up to Leszno Street all went well, but from there the streets were quite empty. I began to wander around the gates of the houses. I felt cold sweat covering me. I was afraid.

Suddenly a German car hurtled past. I dashed into house No. 6 and waited. The Germans had not seen me; the house was quiet. The door was open. That looks bad. I hesitated and went in. It was Aliza's house. I took a few quick breaths and mounted the stairs. There was no one there. The bed linen was scattered all over the floor, everything was topsy-turvy.

"Aliza, where are you?" I stifled my desperate cry. I returned to the stairs. There was no one there either. I went out into the yard and up another staircase. It was also deserted. Pillows undone, feathers flying about, furniture turned over. It was clear that the occupants had left in a hurry. Against my will, I entered the apartments. Here and there I saw remnants of food on the table, an open book, signs of life that had gone on there. I burst into tears. No one saw me crying. It was the first time I allowed myself to mourn. I wept for a long time. I sat there frozen stiff, in spite of the August heat. Now I had to run back a long way.

I fled in horror.

Rut Has Broken Down

We are now in a good "shop," Braver, again thanks to Father's profession. As in the past few days, Rut Heiman, my youth leader, came to us, but she looked different. Her eyes were swollen from weeping, her face was gray. She sat for half the day without saying a word. I sat down next to her, but did not dare ask.

In the end she burst out crying and told me, "They took my parents. Today there was a blockade in Leszno Street, where we lived. We didn't manage to escape down to the shelter because the Germans were already in the courtyard. We ran around in the apartment to find a hiding place. Father hid under the bath, Mother inside the bedclothes on the bed, and my sister and I in the closet. We sat there in deathly silence, each in his corner. We had left the apartment door open, but they already knew these tricks. Cursing and pushing, they dragged Father and us from our hiding places, Mother came out by herself. They led us into the street and we were rather quiet, seized by a strange apathy. They put us into a cart, guarded by Jewish policemen.

"I thought feverishly, I must save myself! By order of the Movement! I must escape, now. Suddenly I saw a policeman I knew. He also saw me and began to shout that I am his wife and ordered them to let me down immediately. After an argument with the Germans, they took me down from the cart. I got off as though in a dream. I don't know what happened next. When I pulled myself together, I saw I was alone and the carts had already moved on. My parents were not with me. Then I understood what I had done: I had let them take them and saved myself. Why did I do it?"

I saw that Rut was crushed and had a nervous breakdown. I couldn't find anything to say to her, I was weeping inwardly. I didn't know how to comfort her. She lay on the bench and did not speak to anyone. She stayed with us for three days, without speaking.

Suddenly she got up and wanted to go away. I asked her to let me go with her. She told me that she had heard that the branch was empty and those who remained moved to the O.B.W. plant in Gensia Street 61. That's where she was going. I went with her.

During the three days we spent shut up in the Braver "shop" and while outside an *aktzia* was raging, great changes had occurred among our members. Most of the surviving Hashomer Hatzair members gathered in some of the rooms of the branch. It turned out that many had parted from their parents and came to live together in the hope that they would soon be able to participate in an armed uprising.

According to the instructions of the fighting organization that was in the process of being established, the members of the Movement were to get together into groups, in anticipation of the struggle to come. I found friends there from the older troops "Tel-Amal," "Banir," "Masad," and younger ones from "Maanit" and "Sarid." The leadership of the Movement had given the following order: Jump off the trains, escape and return to the ghetto, to hide until the moment we are ready to fight.

I spoke with the members. They were all waiting for the day "the order" would be given. I heard that Felek and Rut, the inseparable couple, were sent outside the ghetto to try to make their way to the partisans, and were lost somewhere. Merdek and some others had jumped from a moving train. Members of the "Dror" Movement also gathered in Dzielna Street and we acted in conjunction with them. I heard a rumor that the commander of the Jewish police, Szerinski, was injured. If that is true, it means that the organization is alive and active.

There was no one there from my troop. I was overwhelmed by a feeling of loneliness. From the leading group, belonging to the "In Flames" troop that kept constantly in contact with us, apparently only few had survived. I was in despair. I'll never see them again, never, never. My heart refused to accept it. *By what right am I still here? How am I better than they are?* An intense feeling of being orphaned engulfed me. It was maybe the first time in my life that I mourned deeply, a feeling I shall apparently have to cope with all my life.

Parting without being able to say goodbye, I felt as though a part of me had vanished together with the disappearance of my dear friends with whom I had lived so intensively during the last two years. From the day I heard about the death of almost all my friends from my troop until that terrible *selektzia* called "David," on the seventh of September, I stayed, like most of my friends, at the branch, in a state of apathy, not caring about my fate, feeling helpless. Most of them were pessimistic.

A few called for vengeance and resistance immediately, but the older members persuaded the others to wait and consolidate the fighting organization that was being set up. This was veiled in great secrecy. Most of the members ceased to believe that it was possible to survive and began to prepare mentally for death. Black jokes hung in the air.

One day I saw a scene that moved me greatly and dispelled my apathy. At that time we were hiding in an apartment in Nalewki Street. While sitting there, we heard unusual shouting in the street that was supposed to be quiet at eleven in the morning. It was not a blockade, it was something else. We jumped to look out of the windows.

On the other side of the street, two youths were walking with sacks on their backs. Unfortunately, a car with four SS men passed by. They stopped next to the youths and ordered them to throw the contents of the sacks onto the sidewalk. Pots and tattered clothes fell out.

The Germans chose something, and then one of the SS men with a red face began to hit the boys with a rubber truncheon. One of the boys fell immediately, and then the other SS men joined in. They beat them silently on the face, the belly, the head. One of the boys tried to get up, to say something. The whole of his face was covered in blood.

The German got annoyed and began to kick him all over his body. His friends stood by, laughing. And then, when the boy was bleeding, they ordered the other boy to go inside the house. And at once the liberating shot was heard from there. Their blood ran on the sidewalk. The beasts of prey had satisfied their lust.

A day of mourning. Lazar, my cousin the policeman, came to us with dreadful news: My father's two sisters, Aunt Bronia Dresner and Aunt Mania Vieliczko and all their families had been caught and sent off in the freight trains. How could I console my father when at any moment his other siblings may follow suit, and such fate was also awaiting us? I could not cry. Not yet.

We didn't know anything about Biela and Ignac, my mother's sister and her husband. An acquaintance of ours told us that he had seen Uncle Leon and his family in Shultz's "shop." That was a good place. In the meantime they were safe there.

How was it possible? We were packed off like animals, and why were the Poles silent? Why was the world silent? Why?

Inside a Narrow Crack

Yesterday we were almost caught but saved by a miracle. Another of those miracles happening to us during the last five weeks. Suddenly there was a blockade in the street below. Whistling, shouting in German: "Out! Out at once! If you don't come out into the street, you'll be shot at once!"

Inside the house people began to seize their backpacks, always ready, and flee to the hiding places they had prepared. We have a place in the attic. Actually, it's a narrow crack half a meter high between the ceiling and the tiles, closed from outside by a cover that is lifted. One has to climb up a ladder.

The long, tense moments as we went up one by one and squeezed in seemed to take forever. They could burst into the house at any moment. "Quick, quick," the ones standing below urged those climbing. I was choking with fear, my stomach tight. Another and another one, the time dragged on.

"Too many of us," they shouted from the opening. "No more room, we'll suffocate!"

"You want to live. So do we!" Urging from below.

At last it was my turn and I felt hands pulling me inside. Darkness. *Mother. Father. Mirka. Where are you?* I heard a familiar voice coming from far away.

Shshsh. Closing the cover and pulling up the ladder. We lay there in mortal silence. Impossible to sit, to move. Dozens of people leaning on each other, no air to breathe. Clouds of dust swirling, blocking my nose and ears. I mustn't sneeze! The air is suffocating.

The silence was broken by a low sound from below. We strained to hear until it hurt. The hunters of Jews walked quietly, to create an illusion and surprise. Suddenly we heard German voices quite near. They were coming up the stairs toward us. I bit my lips until they bled. The steps approached. Someone was walking on tiptoe in the attic, coming closer. I shrank into myself—another moment and they'd find us. We heard hands knocking on walls, near us… and moving farther away.

Finally, he had gone. I breathed a sigh of relief. At that moment a child inside our hiding place started to cry. God! Now the man would hear the crying and return. He hadn't left the attic yet. The baby cried louder and louder.

"Stop up his mouth," people whispered.

There were almost thirty of us cramped in the attic. Someone was weeping silently, someone handed the mother a pillow. The child had fallen asleep, maybe forever. The air was more and more stifling. I closed my eyes. I lost the sense of time.

Shots resounded in the street. The noise grew louder. I could hardly breathe. I dozed off into a kind of heavy sleep. I wanted to say "Mother," but I couldn't move my lips. I was losing consciousness and all those around me were lying in a faint.

I don't know how much time had passed. When I woke up, the cover was open, and from outside they called us to come out. No one answered from inside. We had lain there eight hours. Slowly others pulled us out.

In our apartment the scene was terrible. All the bedclothes and other things were lying about on the floor. These were just the remnants; the Lithuanians and Ukrainians had taken everything of any value. We had succeeded in concentrating in the flat the remains of our property, besides the backpacks. Mother stood there helplessly. Now we really only had our backpacks that had been hidden behind the closet.

"Nonsense," said Father, "the main thing is we've made it once more. Would it have taken a lot for us to suffocate or to be found?" Another day gained.

Survivor from Treblinka

I have no words to describe all the blockades, the hardships, and wandering from place to place, the lack of food, the unsanitary conditions, the nights in cellars on the damp floor, the suffering that dulled the senses and led to apathy in the face of the death of others.

At that time we lived like animals, fighting for our lives by means of a primitive urge for survival. This existential urge made us act instinctively. We had shed almost all the veneer of civilization, driven to flee by fear, but defeat in this battle came closer with every passing day.

It is painful for me to write about the behavior of the Jewish police, particularly at the start of the expulsion, about the robbing of diamonds and jewels in exchange for survival, about pushing people into line. True, not all behaved in this way. Many honest ones took off their armband and police cap and became like us. My cousins also did so.

One of them disappeared with his family in the great expulsion, and there will be more to tell about the other one, Lazar. There is no doubt: Those who remained in the police turned into the scum of the earth like the *kapo* [guards] in the concentration camps. They deserved their bitter fate that caught up with them later on.

One day, I think it was at the beginning of August, I came to the branch. I met David Novodvorsky there, a member of the Movement, the only one who succeeded in escaping and returning from Treblinka. It was from him that we heard that name for the first time.

David was tall, blond, light-skinned. He wore large glasses. His story caused an upheaval in all of us. At first he made me lose the little level-headedness I still possessed. For a whole day David lay in a state of shock at the branch before he could speak. He had been caught two weeks before together with a large crowd and herded to the *Umschlagplatz*, the railway station. Here is his account:

> Thousands of people were lying about there with their belongings and their children, waiting for the train in the great summer heat, without food or water. They all relieved themselves where they lay. It was a mass of

people, in despair and apathy. The trains came. No one wanted to get in first, people began to flee to the other side of the platform. The Germans fired into the crowd and pushed the people into the freight cars.

Eighty, a hundred people in a carriage meant for ten horses. Everyone tried to get a place under the little barred window, to get some air. It was hot, terribly hot, and people were wearing several layers of clothing. There was so little room that no one could move a hand or foot. They locked the carriage and an SS man stood behind the door.

I have no idea how long we traveled. All my limbs were aching. Someone was crying hysterically. Two people apparently swallowed poison, cyanide. We knew we had two corpses with us. A wounded man was groaning all the time. A child wept, pleading for *wasser, Mama'le, wasse* [water, Mummy]. He was asking all the time when will we get there? He could not stand on his legs. His mother was sobbing.

Suddenly we heard a scraping sound by the window. It turned out that a youth was trying to saw the bar on the window. The people in the carriage were confused. They advised him not to jump out. It's certain death, and maybe we shall get somewhere after all.

"I'll die here or there. What's the difference," the youth answered. He succeeded in bending the bar he had sawed and pushed out his thin body. People helped, one leg after the other, a shot and his body remained hanging on the window until it dropped. Horrible.

In the early evening we arrived at a field surrounded by a fence. It was dark, Ukrainians were all around us. The doors opened and we fell out, totally exhausted. The Germans shouted and fired constantly. I knew I was going to die, that was the end. "Get up!" was the command. "Get into rows!"

We were marched to a building, men separately from the women and children. I was ordered to the side with a group of men. I froze. I can't describe what was happening around me. The weeping of the children torn from their parents, the desperate cries of the separated families. There was only one thought in my mind: how to seize the German's gun.

Someone jumped on the German. There is no escape from here, this is hell itself, worse than Dante's. I stood there as though in a dream and for a moment I thought I'd wake up in my bed with Rivka above me. No, no! I'll never see her again, and Eretz Israel, I won't dance the hora with my friends. Polish Jewry wiped out before my eyes.

My thoughts were clear and raced at a feverish pace. A sharp existential awareness seized me. At that moment I decided to avenge myself. I'll also jump on a German and will try to strangle him. Then someone approached, apparently a Jew, and whispered to us to keep quiet, we had been chosen for work.

We dug until dawn. The mechanical work calmed us down in some way. At sunrise, trucks approached, and on them, oh, God, distorted, swollen corpses, eyes staring in terror. How horrible! I lost consciousness and fell down. Someone's leg woke me and I jumped up.

We went on digging, some thirty silent men. The German screamed, "Work, work, tomorrow you'll be in the pit."

As in a dream we pushed the corpses into the graves. No one spoke. Someone began to howl like a wolf. They shot him too.

They took us to sheds far from the gas chambers. In the evening a youth came to me, I seemed to know him, my cousin.

"We can escape," he whispered. "Tonight they are loading the clothes of the dead onto the trains they came on and taking them back to Warsaw. We'll be loading the clothes, we'll hide inside and return."

His words and suggestion sounded strange to me. Can one go on living after what we had seen? What for? To slip away and be caught again? Surely this nightmare will never leave me! My cousin realized what state I was in and dragged me with him. I gave in and followed him. I succeeded in slipping back into the train, even though we were constantly counted. Someone will be punished because of us, but what does it matter.

Then, before dawn, we jumped from the train. Four days of hunger and wandering in the forests, and now I am here with you. You must tell it all to the world, tell them the truth. So everyone knows where the transports are going. The same thing is happening in Belsetz and Chelmno. They must escape, fight, take revenge!

And he took revenge. During the uprising David was the commander of one of the fighting units in the area of the "shops." When the fighting died down, he escaped through the sewage canals, tried to get to the partisans in eastern Poland, but was caught and killed.

Again we distributed leaflets. The name *Treblinka* spread quickly. David's testimony was beyond a shadow of a doubt.

Something disastrous happened to the Movement. On the third of September Yosef Kaplan, its founder and leader, was arrested. His arrest was veiled in secrecy. The girls at the branch were unable to tell me what had really happened. Everyone was depressed and in despair.

On the same day Shmuel Breslav, a member of Hashomer Hatzair, was killed. It happened as he was walking along in the street at ten in the morning, when the streets were empty. He was caught by chance by a German patrol wanting to search him. Shmuel resisted. They say that he drew a knife, that he seized the German's revolver. Anyway, he succeeded in hurting the soldier and was shot at once. His body was found in the evening. That is what I was told by a little girl from the "Sarid" troop.

We also lost the first lot of weapons sent to us. It was terrible. Reginka Justman carried the revolvers that Iurek Vilner sent from the Aryan side in a basket covered with vegetables to a new hiding place. It was dangerous to leave them in Mila Street because of Yosef Kaplan's arrest. It was not clear how she was caught. The lovely, gentle Reginka, lifetime partner of Shimon Heller. The all-important weapons were lost.

After a few days Mordechai Anielewicz returned to Warsaw and took over the leadership of the Movement. A short time after his arrival, he was appointed the first commander of the Jewish Fighting Organization (Z.O.B.). Mordechai was respected by all, the Zionist activists and also the ghetto operatives. He was self-confident and radiated determination and intelligence. He was the right person for the role.

The *kociol*—the Great *selektzia*

The *kociol* [cauldron] began on the sixth of September. In the evening policemen went from house to house, from "shop" to "shop," and ordered all the Jews to report the next day until ten in the morning next to the workshops where they were registered.

By then all must be in the area including the streets Mila, Lubetzky, Smocza, Ostrovsk—a small area enclosed on all sides by ropes, secured by the Germans.

"What's happening?" we asked each other. The family members are debating: Should we go, or hide in the hiding place we've prepared? If we don't go and they find us, the order is to kill anyone on the spot. And if we do go, maybe there will be some kind of "selection" and some of the residents of the ghetto will survive.

Father and Mother decided to go. My parents were promised *Ausweis* by the large "shop" of the German industrialist Töbens.

We walked with our usual backpacks to Leszno Street and joined the line of thousands of fortunate people belonging to those workshops. The weather was hotter than usual in the stifling summer heat, and we were wearing everything we were able to put on. Of course, one dress on top of another and a winter coat as well, for who knew where they'd take us from here. Each one of us was afraid, but also believed that we would get through this selection.

I looked at my mother, a beautiful young woman, but her hair had gone white and her face haggard. I had scissors in my backpack and suggested that I'd cut her hair short, to make her look younger. Father, a young man, very thin, his face pale and drawn. He felt the responsibility, he was anxious about his family. My dear father, unable to help his children. My sister, aged nine, but looking much younger. Her hair was fair—she doesn't look Jewish. She was clutching her mother as if she could not exist without her. She believed in her mother and her ability to save her.

I felt terribly hot and thirsty. We were approaching the line forming in front of the German manager. Next to him stood the Jewish manager of the plant, the famous omnipotent Nojfeld, and he whispered to the German, telling him to whom to give the worker's permit. Father and Mother received the *Ausweis*, I and my sister, of course, did not. The endless procession was approaching its destination, on order by the Germans. We were already in Mila Street. Now we were pushed from the lines of the Töbens people, pushed into the crowd; we held onto each other with all our strength.

God! We mustn't get lost among the thousands of people, sweating like us, totally exhausted by the tension, the heat, and the thirst. The silent question was reflected in their eyes: *What do they mean to do with us here, in this cage? In this human cauldron? Why did they concentrate tens of thousands of people here?*

I slipped out of the line, leaving my family in the courtyard of one of the houses in Mila Street and ran to the branch. Quick, quick—what have they all decided to do? What is happening to the members of the Movement? I went up to the first floor. Empty. No one was there. I went up to the second floor and found Erella of the "Galil" troop, hurriedly gathering the things.

"Erella, where is everybody?"

"We divided up into two groups, two hiding places. We decided to survive the cauldron in hiding and prepare for the uprising. We are not ready yet. They even seized the few revolvers we had, did you know?"

"Yes, I know that Reginka was caught, and two of our leaders were killed."

"Several boys, led by Shimon Heller, intend to ignite the entrance to the cauldron," added Erella. "And what about you, Lilit?"

"I am staying with my parents, whatever happens," I said.

I was late. They had all gone to the hiding place. My heart sank. I returned to my parents. I pushed again into the crowd and found them. The commotion in the street increased. The "Töbens people" were called to stand in lines, go through the *selektzia* and then return home. The heat got worse. I threw my winter coat on a pile of things lying in a corner. I went with my family.

And now we were at the large wooden gate built across the street. I went with my father as though in a dream. He was holding the *Ausweis* in front of him. Two rows of Germans stood in front of us.

Suddenly I heard a voice, asking in German, "*Deine Tochter? Ist sie auch eine Arbeiterin?*" [Your daughter? Also a worker?]

"*Ja, Jawohl,*" Father answered. Yes. A hand motioned us to turn back and the same hand took the *Ausweis* from my father. Mother felt instinctively that something was happening to us and dropped out of the line. We were together again, but had only one Ausweis.

Meanwhile the crazy procession moved on. I stepped aside, right up to the fence, and peeped in to see what was happening on the other side: Two rows of Germans, motioning to the people to go right or left. I saw a mother with a little girl. They separated the girl from the mother. The mother to the right, the child to the left. The girl held her hands out to her mother, crying bitterly and calling her desperately. The mother stopped, tried to free herself from the German policemen holding her, and wanted to run to the other side, to the weeping child.

Blows rained on her from all sides, and in the end they dragged her to the right. Now there goes a father with a baby in his arms. The German grabbed the child from his hands and threw it with all his strength on the ground. They beat the father with a rubber truncheon, until he lost his balance. The corpse of the baby was disposed of quickly.

Now I understood that they were taking all the children to be killed. What a miraculous instinct warned my mother so that she did not follow us, but moved back.

Evening fell. The gate of the *selektzia* was closed. They said that most of the people with *Ausweis* had already passed through. Yet tens of thousands still remained in the cauldron.

Mother said to me, "Liza, you are young…fourteen…my darling, take the remaining *Ausweis* and try to get through tomorrow. Maybe people will help you and you'll survive."

Stunned, I looked into Mother's face, grown so old these days. Full of boundless love and willingness for self-sacrifice. "Surely you understand," she continued. "We'll go together with Mirka. Why should you sacrifice yourself in vain?"

I looked into Father's face and saw determination. I saw a nervous quiver distort his face, and then I fell into my mother's arms.

"No! Don't say that! I won't go on my own!"

It was a great relief to be together again. We stopped talking about it. Now my mind started to work, to search for other solutions. I felt that my parents accepted the idea of death; they were quiet. I did not. I had come to my senses and began to think logically.

I wondered, *Why did the German during the selektzia send me back with my father into the crowd and did not order me to the left, as they did with all those without an Ausweis? Does that mean that there will be another selektzia tomorrow, but this time not according to the Ausweis or any other document, but according to some other criteria? He did ask Father if I also worked for Töbens, and Father answered that I did.*

I tried to explain to my parents that we could attempt to get past tomorrow as well, we must not despair. One of us suggested that we empty a backpack, put Mirka inside and Father would carry her on his back. I'd hold the only *Ausweis* we had, as I was still in danger, and my parents would try to get past, declaring they work for Töbens and were late yesterday.

We calmed down a little and looked for a place for the night. We entered an apartment, already full of people lying on the floor. The atmosphere was full of tension, and the people were nervous, but we sensed wonderful friendly warmth. They even made room for each other, and for us too.

Last-minute charity, fellowship of the condemned to death, I pondered. We were all troubled by the groaning of a youth with a wound in his head, lying unconscious in the corner. His mother was bending over him, wetting his lips with water. From time to time he cried out.

At five o'clock in the morning, after a sleepless night, we again stood in rows in the street, waiting for the *selektzia*. The people of the Schultz "shop" passed by, holding out green numbers, attesting to their "kosher" status. Many children were among them, going to their death. Suddenly, in one row, we saw Uncle Leon, Father's brother, his wife and two sons, Adash and Meir. Without their six-year-old daughter.

Father asked, "Where is Hanale?"

"We've hidden her in a hiding place with grandmother," Uncle answered.

"Where is it? Tell us and we'll take Mirka there. Do you know that they are taking all the children?" said Father, agitated.

Aunt Irena answered, "That's impossible, there isn't any more room there for anyone." They strode on in wide rows in the direction of the wooden gate. We stood there, stunned.

We had another significant meeting during that "march" to the *selektzia* in Mila Street. Fate again brought together two brothers—my father and his older brother David and his family. Fate had wished him to meet his other brother as well, before their final parting.

Uncle David was unshaven, emanating despair. Beside him walked Aunt Guta and their two daughters: ten-year-old Helenka and nine-year-old Milka. The two brothers embraced.

Uncle David said, "There's nothing we can do, Shimek. That's the end for us." They had no *Ausweis* of any "shop," so they went along with their little daughters. They went with them to the end. There was nothing to say to each other. We were also going into the unknown. I looked at the little girls. My uncle's daughters had blue eyes, so light blue. *Did they understand what awaited them?*

Father's backpack was heavy for him. He made a hole so Mirka could breathe, and through it he occasionally gave her water to drink from a bottle. I supported the precious backpack from below. *How can the poor child sit there, with her legs folded under her, her back bent tightly, without air? Will she be able to remain like that? And what if they beat Father with a whip, as they often do, and Mirka is hit and, God forbid, cries out and they discover her? And anyway, how much chance do we have?*

We agreed that I'd go first and Father would follow me. If he sees that they order me to go to the left, to those condemned to death, he'll go there too, and Mother will follow him. *But what will happen if I get through and they don't?*

My head was throbbing from the heat of the day. I must remain calm, maybe that's the test Mira Fuchrer spoke about. Mother came close to me and whispered in my ear. I felt her hot breath. She kissed me and gave me strength.

Now it was the turn of the rest of the people belonging to the Töbens "shops," left over from yesterday. Suddenly the people in front of us drew back and we were facing the gate.

Father pushed me to go first. I held the *Ausweis* firmly in front of me and walked straight to the right, pushing aside the rubber truncheon in my way. I turned around. Father followed me with the heavy backpack. *Mother, where is she?* And then I saw her, head held high. Walking erect in a dignified way, she followed Father. We've made it!

A miracle! The people in front of us had drawn back because they began to take everyone to the left, and yet we passed. We stood in a long row with the other fortunate people and watched what was going on: There were no more "shop" people. The Germans let us go to the right for no particular reason. They took others to the left according to some blind game, according to rules known only to them.

At noon, exhausted, we began to move in a long procession back to the ghetto. It was hot, terribly hot. We were covered with sweat and very thirsty. Mirka peeped out of the backpack, and people were surprised that a whole family was able to pass. Most of them had remained alone.

We were escorted by Jewish policemen. They were also tired and worn out. In the streets corpses lay about, of people who were discovered in hiding places and did not go to the cauldron. The roads were strewn with household utensils, clothes, cutlery, undone quilts. The ghetto streets, brimming with life only a few days ago, were deserted.

A deathly silence permeated everything. Only the open windows banged in the wind, and belongings bereft of their owners were scattered around, among the blood of the unfortunate people lying on the sidewalks. Only the stillness greeted us, calling for revenge. Everything cries vengeance!

We dragged our feet in silence, not as though we had been set free, but as slaves granted a respite. A thought reverberates in my head: *Why me and not someone else?* We returned to our street, to the houses allotted to the Töbens workers.

On the next day, when I returned from the "shop," I ran to the branch in Mila Street. On the way I met Lilit from the "Sarid" troop. She was pale and could hardly walk.

"All of them are alive," she said. "We spent five days in our hiding place. We hardly ate anything at all." I breathed a sigh of relief. They are alive!

In the course of time, I found out the extent of the catastrophe: The *selektzia* and the search for people hiding in the ghetto lasted four days. After the *selektzia* the *aktzias* stopped completely. The first stage of the extermination of the Warsaw Jews was over.

During those days they took more than a hundred thousand people, among them almost all the children in the ghetto. The ghetto was now *kinderrein* [unpolluted by children]. Some fifteen thousand people remained, working in the "shops" of Schultz, Töbens, and Helman in our area, in Nowolipki, Smocza, and Nowoliple Streets. They were an island in an area called "wild," which was out of bounds.

Farther away, the Germans left a small ghetto—the central ghetto—with about thirty thousand Jews, and another area near there, in Shwentovierska Street, the brushmakers' district, with factories and workers' lodgings.

At the end of the great *aktzia*, on September 12, 1942, altogether about fifty thousand Jews out of a population of over three hundred thousand remained alive.

5 : Preparations for the Armed Struggle

Back in the Töbens "Shops"

On our return to the block of houses allotted to the workers of the Töbens "shops," we immediately had to look for a place to stay. Everyone hurried to seize an apartment. We found a large room, together with Aunt Biela and her husband, Ignac, whom we met on our return to the "shop." They went through the *selektzia*, not knowing what had happened to us. Now there were six of us in the room, where two young couples had lived before.

The Fischer family lost their little child in the *selektzia*. Dr. Davidson's family had a seven-year-old daughter that they had hidden in a hiding place. We were now eleven people on five narrow beds. Luckily for us, before the war the apartments in Leszno Street had belonged to wealthy families, and there was no lack of blankets, bed linens, and various kinds of household utensils.

On the following day, after work, some of the adults went to "wild," deserted apartments, to collect some clothing and other things. All went out into the empty streets to pick up whatever they could. In the ghetto slang it was called *shaber*.

Ignac, a cynic but a man of principles, was disgusted by it and forbade Biela to go. "Whatever we have must do. I won't take things belonging to people who have been murdered," he said resolutely.

Biela tried to explain to him, "If we don't take these things, the Germans or the Poles will. Isn't it enough that they took their lives, should they also take their property?"

Mother, with her practical sense, added, "We have nothing, just our backpacks. Maybe they'll let those who survived the great *selektzia* live on. Maybe they were given the order to stop the deportation immediately."

I butted in, "Mummy, no illusions. They'll leave us until the next *aktzia*."

"How can you be so sure? Does anyone know what they are scheming?"

I had to admit that we didn't know. That's their method: They create a state of uncertainty, confusion, illusions, and that's how they succeed in leading to their deaths thousands of people without any resistance. We didn't know if they'd wipe out the ghetto straightaway and who would be left alive.

I went to see my former library in Karmelitzka Street. It was a depressing sight. Destruction, like everywhere else. The bookcases were lying on the floor on top of each other, and the books were all over the place, in a mess. Wonderful books, cultural treasures. They have no place in this dreadful world of death and destruction.

I decided to take as many books as I could carry and transfer them to our apartment. For several days I went to the library and dragged piles of books back. Mirka helped me; she also loved to read. And what not to take? I chose mainly Greek tragedies, all of Euripides and Sophocles and Greek mythology that I loved so much.

Later I asked myself why I was so interested in philosophy and ancient tragedies just at that time, after the great calamity, when we suffered greatly emotionally, depressed by the terrible events of the last two months? *Was I looking for peace of mind? Did I want to escape the cruel reality to an unreal world, the world of fiction, or was I desperately seeking proof that civilization existed and would continue to do so beyond the ruthless present, beyond material cares, beyond cynicism and greed?* I read avidly and with devotion, in spite of the crowded and noisy surroundings.

Our apartment was too small for four families. At night I had to listen to sounds coming from tortured souls in their nightmares. All that had not been uttered during the day could be heard at night. Genia Fischer groaned, turned from side to side, her bed creaked. Her husband used to wake up and silence her quiet weeping. Sometimes she got up and stood by the window. Maybe she was looking for her little daughter in heaven, one tiny star, a soul seeking her mother. She had been taken from her during the *selektzia*. Maybe she was tormented by the thought how her little girl was pushed all alone into the freight car and into the gas chambers, without her parents.

No doubt she was tormented by guilt, like many other parents who had let them take away their children. An instant of panic, at the decisive moment, and its terrible result will be with them throughout their lives. I didn't know what happened to the Fischers. They were always quiet, brooding, as though life had gone out of them. Six months later, when everyone was feverishly looking for ways of escape, they were apathetic.

I also heard sounds of lovemaking. People wanted to unwind and could not take others into consideration. Mother knew that we heard everything and asked me to talk to Mirka and explain to her about sex. I, as the elder sister, carried out the task willingly. It went something like this: "Do you know why the grown-ups move and sigh so much during the night?" I asked her naïvely.

"You are telling me they want to make more children, because they took all the children in the ghetto."

"And do you want to know how they make children?"

"Really, Liza! I can tell you! I've known for a long time what it means to have sex."

"Mirka, the words you use! It's to do with love!" (That's what I learned in the Movement.) I saw that there wasn't much that I could teach her. A nine-year-old ghetto child who heard, saw, and was forced to understand things far beyond what would normally be necessary.

Mother used to get up first. It was dark outside with unpleasant autumn rain, howling winds. I woke up without wanting to get up. *What for? What would the day bring? What is there to live for?* In the end I got swept up in the turmoil of preparations for going out to work.

We took Mirka with us. While it was still dark, we slipped her into a little room where she stayed throughout our working hours. It was good that she had plenty to read. Sometimes she would come out of her hiding place and help us.

The work was terribly boring. Forced labor, hated by all. We manufactured socks and uniforms for the *Wehrmacht* [German army]. We were helping them so they wouldn't feel cold on the Russian front. I was thinking, full of hatred: May they all die there in the snow, in the Russian steppes! Although their advance was arrested at Stalingrad, liberation was still far away.

At work, news from the fronts was passed on by word of mouth, and people were arguing about the turn the war would take. We got the news from a group of workers who went out to the Aryan side and returned at night, the *platzovki*. That is the way one can leave the ghetto or return to it secretly. They also traded with the Poles who came near the place where the group was working and would sell them food in exchange for the abandoned belongings, stolen immediately after the cauldron. There were no more stores in the ghetto now, and all the trading was carried out in passing, on the spot.

The people working in the "shop" looked after members of their families who were left without any means of livelihood in the central ghetto, a reduced remnant of the former large ghetto. These people lived in the "wild" area, with no "permission to live" without documents. The Germans left them there, but for how long? *When will the aktzia resume? How long would they allow us to live? What were their devious plans, damn it?*

Bereavement

People began to mourn. During the period following the great deportation, the atmosphere was gloomy. Everyone looked for any family members, friends, and acquaintances still left.

Who had survived?

Mostly young men and women whom the Germans considered useful for their war effort, so they received *Ausweis* and now lived in the permitted area around the various "shops." They joined up in groups and lived together. They shared their grief, the loss of their families. Few families remained in hiding. Those who did not go to the cauldron stayed in the reduced ghetto. These were mostly pugnacious people and some with presence of mind, people who had seen their dear ones seized in front of their own eyes. Men whose wives and children had been ordered to the left, and for whom despair had made them fearless, despising all danger and the values they had believed in. They now considered life of little value. They knew that sooner or later they would also be killed.

In the meantime they wanted to live—drink, eat, and make love until the time comes. Eat and drink, for all is vanity. What is the point of pangs of conscience under conditions of borrowed time that may soon be over? What is the value of morality?

Today I am sitting and writing in the youth group's little wooden shed, perturbed by philosophical thoughts. From the point of view of a normal society, it was a period of moral disintegration, devoid of any civilizing prohibitions that we had adhered to so devotedly during our life in the ghetto before the deportation.

Even then the situation in this respect was polarized: There was corruption, dishonesty, bribery, prostitution, and informing. But the majority of people scrupulously preserved their human dignity. May those who survived judge others? Those men and women, parents of children who had gone to the right and their children were taken from them, how was it possible that they did not go with their children and let them die alone, lonely in the stifling cattle cars and the gas chambers?

My heart throbs when I think about that horror. What did those parents feel? Nothing, apparently. They were paralyzed by fear, and the instinct of self-preservation held sway. People who had succeeded to remain in control and their instinct told them to go with the children, went with them, or at least tried to. Sometimes the Germans tore the children from them by force and they could do nothing. Only later they came to their senses, when, in a long procession, they reached the empty apartments. Some committed suicide, out of feelings of guilt and shame. Very many experienced a bitter awakening, despair, and remorse. Later they transformed their pain into a tremendous desire for vengeance.

Where Is the Melamed Family?

As soon as we returned to the "shop" of Töbens, we found out that the family of Uncle Leon was farther down Leszno Street, in the "shop" of K. G. Schultz ("the little Schultz").

At our poignant meeting, we heard about the calamity in the family. Aunt Irena (Judit) hugged Mirka and sobbed silently: "May God watch over you, may God watch over you," she repeated again and again.

My uncle, Leon Benyamin, was sitting in the room, his eyes red from weeping. I thought that it was our meeting that moved them so. Adash, my age, and Meir, two years younger than I, came in from the other room. I expected to see eight-year-old Hanale, but she did not come. I looked at my father and mother, and I understood.

Uncle Leon told us the story, his head resting on his hands, a glazed look in his eyes: "We were afraid to take the girl with us to the *selektzia*. Irena's mother was also with us. The two of us and the boys had the green numbers of Schultz's shop, they didn't. We went with all the others to the cauldron. In Mila Street I met an acquaintance. He told me that he put his son in the cellar in Mila No. 54. I paid them a lot of money, and they put grandmother and Hanale in there too. We went to the *selektzia* without knowing who would survive—they or we—but we had no choice. Remember, we met there and I saw Shimek with the backpack with Mirka on his back. We couldn't know that we would pass through with the big boys and that they [Hanale and Grandmother] would be discovered."

The aunt interrupted, "They remained in the bunker two days after us. The Germans searched everywhere. They caught another Jew who had hidden his family in the bunker. He handed over to them all those in the bunker, and in exchange they let his wife and son go free. That's what a Jew did to other Jews, and my Hanale went to Treblinka." The aunt wept and we all wept with her.

They were saved through belonging to the Schultz "shop." All his workers with numbers passed in rows through the gate and to the right. Even Meir, who was only twelve, marched among the mechanics in the middle of the row and came through safely. As they went through, none of them knew if those walking behind them would get through. But they were saved. There will be more to tell about them later, because from my father's family, numbering eight brothers and sisters, only our two families survived.

Benek Lechtus, my cousin, succeeded in getting across the "wild" part without Jews, and he told us that his family was saved. His parents, Father's sister Ester and her husband, his brother the doctor and his sister, Helenka Lazar, were all unharmed. At the time of the cauldron, his parents remained in hiding, and the young ones went to the *selektzia* with the "brushmakers."

We also heard that my other cousin, the beautiful Ida Holtzman-Weisberg, went out to the Aryan side after her husband was put on the train, and that she was hiding in the homes of her many friends. But later, in our shared hiding place, we heard the truth from Lazar. Her benefactor was a *Folksdeutcher*—a Pole of German origin, serving in the Nazi army. He was her lover. I was shocked.

Mother said, "A person will do anything to survive. Who knows, maybe he is a German friendly to the Jews."

I thought about it, but her words did not convince me. An enemy's "sweetheart"? She did have a choice; she could have chosen differently. Later, Ida was the one who saved Lazar's life when he jumped from the train speeding to Treblinka, after the great uprising. But she paid with her life for her relationship with the German.

After the war, when I was in Germany, we heard that the Poles had taken revenge on the women who lived with Germans. During the Polish revolt, in 1944, they caught Ida, lynched, and murdered her. I was sorry for Ida, an educated woman, elegant and beautiful, saved only to die just as her life could have started again.

In the Apartment of the Branch, in Mila 61

A few days later I went to the central ghetto to renew my contact with the members of the Movement who had survived after the cauldron. The "shops" of Töbens and Schultz were separated from the central ghetto by deserted streets, called "wild," like the abandoned houses. I was told to cross Nowolipki Street, where the *platzovki* pass through [those work squads going out every day to work on the Polish side of Warsaw] on their return to the ghetto at the end of their shifts.

Through various passages, I got to Novolipie and waited inside the gate of one of the empty houses. The courtyard where I was standing was still full of signs of the life that had ended abruptly. The worst were the feathers—undone Jewish duvets and their feathers constantly fluttering in the air, penetrating every apartment, filling space like pure souls gone astray. My stomach knotted with sorrow. I was not afraid, only sad. Those fluttering feathers. I'll never forget them.

Suddenly I heard Germans and Ukrainians screaming. A group of Jews approached, accompanied by Jewish policemen who had returned to their job. I thought, *I can't get out like this, the Germans will shoot me.* The group was already facing me. If I don't move, they'll pass on.

In a second, straining with tremendous willpower, I detached my legs, turned to stone, from the sidewalk, burst into their rows and went on marching with them. The people around me, tired out, continued to march and did not react to my joining them. Many people used to do it, and it became a way of getting from the "shops" to the central ghetto. They marched in silence in rows through the ghost city.

It was already autumn. The wind banged the windows and made a strident noise. The belongings scattered in the streets bore witness to the tragedy that had befallen their owners. We soon reached the gate where the German policemen were standing. They checked us hurriedly. And I was in the ghetto. From there I ran on my own to Mila 61.

Dozens of *Shomrim* had gathered in three derelict apartments and led a totally communal life. The underground activities were run from there. I knew many of them. We embraced, weeping quietly. They had escaped the cauldron by hiding in two places. We told our stories with agitation. They had all lost their families, and they lived at the branch like one big family.

The atmosphere was gloomy. Supper consisted of a thin soup. They suffered from hunger. It was only later that a group of girls went out to work in vegetable patches in the cemetery, and others got work in the O.B.W. "shop," run by Alexander Landau, the father of Margalit from the "Galil" troop. He placed apartments at the disposal of the members of the Movement and protected them. We had a wonderful friend.

In the evening they all lay on mattresses spread out on the floor in the dark. Someone began to sing the songs of *Eretz* Israel we loved. One by one others joined in from the scattered rugs and mattresses, and the song soon spread from room to room, filled with yearning for that beloved distant land where our people live in freedom and where we were also meant to go. And then they went over to Yiddish songs, lullabies sung by Jewish mothers to their children—and quiet weeping was heard here and there in the dark.

And suddenly a powerful song erupted:

We are unknown soldiers without uniforms,
Around us terror and the shadow-of-death.
All of us enlisted to the end of our days
Only death will release us from the ranks.

In days of pogroms and bloodshed,
In black nights of despair,
In towns and villages our banner we'll raise
And on it—Defense and Conquest.

[The poem "Unknown Soldiers" by Avraham Stern (Yair) was the hymn of the LECHI (Fighters for Freedom), an underground terrorist movement during the British Mandate. It was founded in 1939 and disbanded in 1948. We adopted the words and the tune because at that time they expressed our emotional state. But certain phrases that did not suit us were changed.]

Since then we sang this song on many nights. It became dear to us, in expressing our mood. No one knew nor asked where the song came from. It spoke of determined resistance to the enemy and that was our response, that of the Zionist youth, to the destruction and murder perpetrated against us by the Nazis.

The autumn wind howled outside as distant whistling of trains filled us with a feeling of dread, reminding us of the deportation during the last two months. To this day I can't stand this sound.

When I fell asleep, I had a dream, or it may have been a hallucination. It is a pitch-black rainy night, only the railway lines glisten. A lonely person is standing at a railway station, waiting. He is waiting for his train. He is afraid. And now the train draws near, its wheels pulsating with hope. Its windows are lit and radiate warmth. It hurtles past and disappears in the mist. He runs after the train, crying desperately for help, until he falls into the mud. And again he is alone with the moaning wind and his cry, now mute. This hallucination returned again and again. Eventually it also became mute.

At that time I used to come to the branch frequently. I needed my friends; I felt my place was there. It was there that the fighters began to get organized. It was from there that our Movement's emissaries and those of our sister movement, "Dror-Hechalutz," went out to the Aryan side, to other cities.

One day I met Mira Fuchrer, the former leader of the troop. I could barely recognize her. While among the *shickses* [local Polish girls], she dressed up and put on makeup like one of them, when going to meet her lover. She looked just like a real Aryan. Who would recognize the modest, spartan Mira! We laughed at her new appearance, and Mira told us how she had gone over to the Aryan side by way of the nearby cemetery, where she had met Polish contacts, our friends. Her voice was hoarse, as usual, but her eyes shone with the vitality of someone doing things felt to be important. She did not go out often. Together with Mordechai Anielewicz and other older members, she was busy building up cells of fighters.

That autumn at night, there was a lot of arguing at the branch in Mila Street. The young ones, sixteen and seventeen years old, wanted to be active. They urged the older members to let them take part in actions. Dan from the "Sarid" troop, a boisterous youth, full of life, demanded a weapon and wanted to go out with it into the street during the next *aktzia*. We all knew that the Germans would not let us live in peace. At some point the *aktzien* would resume. The older members also argued among themselves. Some of them thought that we should all leave the ghetto and fight as partisans, as a Jewish unit seeking vengeance.

I remember that Merdek said we should remain there, in the ghetto:

"Our place is here, where our families were murdered. And here we must fight our last battle."

But no one thought only about saving himself. We were burning with the desire for vengeance, and maybe also with shame—ashamed that we had not organized ourselves earlier, while there were still many Jews there. Ashamed of the helplessness, the fear that had paralyzed us.

"What do you want," said Margalit, "and where were the leaders of the parties, and the rabbis? What did they do? They all tried to escape and save themselves. At least we called to the people not to report. We told them the truth. Did the Judenrat do so? Did they warn or help? They did nothing! We have nothing to blame ourselves for."

And Elik, good-natured Elik, who always backed Margalit, persuaded us that it was only now, when the deportations had ended, that we were able to obtain weapons from the Polish underground organizations. He explained that there were two underground movements: a right-wing one, under the authority of the Polish government in exile in London, called A.K. (Armia Krajowa). Many of them were anti-Semites and we couldn't expect any help from them.

The second underground is called A.L. (Armia Ludova), and that is the armed wing of the Socialist Party P.P.R., connected to its leadership in Russia. There we have loyal friends, but it is still in its beginnings, not sufficiently organized, and has few weapons at its disposal. Elik also told us that Jurek—Aryeh Vilner—is in charge of the purchase of weapons on the Aryan side, with the help of other emissaries from the organization. This was all extremely secret, and we were told not to say anything about it to anyone.

The Remnants of the "In Flames" Troop

I found Miriam (Tzelina Hammerstein) again by chance. It turned out that she and her family had also been through the *selektzia* and now they were living in Schultz's area, near me. Her father was still running a bakery. Miriam was a dear friend of mine from age seven; we had been in the same class at the school in Ptasia Street No. 5. We used to gather chestnuts in Saski Park, and we had joined the Movement together.

As I write these lines, I do not know if she is alive or was killed on the Aryan side after the uprising. All our ideas about rebellion and an uprising were born during heart-to-heart talks on our walks and while we were sleeping in the same bed, in the alcove in Ciepla Street. In the beginning we rebelled against our "old-fashioned" mothers, then against the humiliating conditions in the ghetto, against that meaningless life.

We were separated during the great *aktzia*, when we both clung to our families and to the thought of survival. Miriam was a sensitive person, striving for truth. She thought deeply, seeking to get to the root of things. When we met again, she did not join Yaakov and me in our outings in the ghetto and in the tasks we were given. She was a skeptic and not suited to the dangerous life of the underground. But our relations remained close, even though I was unable to share my experiences with her. She, her sister, and her parents succeeded miraculously in getting through the *selektzia*. This is what Miriam told me:

"During the great deportation I was very ill. Gangrene spread all over the lower part of my pelvis. I was lying with a high temperature, hiding in some cellar. I wanted to die. I had no strength left. I felt my life was ebbing. My sister, Halina, urged a friend of hers, a medical student, to help me. And he came to the cellar and operated on me.

"Mother sterilized a kitchen knife in the light of a carbine lamp. They laid me on the table, and he cut off a part of my buttock, stuck in a plug that absorbed the pus and saved my life. He came to the hiding place again twice and changed the plug.

"Another friend of my sister made contact with his friend on the Aryan side and, with the help of an acquaintance in the Jewish police, slipped in a vitamin C injection for me. When the order to report in the cauldron came, my family got me up and told me I must go there, whatever happens. I didn't want to. I couldn't. I begged them to leave me in the cellar. They refused and urged me to get up and go.

"Mother said, 'If you don't go, you are passing a death sentence on all of us.'

"This argument forced me to get up. Halina and Aunt Rosa brought makeup, colored my cheeks pink to make me look healthy, and that's how they dragged me into the lines walking to the *selektzia*. I don't know how it happened, but all of us came out on the right side, with the survivors. They held me firmly by my arms and so, with super-human efforts, we reached the Schultz 'shop' in Nowolipki Street."

After some time we discovered that Shoshana and Alma, members of my troop, had also survived. Alma was a beautiful girl, with blond hair and flushed cheeks. She was left alone with her mother. All the rest of her family had been killed.

One day Yaakov and I decided to go to the central ghetto to meet her. She and Shoshana did not take part in the underground activities because they considered them dangerous and too daring.

At dusk I went with Alma into the noisy street. Alma seemed restless and said she wanted to tell me something.

"Lilit," she whispered, "my mother wants me to go to the Aryan side because I 'look good,' and so I may be able to survive. But we don't have any Polish acquaintances, nor money."

"I don't have any acquaintances either. My mother is trying to make contact with Polish women who worked in our workshop before the war, but…"

"No, no, that's not the point. She knows an old man who was the only survivor out of his whole family. His wife and children were taken to the cattle cars. He can help us."

"If so, that's great. Do it, Alma. We must do all we can to survive," I said.

"All we can?" she hesitated. "Anything? Also to become the mistress of a fifty-year-old stranger, in exchange for possible survival? To give myself to him at the age of fifteen, when I have never yet been in love?"

"Is that what your mother wants?" I was shocked.

"Yes. I can't decide. Help me!" she pleaded.

"Alma, I don't know if I can help you. It sounds terrible, but…maybe."

"My mother is selling me. It's better to die here."

"No, Alma, she isn't selling you. She seems to love you very much. Think about that." We hugged and wept.

I returned to Yaakov, with my eyes still red. He didn't ask me anything, only put his arm around me and hugged me. That was the last time I saw Alma. I understood that she had agreed to do it. I never found out if she had really survived.

When I met Yaakov by chance in Leszno Street, I was dumbfounded. I couldn't believe that he of all people was still alive. Yaakov and I were very close and in normal times we would have become real friends. In those days we were shy about it and did not reveal our feelings to each other. Even now, many years later, I think of him with affection and sorrow. I think he died during the uprising, as he wanted to.

Yaakov was thin and tall for his age—sixteen. His eyes were dark and deep and his features were fine. He didn't talk much, but when he did open his mouth, he would speak with enthusiasm and infect his audience with it. He was a talented writer and played the violin beautifully. He was an artistic type, quiet, but full of turbulent feelings that he kept to himself.

Yaakov was sent with his father to a work camp. They both escaped, but were caught on the Aryan side. Polish informers, thugs, stole all the good clothes they wore, robbed them of everything, and left them helpless near the ghetto. When they returned, they could no longer find his mother and two little sisters. No one knew what had happened to them. Yaakov and his father succeeded in getting into the Töbens "shop" and work there. The lifesaving document provided by the workshop protected them for the time being.

Bella, my friend from my studies at the complet, also joined us. Now we were a group of three living in the same area. Yaakov blamed the older members of the Movement: Why don't they organize reprisals? Why don't we rise up courageously and openly? He was not the only one who felt that way. He wanted to act and so did we.

The first opportunity came soon, before I was ready for it. When we came to the branch, this time through openings in the attic, they called me, Yardena, and Rut and told us to be ready for underground activity in the Töbens and Schultz areas, and that soon Yaakov and I would become involved in various initiatives. I was happy and expressed my fervent desire to do anything I was charged with. As a result, I had to go several times a week on various errands to the branch in Mila Street. My disappearing from home caused my parents great concern and fear.

At a certain point I said to my father, "I can't just sit and work for the Germans. You had better understand that nothing will stop me from being with my friends at this time. I can't tell you what we are doing, but now I belong to them."

Mother looked at me for a long time and said with her lips drawn tight, "You are no longer my daughter, you belong to your Movement."

I could see she had been deeply offended by my words, but nevertheless understood that she no longer had control over me, and in some sense gave up the struggle against me.

I think she will never forgive me for my behavior at that time, even though later we got closer and our relations became normal again. Today, when she has remained in Belgium and I am in this country [Israel] *on my own, I am trying to understand her better. I miss her and my little sister Mirka, and so much want them to come here. In those days, the Movement, the underground, my concern with the Jewish struggle and vengeance were even more important to me than my family.*

By then it was winter. A thin layer of ice covered the ground. It was the year 1943, the beginning of the fourth year of the war. What will this year bring? Life or death? Will salvation come and the British and American armies invade Europe and subdue the Germans? Will there be a turning point on the Russian front and the Germans will begin to withdraw after their anticipated defeat in Stalingrad?

Rut and Yardena came to Töbens's "shop." They met me in one of the apartments there and handed over to me and to Yaakov pages typed on a typewriter. The order was to stick them on the walls of the houses in our area. As at the beginning of the deportation, this time we were also warned about the possible reaction of the inhabitants. We decided to go back together to the branch on the following day.

I slipped away to Leszno Street a short time before the work in the "shops" was over. Yaakov was to stick the posters by Schultz's "shop" in Novolipie. My feet trembled with agitation and fear. I looked around. I didn't see any *Werkschutzim* [guards at the "shops"] or policemen. There were a few people in the street.

No time to waste, quick, I said to myself. I stuck one poster on every house and ran on. Without gloves, my hands smarted from the cold and barely obeyed me. It was well below zero, the sky was overcast. It would soon be completely dark. I finished my row within a short time and was about to turn back when suddenly two young men appeared next to me and began reading.

"Wait, wait, are you from the fighting organization? They have such children there? The organization calls on us to fight and not to go to the Poniatow Camp, but where can we get weapons? And what is this organization? It's sure to be communists and they are not to be trusted. Run along, or they'll catch you and kill you on the spot."

They tore the poster off the wall and threw it on the ground.

"You'll soon see what organization this is. You'll hear about it," I said and quickly slipped away.

On the following day I saw groups of workers from the "shops" standing and reading the leaflets and others tearing them down. I hurried to Dielna Street, hid there, and waited for Rut and Yardena. I told them about the reactions of the people.

They said, "It takes time before people can grasp the significance of an underground fighting organization and stop being afraid of their own shadow. The blood of the Germans is red like ours and they can also be killed."

We walked in the rows of the freezing and exhausted workers. As we approached the guarded gate, they became uneasy. Each one of them was carrying food in his toolbox. Will they get through the search safely?

Suddenly we saw a man being taken out of the line and pushed by the German police into their hut.

Yardena whispered, "He is one of ours. I know him."

We ran quickly to the branch and reported they had arrested someone, apparently a member of "Dror." Later that evening I heard that the organization had acted and freed him. I was glad they had saved him.

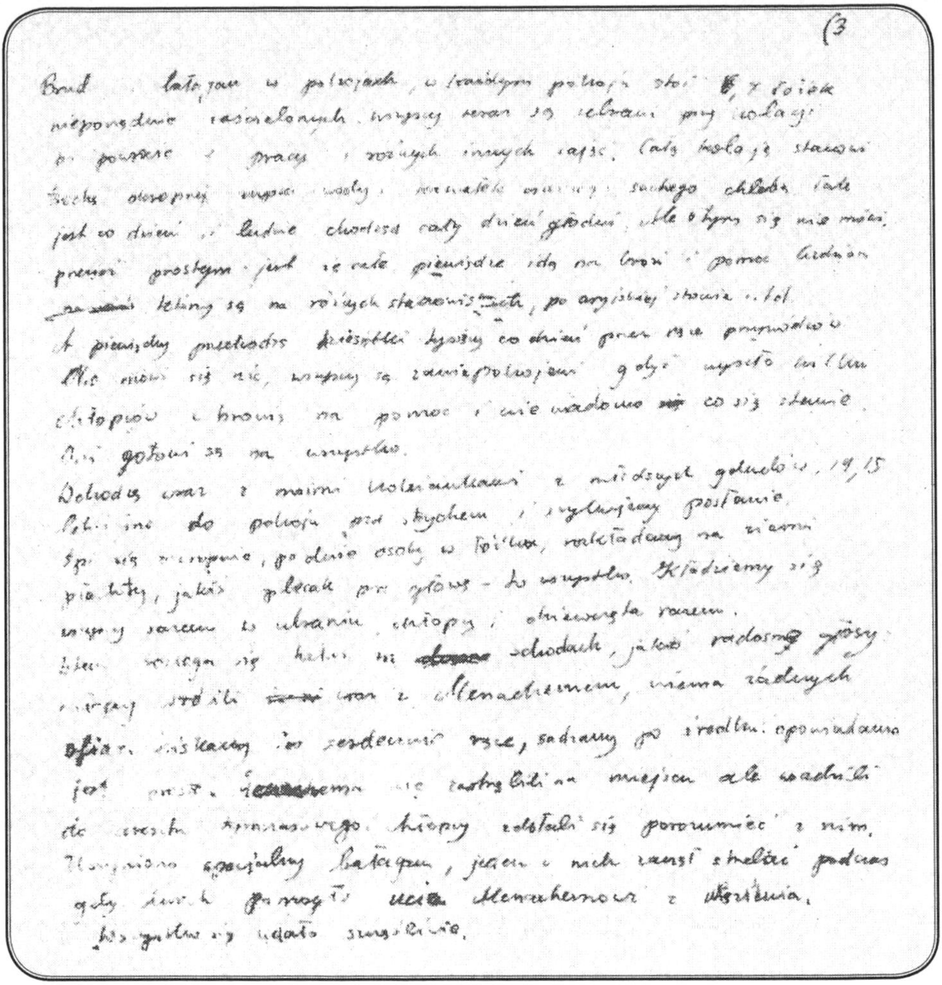

Page from my diary, written in 1943, that I smuggled out.

The Second *Aktzia* and the First Confrontation

Suddenly, on the eighteenth of January, the second *aktzia* in the ghetto began. I was sitting with Naomi in the "Sarid" troop in our "shop," and we were on edge. *What is happening? No one has gone to work.*

In our area it was still quiet. In the evening we contacted Dan from "Sarid" who had been in the ghetto by chance, slipped into the "shops," and told us what was happening in the ghetto. He was on his way and hid together with others in a hiding place there, called Janek.

The first information he brought was confusing and terrible: "They surprised us in the morning. Some of us hid in the hiding place, and the others were taken into line in the street, among them Mordechai Anielewicz. Some of them had weapons. They were on their way to the *Umschlagplatz*. A battle broke out in the street. Elik Rozanski from the 'Banir' troop hid behind the corner of the street and threw two hand grenades. He killed Germans and he himself was badly injured. Later they brought him back to the branch, unconscious, and he died there. I have no idea what happened to the other people," he said, and left us in a terrible state of uncertainty.

A deep sorrow engulfed us. Elik is dead! Eighteen-year-old Elik, tall with long legs and arms, Elik with kind moist eyes. When he spoke about Jewish defense, there was a steel gleam in his eyes. A few weeks ago, I think it was at the end of October, Elik had fired at the commander of the Jewish police, Yaakov Laikin who had replaced Sherinski, and killed him. He was in the same unit as Margalit-Emilka Landau and Avramik Zandman. That death sentence stunned the ghetto, and there were various rumors about assassination attempts. I heard about it, but did not tell my family who had done it.

In the evening we all returned home from the "shop." The atmosphere was heavy. The German manager of the workshops, Töbens, announced by means of his Jewish deputy Neufeld that he had no intention to send off his workers. We are all protected and could continue to work.

In the hiding place the same arguments began. Is Töbens to be trusted, or not? The opinions of the lodgers in our room differed: The Fischer family decided to go to work, and even Ignac and my aunt sided with them. But my mother was suspicious—and I agreed with her.

We decided to hide in the attic. Naomi joined us. I was glad I wasn't alone. Through a little window, we could see what was happening in the courtyard of the house in Nowolopki Street. Suddenly we heard screaming, "*Alle runter, alle raus*" [all down, all out]. No one came out. The Jewish police was not in the area, only Germans, Latvians, and Lithuanians. And now they were starting to pull people out by force and throwing them into the yard.

At a distance I saw a man arguing, holding a piece of paper; the German pushed him into line, an old woman fell down. God, he shot her! Frightened people got into line, but more people were lying in the yard, shot dead.

Mother closed the hatch. Naomi and I clung to each other. There was silence in the hiding place. We remained sitting there all night. On the third day of the *aktzia*, someone went out to see what was happening in the "shop." It turned out that they did not touch Töbens's workers, but took some from the smaller "shops," and even from Schultz. It was early morning, so we decided to go out and look for some of our people, living in Leszno. At the entrance to the house, we met Chaviva Zandman, the little sister of Pnina and Avramik.

She pulled us into the entrances on the staircase and told us in an agitated voice, "Yes, there was a battle in Niska and Zamenhofa Streets. They surprised us, but Mordechai immediately distributed weapons, and most of them came out into the street with those being expelled and slipped into the rows. They were all killed. Elik was wounded. There was a battle, and they threw a hand grenade and bombs with a flammable liquid. Our people fired and shot Germans. The whole crowd dispersed and fled. The Germans were stunned and lay in the street. Mordechai survived miraculously."

"How? Tell us how it happened," we begged.

"Everything is so confused, the people are in shock, still hiding. I wasn't there, they told me. I was sent to pass it on to the group in the 'shops.'" Chaviva spoke with great agitation, swallowed words, and looked around. "It was Jezik (Dan) from the 'Tel-Amal' troop who saved Mordechai," she said and hurried on.

"But how, wait a minute!"

"When the bullets ran out, Mordechai jumped on a German and wanted to grab his weapon. Some other Germans came running. Dan saw it and also jumped on the German. Together they seized his gun and slipped into the house close by, where someone hid them in a bunker."

We knew Dan well. He was the leader of one of the groups in our troop. Sturdy, with fair hair, gray deep-set eyes and bushy eyebrows, a pleasant, somewhat shy smile in a handsome face. An intelligent boy, from a wealthy family, high-minded and brave. I was excited and ran to tell my parents that Jewish youth had rebelled and fought in the street, on the way to the *Umschlagplatz*. They didn't believe it.

"How can you spread such rumors? How do you know such things? Better not talk about it."

Ignac, the doctor, my aunt's husband, said seriously, "The splendid Jewish youth, where were they until now? The Poles who mock us are right. We don't have the strength to resist. They are just bluffing!"

I grew quiet. I was so happy and elated that they had not been afraid, had gone into the street, fought and fell beside the dead Germans.

"And who knows what punishment they'll mete out on the whole ghetto because of the Germans they killed," Father added anxiously, knowing that I wasn't making it up. All the people present thought about that, for it was the way the Germans had behaved to the Jews and also to the Poles until now: indiscriminate collective punishment.

After a few days I got to know more details: Arie Gzybowski, a member of our Movement who was a policeman, was given the task of passing information to the Z.O.B. headquarters and helping out when necessary. Arie brought the news that he had succeeded in helping a group of members of the organization escape when they were on their way to the *Umschlagplatz*, and hid in the attic of the hospital adjoining it. They remained there without food or water until the trains had gone. At night help arrived. The members placed a board between the roofs, rescued the survivors, and transferred them to a safer place.

The Germans learned to fear entering houses, after they had been surprised in various places by a group of fighters from Hashomer Hatzair, "Dror" and "Gordonia." It seemed to them that people were firing from many houses, which was not true. The fact was that the fighters were always changing the place from which they fired.

The Germans must have wondered how come that those *jids*, who had until now gone quietly and meekly to their deaths, had decided to defend themselves. Apparently they had not thought Jews capable of it. Then they declared that those were Poles who had come to help the Jews. That's what we were told later. I didn't know who had been saved that way.

Besides, the Jews learned how to hide. Apart from those who went on January eighteenth to their *platzovka* to work and were diverted to the trains in spite of their documents, the Germans and their helpers could not find people in their apartments. People said that those caught in that *aktzia* were not taken to Treblinka, but to Lublin, to the camp called Lipova 6.

The example of self-defense in the ghetto reverberated in and outside the ghetto and made people feel there was hope. Margalit-Emilka Landau from the "Galil" troop made a name for herself. Many stories about her heroism were passed around in the ghetto. The lovely brave Emilka was the first to throw a hand grenade from within the crowd being led to the *Umschlagplatz*. She was killed on the spot. She and Elik were in love and were also united in death. A boy and girl, aged eighteen or nineteen, the first to fall in battle. We all mourned their deaths.

The second *aktzia* was over and with it the first attempt at resistance. A new era had begun.

The Ghetto Prepares for the Armed Struggle

The Jewish Fighting Organization (Z.O.B.) went through a period of reorganization and of drawing conclusions. First of all, its existence became well known among the people in the ghetto. It included all the Zionist organizations except Beitar. The "Bund" and the communists of the P.P.R. party also participated. The headquarters included their representatives whose names were not known. All we knew was that Mordechai was the commander and Yitzhak Zuckerman his deputy.

["Antek," Yitzhak Zuckerman, deputy commander of the Jewish Fighting Organization (Z.O.B.), one of the leaders of the "Dror" Movement. He was active in the Z.O.B. delegation on the Aryan side, whose task was to remain in contact with the Polish underground movements, A.K. and A.L., to represent the organization after Aryeh Vilner had returned to the ghetto, to obtain weapons and to assist the organization. He survived, immigrated to Israel, and was among the founders of Kibbutz Lochamei Hagetaot [ghetto fighters]. Together with his wife, Tzvia Lubetkin, and others, he founded the museum Beit Lochamei Hagetaot. He died in 1981.]

The secrecy of the organization was stepped up. I knew that the leadership of Hashomer Hatzair included, besides Mordechai, also Tosia Altman, Aryeh Vilner, Mira Fuchrer, and Yehuda Wangrower.

[Yehuda Wangrower commanded a fighting unit. He was poisoned by gas but survived and came out of the ghetto together with Tosia through the sewage canals on May 10, 1943. Together with the other survivors, he reached a forest near Warsaw, where he died of exhaustion and of the gas poisoning.]

The branch in Mila Street 61 was closed down. Only one room was left and a few youths lived there—some of the young ones, not posted with the fighting units. Their role was to pass around leaflets and stick posters on houses and serve as a liaison among the fighting units, living together in an apartment intended to serve as their base when the time came to fight.

I remember some of the young people by their first names only: Lilit, my friend from the "Sarid" troop; Moshe and Sabra from the "Galil" troop; Erna from the "Tel-Amal" troop. Israel Kanal, a member of the "Akiba" Movement, was also there; he was wounded in the leg. In the midst of the great *aktzia*, it was he who shot Yosef Sherinski, the commander of the Jewish police, on August 20, 1942.

Sherinski was accused by the organization of fulfilling the German orders in directing the great deportation at the beginning of the summer *aktzia*. The Z.O.B. sentenced him to death, and Israel was charged with the execution of the sentence. In the ghetto they thought it was the Polish underground that had done it. At that time people did not believe that there was a Jewish underground organization.

[Israel Kanal, one of the mainstays of the pioneer movement "Akiba," fought in the Warsaw Ghetto. He left the ghetto through the sewage canals, but died in Auschwitz.]

The secrecy was so complete that the addresses and names of the fighters were kept secret. Mordechai also used to change his outward appearance. Once I saw him in the street dressed as a *platzovka* worker. He wore knickerbockers, a filthy short jacket, and a cap pulled down over his face. I noticed he had a mustache.

On another occasion I landed in an embarrassing situation. I wanted to cross from Leszno Street to Nowoliple Street. Like everyone else, I had to climb through holes that had been opened in attics. After a long climb up stairs, I succeeded, with the help of a flashlight, in getting to the right hole in the wall. I had to bend right down, but there were a few more people waiting in line to go through. I asked the person standing in front of me, "What's the time?" He turned around, looked at me in the feeble light of the flashlight, but did not answer. To my amazement, it was Mordechai. He was dressed as a student. His neck was wrapped in a shawl, and he was wearing a student's blue cap.

As spring approached, the atmosphere in the reduced ghetto changed. We waited for the final *aktzia*, for the final extermination of the Jews of Warsaw, making it *judenrein*. People began to build bunkers. Experts turned up, engineers who built bunkers with electric light, in wells and toilets. Most of the bunkers were dug in cellars. There were various ways to enter the bunkers from the ground floor: by raising a cover in the kitchen stove or through an opening in the large stove attached to the wall, or in many other innovative ways, according to the fertile imagination of the builders. The ghetto was preparing for a struggle.

At that time, in February 1943, the owners of the large workshops decided, authorized by the SS command, to transfer their large plants from Warsaw to the camps that had been set up for that purpose in the Lublin area: Poniatow and Travniki. The Töbens shop also had to move. All were in a dilemma.

The Germans tried to persuade us "nicely" by sending Jewish representatives to these places. On their return they told us they really are building work camps and wooden huts for the workers to live in. But who can believe them? Nevertheless, a few groups of Jewish workers went out to these camps.

My mother and father did not believe a single word the Germans said. Mother began to think about going to the Aryan side. Aunt Biela and her husband, Ignac Shpak, got ready to leave the ghetto. They both looked "good," in other words, not Jewish. I heard that Ignac even had an operation to remove any signs of circumcision. He went out of the ghetto and remained there for some time. My aunt joined him, but in spring, just a few days before the last *aktzia*, they both returned in despair to the ghetto.

They told us they had exploited all the possibilities; they had no more money or acquaintances willing to risk their lives on their behalf. Whatever will be, will be. At that time Mother and Mirka were no longer in the ghetto. Aunt Biela had lived with us for many years. Mirka was very close to her, and she was sorry to have to part from her. *Why had they given up so quickly?*

It was only later that I understood what tremendous spiritual forces are required to dissimulate, to hide one's identity, to overcome the constant fear of informers and of the eyes of passersby, of neighbors, of every Pole. They had made up their minds: "Our fate will be like that of all the others." After all that happened to me on the Aryan side, I am better able to understand them.

Isn't it a defeatist solution? Giving up, not facing up to the challenge? Accepting one's fate? I was sorry for them and tried to persuade them to try again. Ignac formulated his position in a philosophical way, typical of him: "I accept my certain death approaching, not as God's will or fate, but as the inability to prevail over reality. Out of all the hopeless alternatives, I choose to die with all the others."

Later, when there was no other hope, they went to Poniatow and suffered the same fate as Father.

The mood in the ghetto improved. There was enough food, and the news about the German losses on the Eastern Front gave the ghetto inhabitants courage. Maybe the war will end in a few months, and if another *aktzia* breaks out, we'll hide in the bunkers. The Russians will come and liberate us. We'll defeat Hitler.

Oh, how bitter was their disappointment! Within three months their hopes were shattered and the people annihilated.

Between the January uprising and the final *aktzia* and the April revolt, the remnants of the Jews of Warsaw were feverishly preparing for what was to come: Some for going over to the Aryan side, some building a hiding place, and some to fight.

Again and again posters appeared on the walls of the houses, now quite openly. The battle in the central ghetto had repercussions both among the Jews and among the Poles. The unbelievable had happened! Someone had dared to kill Germans! Not a large underground movement, but those Jews who previously "went like sheep to the slaughter." The bent back straightened up, the Z.O.B. gained in esteem. Now one could openly speak about "the organization."

The Jews of the ghetto stood in groups in front of the posters. I slipped into the crowd to hear their reactions. They were positive, uttered aloud, and I relaxed. I had also added a little to that feeling of elation the sense of self-respect and the will to fight for their lives. Just knowing that we had an organization, daring to come out openly against the villainous Nazis, that there was someone showing the way, and a leadership taking responsibility, contributed tremendously to the self-esteem that had suffered such humiliation during the last four years.

One morning we heard a shot on the stairs. Alarmed, we ran to the door. I saw the figure of a girl slipping away quickly. I recognized her. It was Shulamit (Shoshkova) fleeing, holding a revolver. Several young men also fled. On the staircase lay our upstairs neighbor, bleeding. We knew that he traded in foreign currency.

People lifted him up and took him into the apartment, shouting, "What do they think? That they can also shoot Jews?" It was clear whom they meant. It was a Z.O.B. squad, carrying out an act of punishment called "EX." My parents pulled me inside.

"Don't your friends have anything else to do? Do they have to shoot Jews?" they said harshly.

"They must buy weapons and the organization has no money. Whoever doesn't give willingly will be forced to do so," our neighbor Fischer answered instead of me.

I was silent. I knew that everyone had heard about the organization's forays into rich people's apartments for a contribution to the purchase of weapons, and it was levied from all the wealthy people. The members did not want to do it. They tried to talk to the people, who usually cooperated and gave some money willingly. But apparently there were also cases of keeping "a hostage" in some hiding place belonging to the organization until the recalcitrant agreed to redeem his relative.

At that time we heard about the arrest of two young members of the "Sarid" troop, Dan and Tamar. Both of them had gone over to the Aryan side to help our emissaries. Dan was taken to Zelaznej Street 103, to the *Befehlsstelle*, the SS headquarters. He was brutally tortured and executed.

Tamar was also caught while crossing to the Aryan side. The Polish policeman who arrested her was willing to accept a bribe, but just at that point a German policeman came up. A Jewish girl who wants to run away from the ghetto? He sent her to the Gestapo headquarters in Shucha Avenue. I heard later that she did not admit that she was a

Jew, endured all the torture, and was sent as a Pole to do forced labor in Germany.

At that time we also heard about a Jewish group that had tried to get to the partisans at the time of the great *aktzia*, and its members fell after they had been denounced—among them Pelek and Rut from the "Banir" troop and Nola and Shulamit from the "Merchav" troop. This course of action, fighting with the Polish partisans, was also out of the question.

A Radio?

One day Yaakov came to me with a mysterious smile on his face, arousing my curiosity. "Listen," he whispered, "come with me to the stairs, put something on."

My parents knew him, and Mirka perked up her ears. I put on warm clothes and we went out into the frozen yard.

"I've heard about some people who have a hidden radio. I told Shmuel and he said I should try to get it from them. I have a revolver but no bullets. It will be useful just to frighten them. Will you come with me?"

"Of course," I said. "Will Bella come too?"

"No, no. She looks too young. Tell your parents that you are going to a Movement activity and will soon be back."

The street was dark. We went up to an attic in Leszno. At that time attics had turned into streets. Openings were cut between the attics of adjacent houses, and in this way it was possible to get through almost to the central ghetto. All you needed was a flashlight and courage.

We squeezed into the narrow openings, stepping on various things. Sometimes one even had to go over the roof in order to continue to the next house. Other shadowy figures moved in front of us and behind us. We again came out onto a staircase. I don't remember which street it was. We knocked on the door. A tall young man opened the door. Yaakov entered, holding the revolver; I followed him. Later another strong fellow appeared. The two men looked at us, amazed.

"We are from the Z.O.B. You have a secret radio and we need it. Do us a favor and give it to us."

We looked at the alarmed face of the burly fellow. I suddenly wanted to burst out laughing. How come he is afraid of us, after all, we are really still children? But I know. He was afraid of "the organization." He took us to an opening in the wall, leading to a small attic. It was their hideout. We had to climb up a ladder.

I went up first, the man behind me, and Yaakov followed him. There was just a narrow crack between the wall and the floor, hidden by a pile of junk. The man lifted a part of the wall, and the hideout opened up in front of us. I was covered with dust and looked for the radio. The man did not help me much. I sensed he was frightened.

"If you don't show us, we'll have to come again," Yaakov said.

"There are parts of a radio here, they must be put together. I don't know exactly where they are."

Suddenly I sensed that he was standing behind me on the ladder and could strangle me. *Why did I get myself into this trap?*

I said to Yaakov, "Tomorrow our people will come to take the radio. Assemble it in the meantime, so they'll be able to take it along more easily. You'd better not get into trouble," I added, faking self-confidence.

Yaakov understood that I didn't want to get inside this crack and stepped back. We went down and left quickly.

"Why did you give up?" I sensed his disappointment.

"I had a feeling that the man is making a fool of us. It's better if some older people come and fetch the radio, someone capable of frightening them."

We told Merdek about "our" radio, but I have no idea if they did get it out of there. That was the end of our requisitioning.

The End Approaches: What Should We Do?

Most of the members of the Movement were assigned to apartments intended to serve as bases during the fighting outposts [*bojowki*]. The apartments were on the upper floors of the houses in the main streets. The young ones remained at the branch in Mila Street. The leaders of the Movement did not feel good about it nor did I. We felt that we had been denied our rights; the counselors had prevented us from participating in the armed struggle. We were dejected, even though they explained to us that there were not enough weapons, in particular for young girls. But we also wanted to fight!

Yaakov, Bella, and I decided to get ahold of weapons and ammunition, in addition to Yaakov's tiny revolver. We started to collect clothes and went to sell them to the people who were going out to do forced labor on the Aryan side. In this way we saved up enough money to obtain a revolver for Bella.

One of the experienced smugglers negotiated for us with the Polish owner of the revolver. It was an old revolver, but we were happy. Now we had to get another one. The dealers and smugglers provided weapons for private individuals who had decided to defend their bunkers when the final *aktzia* began. But the course of events ruined our plans.

March passed and April came. Talk about the approaching final liquidation of the ghetto intensified. The ghetto was fully aware of it and prepared. It was a calm before the storm, suffused with energy and tension. Frequent shots near the ghetto and sudden evening searches by the SS command cars heralded what was to come. Sending off the people working for Töbens and Schultz to Poniatow and Travniki caused apprehension, even though they had gone of their own free will. If they are sending out the workers, what will happen to all the rest?

The companies of the SS General Globotznik, in charge of extermination, again arrived in Warsaw. The people in the ghetto became apathetic about danger, insensitive and hardened. We had already experienced maximum anxiety, so fear no longer frightened us, we were immune to danger.

Many people felt and thought, *Whatever will be, will be. So what? I'll die. If not today, then tomorrow or the day after—what does it matter!*

They stopped obeying all kinds of prohibitions enforced by the authorities. They committed offenses, scoffed at punishments. They did not keep the curfew, and acts of sabotage were carried out fearlessly. They grabbed doors and furniture to keep fires going. Everything would be destroyed anyway.

Under the influence of the Z.O.B., which was the dominant force in the ghetto and in the "shops," people became even more determined not to fall into the hands of the Germans this time. That is why the call for an uprising not only did not deter the Jewish population; on the contrary, it drove them to try to devise ways to save themselves.

The bunkers suddenly seemed useless. They spoke about a hideout discovered in the former small ghetto. When they opened it, they found people inside who had died of suffocation for lack of oxygen after staying there for several months, and only one man was still alive, half blind. He told them that the people had gone blind because of the complete darkness in the hideout. Every day someone had starved to death.

The only possibility left was to escape to the Aryan side, dress up as a Pole, and look for acquaintances or people willing to hide Jews in exchange for money. For a few thousand zloty, one could get a Polish birth certificate and a *Kennkarte*, a ration card.

People handed over their children to Christian clerics, to monasteries, and to peasants in the villages. Sacks with food were thrown into the ghetto over the walls daily and openly, at least on our side. People paid ransom to the foreman of the *platzovka* going out to work on the Aryan side—of course, those who were lucky enough to find "good" Poles, also did not look Jewish.

Women dyed and lightened their hair, and created curls by rolling their hair in pieces of paper, to look like *shikses*. But they could not change the color of their eyes—their dejected and pallid look. A Jew could also be picked out by his hesitant walk, his bent back, his eyes constantly darting around him. We were so preoccupied by our aspiration to look like *goyim* that we examined ourselves and others: Does that man look like a Jew? Will they recognize him in the street?

Of course customers were found who were willing to buy Jews. A new profession cropped up among the simple Polish people, the great anti-Semites: *schmaltzovnik*—a person demanding a bribe, an informer, a blackmailer. [The word was derived from the German word *schmaltz*, meaning lard. The expression describes people you can "grease" by bribing them.]

We were deeply disappointed in the Polish people. We thought that as witnesses of our tragedy, our compatriots, sharing the same language and culture, they would hold out a hand to save us. But it did not happen. Few of them hid Jews for large sums of money; these were mostly people connected to socialist activities and the left-wing parties.

Many devout Christians and religious scholars helped us without taking money, out of true nobility of spirit. Many others, from among the simple folk, made a living by informing on Jews to the Gestapo, and they collaborated willingly out of pure anti-Semitism.

From among the simple people, those involved in seizing Jews, individuals or groups, were various types of thugs—petty criminals who made a living by stealing Jewish property, by blackmail. They walked around in the streets close to the ghetto, spied by the gates and the places where Jews worked on the Aryan side, and looked for victims. Thousands made a living this way.

We heard that sometimes they undressed Jews and left them in the street in their underclothes, and also threw them on the Aryan side right into the hands of the Germans.

But we had no choice; there was no other way out. By now we despised our own lives so much that we risked everything like gamblers in a casino. Moreover, we had sharpened our senses and developed agility, creative thinking, and an amazing ability to find our way and to extricate ourselves from seemingly hopeless situations. People were afraid to move away from their houses and hiding places in case the final *aktzia* found them unprepared. Toward the end of April, the atmosphere was feverish and filled with great tension. Everyone felt that borrowed time had run out.

Mother Takes the Initiative

The state of our family grew worse. We began to suffer from hunger. There were no clothes left to sell. We lived on the food we received in the "shop," distributed by the Germans.

Father sent me to his brother, to Schultz's "shop," to get a helping of soup from him, handed out there. David Leon and Irena did not need the soup from the Germans. They had a lot of money and gold, and a great deal of property from their stores, which they had smuggled out to the Aryan side even before the *aktzia*, to their friend Wosz. They could afford to buy food smuggled into the ghetto in large quantities.

I was ashamed to take charity from them, but I had no choice. Father, my kind-hearted father who loved to help everyone, was now forced to accept donations of food from his rich brother. Mother was vehemently against it. She, the proud and snobbish Mrs. Melamed, would take the remnants from her sister-in-law Irena? For years they had not been on good terms, and Mother preferred to go hungry rather than take anything from her. But Father insisted.

My uncle had behaved wisely. His contact person, the Pole Wosz, was employed as a doorman at the Austrian Embassy. My uncle got him into business and, for a large sum of money, obtained for him a permit to enter the ghetto, and in this way he transferred a great deal of merchandise. In exchange he received from the Pole the proceeds of the sales. Wosz was a decent person. He did not exploit their inferior status and continued to pay them their share of the proceeds, and even arranged a hiding place for them at the home of a relative, also a doorman, but at the closed Swedish Embassy. I found out all this later. At that time we knew they were about to leave the ghetto and hide on the Aryan side.

Father was skeptical. Only Mother and Mirka looked Slavic and could be taken for Poles. He and I, we looked very Jewish, pure Semites, with hooked noses, black hair and eyes. How could we hide there? Mother became full of energy and initiative, brimming with suggestions.

"I'll try to get in touch with the women who worked for us before the war. Maybe Janka Vishinievska will hide us. First of all I must get Mirka out."

She would ask, "Do you think they still remember us? Will they be willing to risk their own lives and hide us? You do know that whoever hides a Jew can expect a death sentence. And money, where do we get the money? Do you rely on Leon and Irena?"

And speculate, "Yes, they are going out to the Aryan side, surely they must help us. If you request it, maybe Leon will agree, he won't abandon us."

I listened to these talks, which became more and more frequent. In the end, Father apparently spoke to his brother and received a promise from him that if Mother succeeded in finding a place to hide on the Aryan side, he'd give us the money to live on, as long as he remained there.

In the morning Mother went out to the Aryan side. The process was simple: Payment to the leader of the group going out to work, a bribe to the policeman counting the workers, and then it's all up to you and your lucky stars.

Mother dressed well. She put on makeup and went off. Will she return safely? She had bought forged birth certificates for me and for herself. She looked like a Polish aristocrat: beautiful, tall, slim, and she walked erect. She spoke Polish without any trace of Yiddish (a language she didn't know). She had a chance to be taken for a pure Aryan. She came back a day later with good news: Janka agreed to rent an apartment below ground and move us there with her parents and her crippled son. Mother, Father, and I would live there. A hiding place will have to be dug in the cellar for me and for Father, in case someone suspected that there were Jews living in the apartment.

And Mirka? Mother received the address of Mrs. Marysia Grzybowska, who agreed to take in Mirka as her sister's daughter who had come to her from the country in southern Poland.

Before the war, Marysia and Janka, like many other workers, received from my parents for safe keeping knitting machines to make woolen gloves. At the weekend they were to bring the finished product and again receive wool to work with. They did piecework at home. It was convenient for the women, as it enabled them to continue to look after their children, and also for us, as we did not have enough room for a workshop.

Marysia was a kind soul. She did not have any children and agreed to take Mirka without payment. She would not hear about any compensation. She was a true Catholic and thought it was her duty to help people in distress. She herself was poor and lived with her drunken brother in a miserable apartment, barely able to get by.

The day to part came. They dressed Mirka up as a woman and gave her many instructions how to behave. The parting was hard for me. As opposed to my parents' plans, I did not intend to join them. I intended to remain in the ghetto and to participate in the uprising. I did not tell them anything (for fear of making them unhappy), but I was filled with apprehension that I might never see Mirka again. I was afraid for her, because I did not believe she would manage on her own, far from Mother.

Apparently, I did not correctly judge her stamina and will to live. She said goodbye to us as though we were going to meet again the next day. Mother took her along, and both of them went over to the Aryan side in the same way, by joining a *platzovka*. It was a great moment for a ten-year-old girl. She had to become independent.

Parting, without Saying Goodbye

In spite of my decision, I was in a dilemma. It was a hard period for me, a time of inner conflicts. I had to decide and choose between the possibility of survival and certain death, between loyalty to my parents and to the Movement and ideas I believed in. The dilemmas were my own, and I could not share them even with Miriam-Tzelina, my friend, whose family also intended to go out to a hiding place on the Aryan side. Her parents still had money.

My inner struggle was unbearable. A fifteen-year-old girl forced to choose between life and death.

In the end I made my decision and went to the ghetto to tell my former group leader, Rut Heiman. I said to her, "I am ready to leave my parents. I want to fight with all the others, and if there is no weapon for me, I'll purchase it on my own, as long as they put me into a fighting unit." Rut replied that she must consult others.

A few days later I came again to the branch and met her. The answer was negative. She told me that the Movement had decided that some people should survive to tell what they had seen. There must be witnesses left, particularly among the young ones. She told me that Tzameret from the "Bush" troop was writing a diary and passing it on to the Aryan side, to Irena Adamowitz, a Polish friend of the Movement, and that they were trying to procure a foreigner's papers for Mira Fuchrer, to enable her to get to Switzerland. It was also decided to send several young girls to the Aryan side. Contact was made with one of the monasteries where they intended to send a number of girls who looked Slavic.

About a week before Passover, I met Rut again. She gave me the address of that monastery, in the town of Henrykov near Warsaw, but added that it would be better if I went with my parents, as I didn't look "good." The girls going to the Aryan side were Ktana and Dina from the "Sarid" troop; Chaviva Zandman, the sister of Avramek of the "Banir" troop; Pnina from "Bemaale" and Judit and Erella from "Hagalil." All of them looked more or less Aryan. I was told that in an hour of great need I could turn to that monastery, but not before.

For me it was a heavy blow. Everything disintegrated: my way of thinking, my standpoint. All I had worked out in my mind collapsed. I lost my bearings. I, such an unimportant person, am to save my life, while all those invaluable people I knew must die of their own free will? It was a terrible feeling, and I found it hard to get used to the way charted for me. But time was running out. The date of my leaving for the Aryan side, agreed on with my mother, was approaching.

Father was supposed to leave a week later. Before going out of the ghetto, I went to say goodbye to my friends in the Movement. It was a clear spring day. I went along with a *platzovka*, returning from work on the Aryan side. The streets were deserted. The work squads, *Werterfassung*, were cleaning the streets, and the houses were empty. In the ghetto, tension was in the air. Everyone sensed the imminent danger.

But on that Friday, before Passover, the air was fragrant, as an unfamiliar scent penetrated the ghetto with the rays of the spring sun. Crowds of people wandered about in the streets. Some of them were laughing and chatting cheerfully.

How these streets changed within two days! What an upheaval in the lives of these people, who had tried to forget, if only for a moment, their bitter fate. They had lived and enjoyed the blue sky and bright sun, like people anywhere else.

I parted from my friends. I walked about in the streets, so much a part of my life. Every street had witnessed suffering and changes. *Can one love places where one has felt pain, fear, anguish?* This house is where I hid during the great deportation. On the ruins of this playing field, we played ball and scouting games, and these stones witnessed my inner defiance against my parents, and also against evil and injustice.

In these streets I had spent my childhood. I was supposed to hate this hell, but I couldn't. Ties of great emotional significance bridged the gulf between us. If I hated this place, I would have to hate the whole of my life. And now I was leaving.

What does that mean? Can one really leave this place for good? No! My inner self will remain here, among these gray walls, in these narrow streets, in the courtyards where Jewish children played hopscotch, catch me, and hide-and-seek. Will the body function without the soul, devoid of life, propelled by the survival instinct? Farewell, Warsaw Ghetto! I, a different person, say goodbye to you forever. Farewell my friends, I love you above all else.

Life has its own dynamics and I must go on. It is all over. For me the three-year-old ghetto has ended. I can still hear Mira Fuchrer's words when we parted: "Go on, survive, but you must not forget!"

I went back to the Töbens "shop" the same way. I no longer saw the sun nor sensed its warmth. I felt a great emptiness within me. The emptiness of a well, devoid of water. I was going off alone to fight for my life, to confront an unknown endless struggle. The critical hour had come.

Leaving the Ghetto

I remained with Father in the apartment. He was very tense. Uncle Leon and his family were already on the Aryan side, in a hiding place at the Swedish Embassy. Out of all his siblings, only his sister, Ester Lechtus, her husband and sons had survived. They were with the "brushmakers," and rumor had it that they had prepared bunkers for themselves.

People did not ask each other about their hiding places. Everyone kept it secret. Aunt Biela and Uncle Ignac said, on returning from the Aryan side, that they would probably go to the Poniatow Camp when the Töbens "shop" was finally transferred there. When the two sisters, my mother and Biela, parted, they wept bitterly. They may have sensed it was forever.

At the beginning of April, even before Mother went to the Aryan side, we suddenly had a visitor: Uncle Shlomo Schweitzer, the husband of the third sister, Ida. He came from the summer resort of Otvock, where they lived. He was a broken man, in despair, and had come to tell us terrible news: My grandfather, the father of the three sisters, was caught together with Ida and the two little girls, when they were hiding. Grandfather was killed on the spot. They put Aunt Ida and the girls on the death train. He, my uncle, happened not to be with them at the time and thus survived. He sat in silence. Suddenly he recovered, said goodbye quickly, and went on his way. Later I heard that he had also died.

There was no time to mourn. We had to act. To enlist all our will to live for a single purpose: escaping the murderers, the death sentence they had passed on our people. After my last visit around the ghetto, I hugged my father who looked pale and whispered to him, "Daddy, don't worry. I've decided to go to that apartment, to Mother, and you'll follow us, won't you? We'll be together again, for better or worse."

"Yes. I didn't tell you that Mother sent a note with Goldman. You know, the man who helped her bribe the leader of the *platzovka*. She wrote that Mrs. Janka will come and fetch you on April 17 in the morning."

"What, so soon? It's in two days!"

"Yes, Lizunia, prepare the clothes you want to take with you and wear as many layers as possible. "

"And when will you leave?" I wanted to know.

"I sent a message to Mother that a week after you she should come and fetch me at the group's workplace, also early in the morning, at the end of the night shift."

I felt tremendously excited. On the following day I took a tin box, put in the pages of the diary I kept in the ghetto, dug a hole in a hiding place, and hid them there, promising myself to return there after the war.

The day came to say goodbye.

In the evening I went with Father to the house from where the group on night shift was to leave. I had only a few things with me. I knew that on the Polish side, around the walls of the ghetto, bands of informers and Polish thugs, called *schmaltzovniki*, wandered around, and I was to bring a large sum of money to Mother. I hid it in an intimate place. Another sum of money, not very large, was sewn into the fold of my dress, and a few coins were in my pocket. I wore a pretty woolen kerchief on my head, and I put on makeup to look like a Polish girl.

We stood at the entrance of the house. Father was to leave me there and go off. He was tormented. He could not move. He hugged me, kissed me, and went off. He came back a moment later and we embraced again. I did not cry. I clung to him. Again he left. No, I saw him come back to me once more. I felt I wanted him to leave, I couldn't bear it any longer.

"Daddy, goodbye, see you again. You'd better go!"

One more hug and he left.

A long time has passed since I saw him disappearing into the distance, turning again and again to look at me. I was naïve enough to believe we would see each other in a week's time. I did not know, nor did Father, that at that very moment the order to surround the ghetto before the final liquidation was already in the works.

I went to my fate. All that night I could not close my eyes. The people around me were working on the knitting machines, and I lay awake on one of the tables and fought my profound anxiety. In the morning I was no longer afraid.

The moment the group got into line to return to the ghetto, I slipped out of the gate into the street. This street used to belong to the ghetto, now it was deserted. Mrs. Janka was waiting for me on the corner by the gate. We walked quickly away, arm in arm. We did not have time to get away. We felt we were being followed. We went on walking and talking, pretending not to notice anything. Mrs. Janka began to tremble. The steps came closer and closer, and now three thugs surrounded us.

"Hey, Jew girl, stop! You won't get away from us!"

"What Jew girl are you talking about? Scram!" I said in pure Warsaw slang.

"Don't talk nonsense! You've just left the ghetto. We saw you."

One of them, a fat man, blocked our way. The other one turned to Mrs. Janka: "You, a Polish woman, aren't you ashamed to help these disgusting Jews? Come with us to Shucha Avenue. There you'll stop bluffing."

I knew that in Shucha Avenue were the offices of the Gestapo and their torture cellars. At that moment I made a decision. I turned to a side street, I think it was Ogrodowa, and they followed me. I entered a gate and stopped and said, "What do you want? I've got some money."

We continued to go up the stairs. The house was empty, the Poles had not yet managed to take it over. I saw they were whispering among themselves. I calmed down; I understood they were *schmaltzovniki* and wouldn't take me to the Gestapo.

Mrs. Janka stood next to me, white as a sheet and trembling all over. I was calm. A strange self-confidence engulfed me. I knew things would be all right. My confidence may have made an impression on them. They searched me. They found the money sewn in my dress.

"Is that all the money you have?"

Suddenly Janka opened her mouth: "Don't you see she is an orphan, you godless people, attacking her. You wicked scoundrels!"

At that moment they came to the conclusion that they would not get much out of me, seized the pretty kerchief from my head, and disappeared quickly down the stairs. We breathed a sigh of relief. We went into the street and quickly got on a tram.

During the journey I remained standing, while Mrs. Janka hid me with her body. We fell straight into my happy mother's arms in the cellar of the house in Podchoronzich 47.

6 ∶ ON THE ARYAN SIDE

How to explain

How to explain my life
if not by way of miracles
impossible coincidences
made possible—
uniquely
integrated.

Eli Netzer

Like a Mouse on the Run

Excerpts from My Diary, 19th April 1943

I've landed here and here I am. It's like falling into a ditch. What is happening and what happened "there" seems far away, as though it no longer had anything to do with me. I am apathetic, in a state of stupor. I spend the whole day motionless, doing nothing. I do not belong in the world. I am aware of the spring as though seeing it through a semitransparent veil. If only I could go outside. I feel I am overwhelmed by apathy. I am trying to understand myself. One thing is clear to me: I must survive, I must go on living!

In the morning Mrs. Janka, the owner of the apartment, came into our room and told us that the ghetto is besieged, tanks hurtle through the streets, and airplanes circle above it. Inside the ghetto a battle has broken out. The Jews are defending themselves! The Jews are fighting? She repeats it in amazement, tinged with admiration. She isn't an anti-Semite, she is our friend. I tremble inwardly and grow pale. I look at Mother's face; she is thunderstruck by the news, uttered with real appreciation, without grasping the enormity of the tragedy. If so, then it's the end, the very end! Tanks, planes are destroying the ghetto. Bombing, killing, poisoning cellars, and my friends are there…fighting!

On the first day of the fighting, a few dozen Germans were killed. The war of the Jews against the Germans. Where are the Polish fighters? They did promise to help when the uprising breaks out. Where are their promises? Without their help, all the defenders will die, no one will survive. And why am I forbidden to go out and join them, to fight side by side with them? I just can't sit here the whole day, doing nothing, while I hear firing, the echoes reaching even our neighborhood. Father is there. He was supposed to come to our hiding place within three days. He couldn't make it.

23rd April

A message from Father to Wosz, our contact person. Mother met Mr. Wosz and he gave her Father's message: He has no choice, he and Aunt Biela and her husband have decided to go to the Poniatow Camp near Lublin. This option has remained open. And in the end, something baffling—"On the forbidden way to you!" What does that mean? Maybe he intends to jump off the train and try to get to us, to the Aryan side. God! In the evening the sky is brightly lit by flames. What is it?

Mrs. Janka returned from work and said that they were setting fire to the houses in the ghetto. It can't be! No one expected that! What, are they burning people alive? Are they burning people who are alive and well, shut up in their hiding places, as though they were lice swarming in bed? I stand at the window in the apartment cellar. It is covered by a dark curtain. I've made a hole in it the size of a cigarette to be able to see a little of the sky. The whole sky is red, orange, clouds of black smoke envelop the city, penetrate the houses.

Sleep Aryan Warsaw, pure Polish Warsaw, sleep well, cuddled by Jewish smoke. Sleep, and dream of the day of vengeance when we shall burn them alive! We'll crush their bodies, wipe them off the face of the earth! Yes, but who will be left to avenge us? Who? They are exterminating Polish Jewry, and Russian Jewry, German—throughout Europe. Does this other Warsaw, fast asleep in bed, feel fear or apathy? Do the Poles care enough to avenge us? Who will avenge the helpless Jewish children, burned together with their parents? Who will avenge the blood of the fighting pioneers, the dreamers of dreams, who seized arms and decided to sacrifice their young lives for the honor of their people, trampled on by brute force? Who? I swear, if I survive, I shall strive to avenge their blood!

26th April

This evening we'll get exact information from the ghetto. My cousin Lazar jumped off the train and is supposed to come to our hiding place. My Aunt Ida came to our apartment in the morning, elegantly dressed. She has been living on the Aryan side for a long time. Her husband, the lawyer Holtzman, was killed, and she made use of her contacts on the Aryan side and lives here with forged papers. She agreed with Mother that Lazar would come to us straightaway.

He came in the evening. I look at him. My cousin, a young man of twenty-eight, married to my cousin Helenka Lechtus. Sunken eyes, a thin pale face, eyebrows and his hair singed. His hands covered with blisters from burns. I wrote Lazar's story in hopes that maybe someone will find my diary.

We lived in the brushmakers' area, separated by a wall from the central ghetto. It was a German "shop," producing brushes. The Jewish slaves, working for them, lived in blocks of houses spread over three streets. Everything was ready for the Passover Seder, which was to begin the next day, on Monday, 19th April. But on Sunday night we heard a stamping of boots on the sidewalks. When my father-in-law went out to see what was going on, several neighbors rushed in, their faces pale: "The Z.O.B. guards told us that the ghetto was surrounded. On the roofs of the houses all around the ghetto we can see machine guns and suspicious movements around them."

The clock struck midnight. So that's it. The last, final *aktzia* will probably start tomorrow morning. We got ready quickly. Our hiding place was in the cellar. We had prepared two rooms under the cellar, with the entrance well camouflaged. We had an opening for air, a well for water and even electricity. In one room there were personal belongings and food, in the other wooden bunks to sleep on. We intended to survive for two or three months in this way; maybe the war will have ended by then. All the occupants of the house ran around, gathering their essential belongings. People were not afraid to go out into the street to visit their families and friends, to say goodbye.

In the morning we heard dull sounds of firing and explosions. We sat in silence, one day, maybe two—I don't remember exactly. People's nerves were so stretched that they preferred to keep quiet. Some of the young men in the shelter had weapons. They did not belong to the organization. At night they went out into the yard. In another house, in Swentojerska Street 34, the Z.O.B. had their positions. People from the organization told us about a mine they had detonated when the Germans decided to penetrate into our area, about battles leaving ten Germans dead, about a "peace delegation" of SS officers who came with a white flag asking for an armistice to pick up their wounded, and how they fired at them at once. The fighters were elated, exhausted but looked happy. The battle in most of the houses in that area lasted two days. They ran from house to house. The leader of the group was the commander Marek Edelman. Dozens of fighters took part in the battle, some of them were killed. They went out at night to try to make contact with their friends. They told us that the battle inside the ghetto was still going on, that the fighters had delayed the entry of the tanks and set fire to them with home-made Molotov bottles. They were stationed at windows and changed their positions by walking on the roofs. We in the shelters decided to open fire only when they discovered us. We made up our minds to defend our families to the end, not let them take us to Treblinka.

On the third day fighting also broke out in the area of the "shops" of Töbens and Schultz. At the last moment many people preferred to move to the Poniatow Camp. In the meantime the Germans began to set fire to the houses. On the second day of the uprising, the fighters told us about fires in the ghetto. We sat in the crowded shelter, praying that they wouldn't get to us. We had expected the worst, but not fires. The people in the shelter said goodbye to each other. We were in despair, expecting certain death. We could already smell the smoke. Someone came from the neighboring house; people were fleeing from adjacent houses. There were no Germans around. After a night full of dread, just before dawn, we did hear German voices in the yard. They were calling to the Jews to come out at once, or else they'd burn us alive.

The artillery were constantly firing incendiary bombs. The whole block of houses in Swentojerska, Volova, and Franciszkanska streets was on fire. The shelter was not damaged, but the water stopped running. The electricity went out. The walls of the shelter became unbearably hot, smoke penetrated the cellar. We sat there, coughing, wrapped up in wet sheets. My mother-in-law fainted, other people also lost consciousness. It became unbearable, we were engulfed by thick smoke. We couldn't breathe! In a second we would die of gas poisoning. The men with weapons took over command of the shelter, they went outside. People wept, dragged themselves to the yard with the last vestige of strength.

We had no choice, we would defend ourselves in the yard. The men cleared the opening and gave the order— "wrap yourselves up in sheets soaked in the remnants of water, lie in the middle of the yard, in the garden."

The yard is full of people, smoke covers everything, the top floors are in flames, the fire is running wild without any interference, parts of walls are collapsing and falling into the yard. There are no Germans to be seen. A young girl rushes into the flames. A man, on fire, runs about like mad, a flaming torch, his hair and clothes engulfed in flames. People lying on the ground are groaning with pain. I am lying next to Helenka, my wife, and I see her parents beside her. It is indescribably difficult to breathe. Smoke blinds my eyes and chokes me, my tongue is dry like a piece of wood. The asphalt in the yard has become unbearably hot. *We are going to die*—penetrates into my consciousness. *Die in the most horrible way, without defending ourselves. We must survive!*

The fire begins to die down. Next to me Helenka lies unconscious, she may be dead. I heave myself up. It looks as though most of the people are already dead. I lose consciousness. When I wake up, it is already dark; parts of the house are burning quietly. The place where our cellar was is now in ruins. I begin to look for my family, to try to revive them. My mother-in-law doesn't react. There were four hundred people in that house yesterday; only a few dozen have survived. Suddenly we hear German voices in the street. God! We thought it was all over, that they've left us here. What shall we do? Several Germans burst in through the gate. I lift up my wife and push her in the opposite direction, toward the third courtyard, from where one can get to Bonifraterska Street.

I remain with a few young people at the bottom of the staircase. The Germans have already gathered all the people from the yard and driven them outside. Now they are sure there is no one left here. I fire. I hit someone. Others are also firing. Shouts and machine gun fire. They burst into the yard like a pack of dogs let loose for the hunt. I fire again and retreat. My mind is empty, I don't feel anything, I keep on firing. Suddenly I press the trigger—and nothing happens! I've run out of ammunition.

Three Germans jump on me and seize me. They beat me all over my body and throw me into the line of Jews. When the line starts moving, I see my father-in-law standing over the body of his young son, Beniek. He also fired, I knew he had a weapon. My father-in-law bends down and sees life ebbing out of his son—and then they pull him into the line. My mind captures the picture of Beniek lying there, a thin stream of blood spurting out of his mouth; his eyes are smiling. That's how I'll remember him. We were dragged to the *Umschlagplatz*.

He stopped and his voice broke down. I waited silently for him to go on.

On our way we passed Nalewki Street, totally in ruins. Remnants of houses were still burning or the flames were crackling under piles of cinders. We constantly came across corpses. Shots were still echoing from somewhere, the fighting was still going on. Thousands of people were on the *Umschlagplatz*, scorched, half burned, their eyes crazy with dread and pain. The Germans were searching them thoroughly, grabbing the gold and silver people had hidden on their bodies. I managed to save my wife's ring by holding it in my mouth, and a few more valuables.

I am incapable of describing that journey to you, in the cattle cars to Treblinka, together with the wounded and the dying. How we fought each other to get a place next to a tiny window, to get a little air. It was night, completely dark. I decided to jump out. Together with another man, I succeeded in bending the iron bars. A moment of hesitation. If I jump, the guards sitting on the roofs of the cars will fire at me, and if I succeed in slipping away, the Poles will pick me out by the look of my body and clothes. But the other alternative is Treblinka. I jumped.

I must have lain for a long time in a ditch I had rolled into from the embankment. I raised myself up with difficulty. My body hurt all over. The pain was worst in my head and my ankle. A few dozen steps in front of me I saw the glimmer of a flashlight. Guards. I crawled quickly toward the forest and collapsed on the ground. Poles, looking for escapees, passed by. I knew I was still in the vicinity of Warsaw. I must get to the city, that's how I can save myself. I remembered my cousin Ida's address. I must get to the station before dawn, while it's still dark.

My head swam, I saw flames before my eyes and my wife, Helenka, lying unconscious. What's happened to her? Did she get away? I walk on, bumping into stones and tree stumps. Every little noise terrifies me. The whistling of the train makes me shudder, the branches stretch out their withered arms to me as though wanting to seize me. I sense that the dead Beniek is walking behind me, asking why I had abandoned him, why I hadn't saved him. I am feverish and hallucinating.

The sun was rising and I saw the shadow of a wooden hut in the distance. When the inhabitants saw me, they were frightened. I told them that I am a Jew fleeing from the burning ghetto. I asked them to show me the way to the railway station, to help me buy a ticket. I gave them a silver cigarette box. They were afraid, but behaved in a humane way. They washed me and helped me clean my clothes. I knew it was extremely risky: Anyone will immediately realize that I am a Jew. Will I succeed?

The conductor stared at me and said nothing. At that early hour the station was almost empty. The people in the carriage moved away from me fearfully. I hid my face in a newspaper. I reached Warsaw, the eastern station. I mingled with the crowd and managed to get out of the area of the station, swarming with informers. People passed me, looked at me, and said nothing. That's how I got to Koszykowa Street. An acquaintance of mine lives there. She went to call my cousin Ida.

I saw a different Lazar before me. He used to be arrogant, to show off. The person sitting there was thin, withdrawn; he stammered slightly when he spoke. We'll have to live together in that small room in the cellar. Who knows how long. Until the damned war is over?

The beginning of May

The flames in the sky can be seen day and night. Mrs. Janka told me that, according to the rumors in the city, the fighting by the Jews is dying down and that a handful of Jews tried to get out through sewage canals to the Aryan side, and some succeeded and some were caught. They say that the Socialist Party is helping them to get to the partisans in the forests.

The people in the street generally sympathize with the Jews, but Mrs. Janka has also heard expressions of hostility and hate. She did not want to tell me about it. There were also cases of Polish policemen being wounded and killed in the street. It happened when they went up to someone they suspected of being a Jew, and the man drew a revolver and shot the policeman. And I thought that those who fired at policemen must be members of the Z.O.B. who had managed to escape from the ghetto and were defending themselves when the policemen wanted to arrest them.

It seems that a few more bunkers are still holding out. My cousin, still able to walk about freely, told us that the events of the last few days made a great impression on the Poles. Many changed their minds about the Jews. Some looked with envy and admiration upon Jewish self-defense. Self-righteous women wiped their eyes with a handkerchief, saying, "Even if these are Jews and it's the right thing to get rid of them, but why in this way, burning them alive? That's terrible."

But whether they express admiration or pity, they all stand by without lifting a finger. It does not occur to anyone to provide assistance.

A Lilac Branch

The conditions on the Aryan side are unbearable. There are constant rumors about informers and blackmailing of Jews hiding on the Aryan side. They are helped by Jewish collaborators—the hounds of the Gestapo. They say that Franceska Maan, a famous Jewish dancer, is working for the Gestapo and in particular looking for Jewish children in monasteries. The name of a Jewish agent, Konigsberg, is being bandied about. And there are many others.

It's something I can't understand. Are they really so stupid to believe it will save them? Wasn't it convincing enough for them that the employees of the Judenrat and the Jewish police, who had been promised they would not be sent off with the others, were deceived and put to death together with their families?

They say that the ghetto no longer exists. The wreckage of the houses is still standing, the piles of cinders still crackle, and at night shadowy figures, seeking food and shelter, still move about in there. But the ghetto no longer exists; nearly a half million people have gone up in smoke. And those still alive bleed inwardly, their deep wounds will never heal. And maybe there will be no one left when freedom comes. Does life go on? Do those who have seen such things with their own eyes eat and drink and live on, as usual? As usual?

Someone has brought a branch of lilac to our cellar. They say that lilac is in bloom in the gardens, fresh grass is peeping out of the frozen winter soil, and young leaves cover the trees. And the air. The air that we cannot breathe. Wonderful spring air, crystal clear. The blue sky, dark blue like smiling, happy, loving eyes. And the sun enfolding the world in its golden mantle.

A branch of lilac. I delight in its delicate scent, its magic fragrance. Life is so beautiful, nature is marvelous beyond my understanding; only one creature is full of evil: Man!

But youth is the most beautiful of all. I want to feel the full force of happiness, the pulse of life, the will to struggle, to work, to pursue lofty ideals…to sense the strength in my arms, yearning for movement and for love…to feel the powerful forces of nature, making the blood surge through my body, my legs feel strong. They want to walk, to run. To run far away from the noise made by people. To be free like the birds without the ropes, the chains locking forcefully my fifteen years.

Why are human beings so cruel and evil? They speak about the future, about truth, about Man as proof of God's great wisdom, and it's all lies, lies.

I know there are also good people, but they are persecuted, and society rejects them as weaklings. Why am I prevented from seeing the wonders of nature and the world, from breathing fresh air? Why must I stay here, without even

Jews captured during the Warsaw Ghetto uprising, led to the *Umschlagplatz* [rail station with trains to concentration camps], April 1943.

knowing if I'll survive? How horrible! I am missing out on the best years of my young life. I haven't learned anything yet. I know so little, I can do so little, but I must find out so much, I must learn!

What is this cruel, brute force preventing children from learning and developing? It is the wild, unbridled beast within Man.

From David Leon's contact man, Mr. Wosz, Mother found out that Father is in the Poniatow Camp near Lublin. Aunt Irena's sister and her son are there too. Uncle Leon sent a Polish messenger to try to get them out of that camp. And what about my father, his younger brother?

24th May

Living with Lazar in the hiding place, in the room in the underground apartment, is becoming unbearable. The caretaker of the house is apparently suspicious. I am beginning to think about going to Henrykow, the monastery where five girls from our Movement are hiding. I received the address from Rut Heiman before leaving the ghetto.

I must find inner composure, steel my nerves, in order to be able to face the unknown. Will I have the courage to confront the great dangers? The stoicism of the ancient Greeks? I must be capable of despising death, of acting with iron self-confidence.

My intention to travel to Henrykow is becoming more concrete. I must take with me the following: a small pillowcase, a towel and a toothbrush, a change of clothes, needle and thread, a notebook and a pencil, soap and a hairbrush.

I am going out into the world to meet my fate, to the great test facing me as an independent person.

Yesterday...

The room was dark. I moved the heavy curtain just a little and saw through the iron bars of the gate into the yard, a wonderful green color against the background of a spellbound blue. I felt deeply insulted by the enormous injustice; I wanted to cry out: Why? How have I deserved this?

I longed for human beings who seek knowledge and justice. I thought that, actually, all the ideologies with a humane vision aspire to a final goal—to make Man better, more just, educated, and create a society where people live in peace with each other and seek the truth. The planet, this world of ours, seems to me like a huge ant hill, where people are running about constantly, busying themselves with their paltry affairs. They quarrel and fight, then they make peace; work, get up, and in the end they die. And this goes on and on. And God looks down on this ant hill, watches, and does not interfere.

Every person in this small world has the right to go about freely. Only we, owing to the stupidity, absurdity, and envy entangling us, we ourselves condemn humankind to injustice and suffering. If only I survive, I'll seek justice and help the weak with all my strength. I'll not break down, for I firmly believe in the ability of mankind to find the way to justice and truth. I have drawn this belief from the Movement, and it will be with me always, wherever I go. I shall always remember Mira's words about my real personal test.

[Here I stopped writing my diary, because Mother said that in our present situation, when we are on the run, someone might discover the diary and it would give us away. So I had to hide it for the time being.

I am continuing the story of my life two years later, after my arrival in Israel, but here and there I shall include passages from a diary I continued to write on little pieces of paper.]

One day, the woman caretaker of the house where I was hiding with Lazar in the cellar began to suspect us. I don't know what caused it: Had I moved the curtain and peeped out at the gate opposite and at the sky through the bars? Maybe she heard noises from the apartment, at a time when the lodgers were, so to speak, not supposed to be there; or maybe she was influenced by the hysterical search for Jews who had escaped from the ghetto.

Later I found out that the police had enlisted all the caretakers of the houses and the watchmen for that sacred purpose, and they were rewarded for their cooperation in handing over Jews hiding in the houses for which they were responsible; they received a reward for every Jew.

One day her son, a boy of about twelve, knocked on the door. We were all in the apartment at the time: Mrs. Janka and her disabled son, aged thirteen, and her old parents, my mother, legally listed as having rented the apartment from Mrs. Janka, and Lazar and me. I immediately looked for a place to hide. Lazar got under the bed, and I hid behind the door with many clothes hanging on it.

The boy walked about the room on some pretext, as though he had come to play with the crippled boy, turned here and there and then, suddenly, threw a marble into the next room, behind the door where I was hiding. He wanted to run and open the door, as though to get the marble, but Mother seized him by the hand and turned him back. He smiled, said goodbye, and went off. We understood at once that he suspected there was something forbidden behind the door.

A while later there was another knock on the door. It was to be expected, but we had not even had time to consider what to do when the caretaker herself came in. A middle-aged woman with a coarse face, wearing an apron. Without further ado, she said, "You are hiding a Jew here. He must leave this house at once. If not, I'll hand him over to the police."

Mother and Mrs. Janka tried to convince her that it wasn't true, but she insisted, "I saw him with my own eyes. They'll execute you as well, not only him."

I heard her from my hiding place and understood that my fate was sealed. Mrs. Janka offered to bribe her with a sum of money, but the woman did not give in: Mrs. Janka must get the Jews out of her home! It wasn't clear if she had really seen one of us or only heard some noises.

On the Aryan side, 1943 sister Mirka (right), Liza.

Mrs. Janka said, "All right, but give us till tomorrow morning, it's already getting dark."

The caretaker agreed and went out, after first warning us that the Jew must be out by seven in the morning, repeating her threats.

At that moment I made my decision. I told Mother I would leave and go to the Henrykow monastery, where the girls from the Movement were hiding. My mind raced on. I said, "I have a chance to survive, but Lazar is a man and he'll be caught at once in the street."

We were still debating when there was another knock on the door. Lazar managed to slip again under the bed, and I went behind the door. The caretaker was standing in the room with a man who looked like a police detective. Mother stood up, pale and bewildered, and Mrs. Janka collapsed into a chair.

I was discovered. I looked at Mother. She looked petrified, but I motioned to her to keep quiet. We both knew that if she opened her mouth to protect me, she would not be able to conceal that she is a Jew. And what would happen to Mirka?

I looked around, said thank you, and went with the man. We went out of the gate. The fresh air hit me. I asked, "Where are you taking me?"

"Either to the police or somewhere else, you *dupa*," [butt, in Polish, very humiliating], he said.

Suddenly it occurred to me that he was just a *schmaltzovnik* [blackmailer], not a policeman. I was no longer afraid. A torrent of words came from my mouth:

"What will you gain if I die? I am only fifteen. Are you a Christian? You'll burn in hell if you hand me over to the Germans."

Suddenly he stopped and pulled me to the gate of one of the houses. "Have you got money?"

I had a thousand zloty sewn into the fold of my dress. A considerable sum, for any emergency. And now the time had come. I gave it all to him. He looked at me and gave me five hundred zloty back.

"Take it, in case they catch you again. And where do you want to go now?"

"I want to leave the city and go to Henrykow. I have friends there," I answered.

"So come with me to my sister. She is kind. I'll take you to the railway station tomorrow."

I couldn't believe my ears. I didn't think he was deceiving me. I believed him and walked obediently beside him. He took me to a modest apartment with two rooms. A smell of sauerkraut and sausages filled the air. I was hungry. The woman and her husband didn't pay much attention to me. Apparently I wasn't the first person her brother had hunted down, dividing the spoils with her. They gave me food separately and didn't speak to me.

I was worried: What happened to Lazar? How shall I let Mother know that I am still alive? I was afraid what would happen the next day. How would I get to the railway station? I knew it would be swarming with blackmailers and police detectives.

They let me sleep on their kitchen table, and I spent the night dozing off and on. On the following day "my man" came, while it was still not clear if he was acting out of charity or precipitating my end. He immediately asked me, "Where are your belongings?"

"At the apartment of the good Polish woman who saved me," I answered, in disbelief.

"All right, write them a note that they should give me a package for you and let's go to the station."

Now I was thinking, either he really means it, or he wants to get something else out of me, my clothes. But how shall I find out unless I try it? And a note from me to Mother will be a sign that I am alive. I wrote a note to Mrs. Janka immediately, asking for my things, as I was going to Henrykow.

And in fact, in the end this non-Jew turned out to be humane. He brought my belongings and greetings from my former "hosts." I was happy that Mother knew about me, and maybe she even calmed down a little. I combed my hair and parted it in the middle, which made me look a little more Aryan, but my Jewish nose still bothered me. In the end it will give me away, I thought, and also my sad dark eyes.

Going along with Mr. X (he didn't tell me his name), I got into the carriage safely, after he had lined up to buy my ticket and taken me by a roundabout way to the train station.

"Well, goodbye, my young lady, good luck!"

"Thank you, thank you for being kind to me in the end."

The train moved. After a short journey, I arrived in Henrykow. I went up to a woman and asked her how to get to the monastery where young girls study. She pointed out a dirt road on the side.

The monastery was surrounded by a lovely garden. I immediately asked to see Mother Superior, Irena Adamowicz. In the ghetto I was told that she helps Polish scouts join the underground, so I did not expect any great problems.

Unfortunately, Mother Superior was not there, and I was received by her deputy. I didn't know if she was in on the secret. Her face was stern and dignified. She was sitting behind a large writing table and spoke to me in an unfriendly tone of voice, "What do you want?"

I explained my desperate situation and asked her to let me stay. I didn't hint in even the slightest way that there were other Jewish girls there.

"I am sorry, but we do not hide Jews here. Only two days ago they found Jews in this area and executed them. I shall not endanger our institution in order to hide you."

Her answer was unequivocal. "You had better leave this place."

I had no choice. I went out crestfallen, defeated.

I sat down on a bench in the garden and fell into despair. The nuns in the courtyard advised me to go and sleep at the house of the head of the village. I told them that I had run away from home because my father beat me, and my mother as well. I have nowhere to sleep.

Of course, I didn't intend to go to the head of the village. I was hungry. It was late, about six in the evening. I left the monastery and looked for a store to buy bread. Nearby was a little village store.

When I entered, everyone stopped talking. They stared at me in silence. I bought a round loaf of bread and left quickly, before anyone would call the police. I walked along the railway tracks without knowing where I was going, pinching pieces off of the loaf. I became tired and sat down to rest on a stone. At some distance ahead I saw a railway worker in uniform. I went on sitting there.

He stopped next to me, looked at me, and said, "Girlie, you are sitting exactly on the same stone where three Jews were killed a few days ago. Don't stay here. German guards go past. Run away! Do you see the black strip on the horizon? Those are forests. Go there, hide!"

I thanked him warmly and ran away from there at a crazy speed. I went into a wheat field. It was already the end of May and the wheat was high, almost my height. The sun was setting. I walked on and on toward the black strip on the horizon, but the farther I went, the farther it seemed to be. My legs would no longer carry me. I felt as though the skin on my face was burning.

After spending so long in the cellar, my pale face was hot and surely also red. Luckily it became dark so I could go on walking and avoid meeting the peasants' dogs. Walking in plowed fields or through the wheat was hard.

As night fell, with the last remnants of my strength, I reached a little wood. I was thirsty, and I sucked the stems of plants. I stayed there two nights. During the day I daydreamed. I saw our house in Warsaw and my father's face. He spoke to me and comforted me, but could not save me. I was careful with the loaf of bread and measured each portion I ate.

On the third day I decided to go back to the monastery and try to get to the Mother Superior. She was the only one who could help me, not her deputy, who didn't seem to be in on the secret. I must go on fighting.

I plucked up courage and my strength returned. I can't imagine how I managed to get back all those kilometers, bypassing villages and farms, careful not to encounter peasants working in the vegetable gardens, nor other people on the way. It took me many hours to get to those railway tracks and the stone I had sat on, on my way to the wood. From there I reached the monastery easily.

I sat down for a while to rest. A young woman came up to me, holding a milk can in one hand and a little girl of about three with the other. She stood still, looking at me with pity in her eyes.

"Miss, I can see she is a Jew. [In Polish one doesn't address people directly.] Why is she walking around here, what is she looking for?" Her voice was tinged with sympathy.

"I am looking for Mother Superior of the Henrykow Monastery. They told me that she is compassionate."

"In Henrykow? But this isn't Henrykow, you've been misled. This monastery belongs to our village. Henrykow is about two kilometers away. There is a monastery there too, larger than this one."

What's happening to me? Did they show me the wrong place or is she pulling a fast one on me? What shall I do? I looked around and saw a sign at the entrance to the village. No, it isn't Henrykow; the woman is telling the truth.

This discovery filled me again with hope. All is not lost, I can try again.

"Come with me, I am going to the town, I'll show you the place." I got up. "It's not a good thing that you are holding such a package. It shows you come from the city and makes people suspect you at once. Take the milk can and I'll hold the package."

It seemed logical and we exchanged items.

We walked together until we reached the little town and the main street. It was paved and cars were driving along it. I saw the sign "Henrykow" on the way. The large somber building of the monastery rose before me, and on the opposite side of the street was a post manned by German police. We stopped in front of the ancient gate with a little peephole.

The woman quickly took the milk can, but when I wanted to take my package, suddenly the expression on her face changed. She turned around and said, "You won't survive anyway, what do you need the package for? Today or tomorrow they'll shoot you, and I have a child."

"At least give me the bread that's inside, please," I pleaded, stunned.

I saw the Germans on the opposite side and let her go. She walked away quickly, pulling the child behind her. I was left alone in front of the gate, with the Germans behind me. I knocked on the gate, once, twice.

Someone opened the peephole. A face looked out at me. Unbelievable! It was Erella, from the "Galil" troop, one of the girls hiding there. Obviously, it happened to be her turn at the gate.

"Erella, it's me, open quickly, I have nowhere to go," I whispered through the peephole.

"It's impossible, I can't. They already suspect us," she looked at me, stunned.

"Erella! Just for tonight. Tomorrow we'll think of something. Open quickly! Where are our people? Did any of them escape from the ghetto? Tell me."

"Only Merdek's group is in the forest. All the others died during the uprising."

"Which forest, quickly, the Germans are on the other side."

"I don't know, don't look for them. Here they are following us, they suspect us. Run to the forest."

The peephole was slapped shut, and with it my last hope vanished. I was again alone in the growing darkness. I walked away quickly in the direction of the hills outside the town. The lights in the town lit up. It was Saturday night. It started to drizzle unpleasantly.

Who will notice me standing alone in the increasing rain, full of despair? I reached the sands. They were covered with thick bushes. I lay down on the wet ground, water trickled down from the branches onto my body and I felt nothing. Scenes from the past, horrible images of people being expelled, screaming, passed before my eyes. *Is there no way out?*

I tried to recall all the lovely things I had said to myself in the cellar: *I mustn't break down, I mustn't give up. I must survive!* I suppose I fell asleep.

I was woken up by the first rays of the sun and suddenly felt I had regained my strength. What can be worse than death? Torture, of course. Death can wait. I myself will decide when to die. I'll return to Warsaw. I'll look for Mother, and we'll try to find another place to hide. If not, I'll go to the river Visla and drown myself. Fear? Nonsense. There is nothing to be afraid of. What's so terrible about death?

That decision seemed so simple and natural, and I wondered why I had not thought of it before. To find salvation in death. I felt relieved. The only problem was the way I looked on a Sunday morning, in my creased blue dress.

Where shall I wash off some of the sand sticking to me? I don't even have a comb for my hair. They'll realize at once that I am a Jew running away or a miserable beggar, or maybe they'll think I am a madwoman walking about in the street.

I cleaned myself as much as I could and went downhill into the street. It wasn't difficult to find the railway station in the little town. I bought a newspaper and entered the carriage. An inexplicable feeling of self-confidence led me on. I felt full of courage and energy.

I began to talk to the woman sitting next to me. At that early hour the carriage was almost empty. Maybe that's what saved me. I spoke Polish, using the Warsaw street slang.

Only once did I almost slip up. Later a peasant woman sat down next to me and asked where I came from. I told her I had been visiting my family in southern Poland.

She said, "The situation is hard because of this war and the black market is flourishing. How much do eggs cost there?"

God, who knows? I told her the truth, that I hadn't bought any eggs, only my aunt had. We went on talking about the situation until we reached Warsaw.

It was a cloudy morning, and there were few people in the street. During those three years I was locked up in the ghetto, I had forgotten those Polish areas completely; I had hardly known them anyway. Disoriented, I walked about in the streets, looking for the address of Marysia Grzybowska, where my sister was staying. I asked passersby, and they answered willingly, but each one pointed in a different direction. I found myself in a German neighborhood. A column of the Hitler Jugend marched past, singing.

I ran away from there and again wandered about. How I hated this city and its inhabitants! A group of Polish girls my age passed me by, holding their school books, laughing and chatting cheerfully. *Why can they, and not me? How am I different?*

I saw that no one paid attention to me. My self-confidence grew. I walked erect, looking into the faces of the people I met. I even went up to a Polish policeman, maybe he'll show me the way at last. I got to the house and went up the stairs to the apartment.

Mrs. Grzybowska grew pale when she saw me. Mirka hugged me. We clung to each other. My beloved little sister is with me again! I am not alone. I told her to go to the apartment where Mother was staying and tell her about me. Mirka had never gone there until now because she used to meet Mother in a park. She cried when she saw me. Later I realized that my face was red and swollen from the sun.

All that I had kept within me burst out in tears of joy when I was able once more to fall into my mother's arms. My brave mother said we would never part again—whatever happens to the three of us. She was not prepared to endure once again what she went through, standing there helplessly, letting them take her daughter away. She left me and Mirka with Marysia and went to look for a new place to hide.

I lay down, tired to death. My face burned, my legs were also swollen. Mirka put a wet towel on my face. I had not seen her for three months. Marysia lived with her drunken, frightening brother. Mirka slept in the same bed with Marysia, went with her to church every Sunday, and had even learned all the prayers well. She also knew how to cross herself. She played in the yard and was always careful not to drop a word about her real identity.

Mother returned at dusk. She had found a place with the Koligowski family, living outside the city. The woman had worked for us in our workshop before the war and agreed to take us in for a time, without pay, until we found a permanent place. That same evening, under cover of darkness, we went by tram to her home in Sluzev.

Excerpts from My Diary

12th June 1943

I spend my days in a field of high wheat. One day, motorcyclists came to ask questions, to investigate. Luckily, Mother wasn't at home, and my sister managed to run away to me, into the field. I made a hiding place for myself inside the wheat, and I can dream there all day. I have nothing to do—the dreams help me pass the time. I feel like a hunted animal. Some day I'll avenge myself!

I feel better. The main thing is that there is fresh air. The sky is mine again too. I haven't enjoyed nature for three years. How wonderful to see green grass, to breathe air suffused by the scent of flowers! You who are free, do you appreciate it? Do you know that heavenly feeling when one is running against the wind, with hair flying? Or the pleasure of standing in the middle of the wheat field with a garland of cornflowers on my hair, with my eyes shut, sensing the sun disappearing, hearing the rustling of the ears of corn, saying farewell to the sun?

You hunters, you butchers, what right have you to bar me from the beauty of nature, created by God for all his creatures?

And if I am able to be here and enjoy all this beauty, it is thanks to lies and deception. I have to hide my face, marked by the sin of my origin, the shame of my parents who brought me into this world. I'll never believe in people again. At my age I mustn't be naïve. I mustn't believe in truth, in mankind, in lofty ideals. All of them lie, and now I also have to lie.

It's hard to be a member of the Movement under these conditions. At that farewell meeting in the cellar, when Mira spoke to us and urged us to remain free human beings, and wherever we are to believe in the values the Movement has taught us, I swore to myself—as did many of my friends—to make the principles of the Movement guide me in my own personal way of life, when I am alone. But it is hard. If only Rut were here to consult, or my good friend Miriam to talk to, to share with her the heavy burden of my tormented spirit.

Where are you, Miriam? Did you manage to get out to the Aryan side, or are you there, in the ashes at Treblinka? Shall I see you again, shall I see those I love? The wound is bleeding in my heart, merciless sorrow is blocking my tears. I cannot weep. I am trying, but I cannot.

My friends in the Movement, I belong to you wherever you are. Are you alive, has anyone survived the uprising? You sacrificed your young lives. You did not try to escape, to hide. My spirit is with you!

17th June

Last night I had a dream: The war is over and the members of the Hashomer Hatzair Movement gather in the city square. Gradually one survivor after another appears, and soon we are several dozen, and among them almost all the girls of my group. The older ones dance the hora. Rut, our leader, puts us all into one row.

We go up to her and ask, "And what about us?"

She answers, "You don't belong to the Movement any longer, but I'll continue to be your leader."

The dream left me with a bitter feeling. God! How I wish my dream would come true and I'd at least see them alive.

24th June

We have fled again. The day before yesterday Mrs. Koligowski came and begged us with tears in her eyes to find another safe place, because in the village store they told her straight to her face that she was hiding Jews. The women warned her that someone intends to inform on them.

We immediately packed up our few belongings, and Mirka and I ran to our hiding place in the field. Mother traveled to the city; she said she had two more addresses of her former workers, and she would try to find a hiding place. Where does she find her strength? We were terrified all day. We lay in the wheat, and I stroked my little sister. *What are we going to do if Mother doesn't come back?*

She came home at dusk. She had found a place for a limited time at the home of Mrs. Maria, a young woman married to a Pole of German origin, a *Folksdeutcher*. They live in the area allotted to them, and Poles are forbidden to live there. Nevertheless, in spite of the dangers involved, she agreed to take us in. Under cover of darkness, we came out of the field, went by tram to Warsaw, and slipped into her house in Poznanska Street No. 6.

We have been here since yesterday. The apartment has two small rooms and a kitchen. She is young, in her twenties, and has a child of four. Her husband is a soldier on the Eastern Front. We are allowed to walk about the apartment. She doesn't have visitors, but told us that if anyone happens to come, I am to hide in the little cupboard under the window, and Mother and Mirka must get into the closet.

Maria has blue eyes, radiating kindness. She seems embarrassed when speaking to Mother. Mother was her boss and belongs to the master class, and she, Maria, to the simple folk. She speaks to Mother in the third person and keeps the customary distance between the working class and the upper-class people who provide the work. To her, Mother is still a lady, and the new situation, humiliating us by law, does not affect her. How noble-minded this simple woman is. I can't believe she doesn't know the risk to herself and her son.

We don't have enough money to pay her. Mother gives her only a little for the bare necessities, and Uncle Leon, who is hiding somewhere, gives Mother money. She meets Mr. Wosz once a month, and he hands her a small sum on our behalf. We have nothing left. We have few changes of clothes. I feel bad about our future. How long can we stay here and exploit this woman's generosity? I think I'll hide my diary here until the end of the war. The notebooks from the ghetto remained there, in the yard of the house in Leszno Street. I dug a hole by the tree and hid the notebooks in a wooden and a tin box. I expect they were burned together with the house. But in spite of the almost hopeless prospects, I believe that we'll survive.

8th July

Staying in this apartment is dangerous. Yesterday we heard a key turn in the lock. We ran to our hiding places. I had barely managed to squeeze into the little cupboard when the door opened and Maria's sister came in, with a German soldier. Maria had told us that her sister had a key to the apartment, but she hardly ever visits her. It turned out that she had come here to make love with her boyfriend.

I heard their voices through the cracks of my little cupboard, and I almost died of fear. I calmed myself by recalling my decision not to be afraid of death; I'll share the fate of my friends…after all, there is no reason why I should survive them. I was only afraid of torture, not of death itself.

Then they were through. The woman said to the soldier they must get out quickly before her sister returns home. I was not shocked by what they were doing, I had heard those sounds during the last period in the ghetto. When we were working for Töbens and living four families in one room, we often used to hear the sounds of lovemaking.

I think we'll have to flee from here as well.

Today Mother met Mr. Wosz upon his request. He told her some exciting news. Jews, hiding in various places on the Aryan side, are gathering in Hotel Polski. It is not clear who is organizing it. It appears that the Germans have a certain number of permits to go abroad. They are selling them by means of Jewish middlemen, and for a large sum it is possible to obtain a "promesa"—an entry visa to a South American country. There are also "certificates" to Palestine, and for these one can register for a smaller sum.

All the people who register will be exchanged for German citizens living in those countries, and until then the Jews will be kept in camps for foreign nationals. One group has already left to Vitele in France, and now other groups will be sent out.

Uncle Leon is letting us know that he, Aunt Irena, and their sons, Adash and Meir, want to register for that group. They suggest that we join them, but we ask, "What about Father? Are we going to leave him in the Poniatow Camp?"

Apparently, Uncle sent a Polish middleman to Poniatow. He was to get Father (his brother) out for 10,000 zloty after that same middleman had succeeded in getting out Aunt Irena's sister and her son and smuggling them into Warsaw. The man took with him, for Father, the uniform of an official working on the railway, and that is how he intended to bring him from Poniatow to Warsaw.

We are in a great dilemma. Should we believe the Germans and hand ourselves over to them of our own free will? It may be a deception, intended to expose the rest of the Jews who are hiding in Polish homes and send them off to the gas chambers. On the other hand, it was clear to us that if Uncle Leon was leaving, we would be left without any means of livelihood and would starve, and sooner or later we would also have no hiding place.

And what about Father?

11th July

Something very important has happened. We've decided to go to Hotel Polski. Uncle Melamed and his family are already there. We are taking the risk, of our own free will. Shall we get to Eretz Israel? Who knows? If it were true, I would be happy. I am dreaming about that country, about freedom, studies. I am sure there are hard times ahead until then, but I am ready for it. The main thing is to be free! Everything will work out somehow. At least we'll finally be doing something. No longer sitting around doing nothing in these hiding places, in apartments belonging to good people, who, with all their kindness and courage, look at us anxiously, begging us silently—leave, leave soon.

The tragic part is that we have not been able to bring Father out. The railway worker did not succeed in getting into the camp or in making contact with someone inside. He came back alone; he did not give back the money. Leaving without Father, abandoning him there, that's terrible. What should we do? What can we do?

12th July

We are already in the hotel. We parted, weeping, from young Mrs. Maria and thanked her from the bottom of our hearts. Maybe her God, Jesus, will see her good deeds and reward her for saving a family belonging to our people.

There are many Jews here. They are all running about, excited and tense, talking loud. I've seen many bewildered eyes here. We have registered for a "certificate" to Palestine, shared by two hundred fifty people. Uncle Leon has apparently paid for us. The excitement is tremendous. We are allowed to speak Yiddish as people are meeting acquaintances and friends, telling each other their experiences, how they escaped from the ghetto.

To my great surprise, I met all the five girls who had hidden in the Henrykow monastery, and among them Erella, who had not let me in. She avoids me and I ignore her. What can I say to her? I am sure she is glad I am alive—and that's all. These are hard times, hard decisions to make. Should I pass judgment on her? I found other people belonging to Z.O.B., but I haven't spoken to them yet. They say one transport left a week ago and we may leave tomorrow. Another transport will leave next week.

Uncle Leon said he sent a truck to bring Father, and he may come tomorrow. If so, he'll go with the next transport. Who knows? I don't believe it. I am distraught. And if he comes too late?

It's terribly crowded and noisy here. All the people are excited, nervous, talking loud. Mirka is happy. We are all together again, not afraid, not having to pretend. We are all Jews here. She doesn't realize the risk involved in this journey. We may be saved—or end up in a deathtrap.

Jews are standing in the hotel courtyard and arguing.

"It's a deception," says a very Jewish-looking man. "We had a good hiding place at the home of our acquaintances; we paid a lot for it. I didn't want to leave it, but my wife got excited about the idea of being exchanged for foreign citizens. All I want is to save my son. I don't care what happens to me."

"I heard from Engel, that even Lolek Skosowsky has brought his family here. He is a Gestapo agent, the rotten fellow, but this time we can believe him," a blond lady with lightened hair said.

"Lady, lower your voice, it's better not to talk like that," someone says. "As for me, I had no choice, I had already got 'burned' three times. The Poles robbed me of everything. I've lost my family. Whatever will be, will be. Maybe I'll survive."

I listened to everything and believed our luck. It may have been just childish.

Apparently there is a whole group of Z.O.B. people here. I don't know them personally, but I've found out their names and what they had done: Israel Kanal was the commander of the central ghetto. Eliezer Geler was the head of the "Gordonia" Movement. Hela Schipper and Shoshana Langer are here too, and the girls I walk around with all the time: Dina and Ktana of the "Sarid" troop, Chaviva Sandman, Erella, and Judit of the "Galil" troop. Arie Gzybovsky and Ayala, also members of Hashomer, left in the first transport.

[Eliezer Geler left the ghetto through the sewage canals and later died in Auschwitz. Hela Schipper, member of the "Akiba" youth movement in Krakov, a liaison between the ghettos, left the ghetto though the sewage canals. She lives in Israel.]

Israel limps, maybe he was wounded. Eliezer's hands are bandaged and there are traces of burns on his body. I heard that he commanded the area of the "shops" during the uprising. How did they survive? They are all pale, tired, exhausted. But what happened to them in the ghetto? How did they survive? How did our people die? How can I find out? They are silent and there is a dejected look in their eyes.

I am choking with tears, but I cannot weep. The best of Jewish youth fell in the uprising. I am brokenhearted. Even though we knew that there was no hope of victory in that battle and the end was to be expected, what I hear is terrible.

David Guzik, the manager of the Warsaw "Joint," is in the hotel. He is a trustworthy and respected person. He took under his wing the group of Jewish pioneers and fighters. [Guzik Katznel-David was known as a loyal blameless public servant, devoted to providing help. He was a friend of the Z.O.B. and a member of the national council on the Aryan side after the uprising in April 1943. He survived the war but later was killed in an airplane accident in 1946.]

Two Jewish Gestapo men are also here. They are dealing with the sale of the foreign papers. Will it ever be possible to publicize their names and their disgrace—or maybe acquit them for having saved hundreds of Warsaw Jews? If they survive, history will pass judgment on them.

My cousin Lazar is also with us. He has registered in the group of foreign nationals going to South America. He was lucky to survive after the woman had discovered us at the hiding place.

I dare not go up to the older members of the Z.O.B. They look very secretive. The rules binding the members of the underground are still mandatory. There are informers here. I admire them for their heroism.

I urged Dina and Ktana to tell me all they know. I asked them why they had left the monastery.

Dina said, "The Christian girls at the monastery whispered that there are Jews among them. We were forbidden to speak to each other, and we certainly wouldn't have dared to meet. We exchange notes in secret. The ground was burning under our feet. We sensed their malicious looks and heard their remarks about stinking Jews, exploiting the name of Jesus. We were terribly afraid.

"One day Mother Superior called Pnina and said that the underground wanted to transfer us to Dluga Street 29, to the Polski Hotel. I wanted to see the messenger, and we did meet a Polish woman. We knew her name. It was Irena Adamovicz, our contact person with the Polish underground. She had done a great deal to save us; she had arranged for us to be accepted at the monastery. We had no choice, so we came here. What could we do? Walk around in the streets?"

Dina finished her story and after a moment of silence, she added, "You are lucky, you are with your mother."

In her voice I could sense her sorrow and her envy. True, I thought. What would have happened if Erella had let me into the monastery? Maybe because of my Jewish appearance, we would all of us have fallen victim to informers.

On the last evening before leaving Warsaw, I finally found out a few details about the fighting in the ghetto. The stories I heard from friends who survived were confused and contradictory, but I thirst for any hints at what they have gone through.

During the first few days the Z.O.B. units fought constantly, from time to time changing their positions. They killed dozens of Germans and took their weapons. The Germans brought in auxiliary units from among the Ukrainians. They placed cannons and machine guns on the walls and in the streets and drove tanks into the ghetto. The first tanks were pushed back and even put out of action. The fighters destroyed them with bottles filled with inflammable chemicals.

The fighting units were scattered in the "wild" ghetto, and the fighters moved from bunker to bunker in the night, looking for food and water, and trying to make contact with other groups.

The Germans did not dare come out at night. When they started setting fire to the ghetto, and the whole ghetto went up in flames, the situation became desperate. They decided to send a delegation to the Aryan side to make contact with the messengers of the organization, Tadek (Tuvia Szaingut) and Antek (Yitzhak Zuckerman). Zygmund and Kazik (Simcha Rathaizen) also went out.

It was only on the third occasion that they succeeded in reaching the P.P.R. messengers [the Polish Socialist Party], and the people willing to help the fighters. These were Kostek [also called Krzaczek], and Rysiek, a P.P.R. activist, who had enlisted two sewage canal workers. They went to look for the fighters.

On May 7 the messengers went to the ghetto, but they failed in their task. They went there again on the next day, with Tadek and Kostek waiting above the opening of the canal in Prosta Street. Kazik looked in vain for the remnants of the fighters in the ghetto, and he returned to the canal in despair. In one of its ramifications he met ten fighters, lost and exhausted. Some of them decided to return to the ghetto and get all the members out, but a terrible disappointment awaited them.

On reaching the H.Q. shelter in Mila Street 18, they found out that all the fighters there had fallen on the previous day, one hundred twenty people, among them Mordechai, Mira, Aryeh Vilner, Shimon Heller, and many others.

When the Germans, who had surrounded the shelter, realized that the fighters were not prepared to come out and surrender, they poured in gas. Shimon Heller came out armed with two revolvers and killed three Germans before he fell. Jurek (Aryeh Vilner) was the first to call for mass suicide, and the members began to shoot.

Others wanted to defend themselves to the end, still others soaked their faces in water and in this way they managed to get to the other opening (there were five openings), which was unguarded. The members who arrived in the evening found half-conscious shadowy figures, among them Tusia Altman and Yehuda Vangrover, and took them to the canal.

Tusia and Yehuda were transferred to the Aryan side through the sewage canals in a state of exhaustion. But Tusia's luck failed her, in spite of the miraculous way she had been saved from the H.Q. bunker. She, Eliezer Geler, and other members were hidden temporarily in a hiding place outside the ghetto, in a factory making celluloid, in the upper floor of the house. A fire happened to break out there. Eliezer succeeded in jumping down and slipping away, but Tusia was badly burned. Firefighters brought her to the hospital, where she died after great suffering.

The leaders of the uprising committed suicide. Some sixty people got trapped in the sewage canals, exhausted, hungry, thirsty, shuffling dejected in the water full of feces, unable to sit down or rest. Lilit of the "Banir" troop excelled in guiding them, going back and forth to bring others.

For a whole day and night the members waited for them to come out, and the trucks did not come. In despair, Kazik, Kostek, and Rysiek succeeded in bringing a truck, and in broad daylight, on May 10, at nine in the morning, they pulled four ghosts out of the canal in Prosta Street. Driving quickly they succeeded in reaching their destination in Lomianki, seven kilometers from the city. Then they discovered that about fifteen members still remained in the canal, at some distance from the opening; waiting for them was fraught with great danger for all of them.

Meanwhile a rumor spread about Jews coming out through the canal. A large crowd gathered in the street. The organizers could not pull the rest out of the sewage canal. Two heroes, Rysiek and Jurek, were killed while getting the fighters out; a woman who knew them had informed on them. The members of the group remaining in the canal apparently succeeded in getting out. They fought openly against the Germans and died, weapons in hand.

At the end of their account, there was a deathly silence. The hearts and souls of the survivors remained there, in the ghetto, with the dying in the canals and the shelters. I listened to the story with dry eyes. The day will come when I shall weep for them, if I shall want to live after what I have found out. From what I heard, I understood that informers had been involved. The Germans searched in the bunkers where people were still alive. Maybe they caught a Jew and promised him they wouldn't kill him, if he revealed the bunker to them, maybe.

The rescue mission arrived a day too late. One day too late.

I'll always remember Tusia, that wonderful girl. A brave liaison, wise and full of life. She was sent by the top leadership to the country towns and to the communities. She crossed borders disguised as a Pole. Everywhere they loved her and admired her, she brought greetings in person and activated groups of youth, renewing the activity of Hashomer.

I met her several times, and the pioneer youth in the ghetto spoke of her with admiration. What a cruel fate. She was in the delegation acting together with Antek, Tadek, and other members on the Aryan side, and went back to the ghetto shortly before the uprising, just for a visit.

On hearing of the death of each of the fighters, a part of my own soul seemed to leave me, to die. I see with my mind's eye the torment they suffered and their supreme heroism. They will continue to live in our memories. And if we happen to survive, we shall ensure they will be remembered forever.

On 13th July we set out. We went on trucks to the railway station. We passed the walls of the burned ghetto on our way. We were able to see the destruction and hear the deathly silence.

On leaving Warsaw, a large group of fighters, led by Merdek (Mordechai Grobas) still remained in the Lomianki forest. Other fighters were hiding in the homes of helpful Poles. Some of them continued their underground activities, saving Jews who were hiding and trying to get to the partisans. Among those active were representatives of the National Council, Dr. Bergman, Antek Zukerman, and his friend Zvia Lubetkin.

We traveled in silence. We all parted from the life we had led there, in the city of our birth. I also said goodbye to the ruins of burned out houses, the place where I had spent my childhood, a time never to return. I left my weeping soul among those ruins, still issuing a terrible smell, as I parted from the courtyard in Ciepla Street No. 19, from my friends in the Movement and my youth leaders, Rut and Mira; my aunts and uncles; Tzameret, my teacher; Miriam, my friend—a huge graveyard of half a million of Poland's Jews. Wait for the avengers, for the day of reckoning, you damned ruins! Germany will never be able to atone for its responsibility for the death of hundreds of thousands of innocent people.

Farewell Warsaw, the city of joy and anguish, we shall never return. You stood uncaring when we cried to you for help in our despair. I hate you. You let a third of your inhabitants die before your eyes, without a word of protest against that terrible injustice.

The ghetto was lit from above by the bright summer sun, but darkness, the smell of burning and stench of corpses, reigned inside.

Many years have passed since I wrote those sad words of parting from the city of my birth. I always felt a powerful urge to revisit it, to see the ruins once more with my own eyes, to connect again with the period of my life that had become so important to me. To connect, and maybe to find relief from that heavy burden.

Throughout all those years I wanted to find out—I craved to hear and read—all I could about that final *aktzia* and the heroic uprising. It was only in 1983 that I went with my sister to Warsaw with the first delegation to participate in the official Remembrance Day held by the government of Poland in memory of its Jewish citizens.

By now an elderly woman, I told my story to youngsters who were at the age I was when I experienced those events. I looked into their eyes: Do they grasp what happened here? Does our story touch them? Are they capable of identifying with it, or maybe they find it repulsive, too strange and horrible?

7 : IN BERGEN-BELSEN

On the fourteenth of July we arrived at Bergen-Belsen by the town of Celle, not far from Hanover, in northern Germany. We were met by barbed wire fences and shouting in German: "*Schnell, schnell weiter laufen*" [quick, quick, run on].

The women were separated from the men. It was a rainy night when we came to the large and menacing camp. We were about 2,700 men, women, and children. We were meant to be "exchanged" for German citizens, living abroad.

Our "transit camp," set up for foreign citizens, was part of a very large camp. We were all given names of dead people whose papers had remained at the offices of the Gestapo, or sent from South American consulates with the purpose of saving Jews. That is what we were told. Our name was now Kopelewicz: My mother, my ten-year-old sister, and I were told to remember the name well.

On the Aryan side of Warsaw, I was called Halina Grzybowska. When shall I become myself again, Liza Melamed? They put us into huge wooden huts full of two-tiered bunks we called *prycza*.

On the next morning we went outside, we had to stand in rows of five. The Germans counted us repeatedly for hours. This ritual, called *Appell*, is repeated twice every day. In front of us there is a wide road crossing the whole camp. In the middle of the road is a building with a tall chimney. No, it is not a crematorium as we at first suspected; it is a kitchen. We look at it hopefully. They serve us coffee-like water, a daily ration of bread, and a thin soup at noon. (The children are given in addition some porridge with milk, margarine and an egg once a week.)

Behind the kitchen is a camp for Russian prisoners of war. In the evenings we hear familiar sorrowful melodies issuing from there. The people in our camp raise their fists in their direction, as a sign of workers' solidarity. They see us from a distance and respond gladly. We are in the same boat. My heart is full of admiration for them, the soldiers of the Red Army. They did not stay there long. After a few months they disappeared. They were replaced by Jews from Holland.

Life has acquired a certain routine. The tremendous survival instinct of the Jewish people, the will to survive whatever the cost, has led to the development of cultural life in the camp. People have set up a synagogue and hold study groups, lectures, and literary evenings, until the start of curfew at nine in the evening.

There are many assimilated Jews here, who were hiding at the homes of their Polish friends. They say there are some informers and collaborators with the Nazis among them. There is a considerable group of intellectuals here too: Brand, Raskin, Lusternik, Ritowsky, the actress Czervinska, and others.

People quarrel a great deal, they are tense and nervous. They are only now beginning to grasp the loss of their loved ones, until now there was no time to mourn. They are gradually starting to realize the extent of the tragedy.

The most unpleasant experience for me until now is relieving myself. On the edge of the camp they have put up two huts with latrines—for men and for women. In the middle of the hut there is a long shelf with holes to sit on, so that people sitting back to back almost touch each other. Everything is in the open, seen by all, women sitting together with their children.

How can the Germans, such a "cultured" nation, humiliate people in this way? I feel demeaned, helpless, almost a nonperson. Do they want us to lose the sense of shame—differentiating us from animals—so they can do to us whatever they wish, and we shall not be capable of resisting? Yes, that is their method. To them Jews are subhuman, that's clear. How shall we ever be able to avenge ourselves?

The Fear to Lose Again

Between two *Appells* we were allowed to move about outside, in the little space between the huts. It was crowded there. A few days ago something happened I'll never be able to forget.

Mother left us outside and went into the hut for a few minutes, asking me to look after Mirka. When my sister realized that Mother was not with us, she became frightened and began to scream hysterically, her whole body convulsed, not hearing what I, and the people around us, said to her to calm her. The whole camp froze at the sound of her screams. Her dread almost made her lose consciousness. Mother must have heard her and came running and took her in her arms. I couldn't calm down. Since then Mother did not leave Mirka even for a moment.

How did the child manage to live for months on the Aryan side alone with a strange woman and pretend she had no parents, say she was Polish and suppress all her fears, lest they give her away? Now everything erupted. [Maybe this is what has led to her complicated relationship with Mother throughout her adult life: her endless attempts to stress she is grown up, independent and different, at the same time being close to her and influenced by her.]

I was already fifteen and had long escaped from Mother's influence. I had gained my independence in a drastic, painful way. I know I hurt her in the ghetto when I belonged to the underground and used to disappear without telling her where I was going, and stayed away all night. One day she had said, "You do whatever you want, I have no influence over you."

But in moments of crisis, she was with me and cared for me lovingly. When my sister got diphtheria and her life was in danger, she plucked up her courage and went to the camp commander, Haas, and in her broken German begged him for the lifesaving serum. It was an extraordinary thing to do.

I was afraid they would arrest her. I knew her determination well and that she would insist, but the decision was up to the German. He was impressed by her dignified appearance and her beauty and ordered that the medication be given to her. So she saved her daughter's life. He also had Mirka moved to the small hospital and let Mother stay by her side.

At that time diphtheria was a children's disease that could end in asphyxiation, if the serum was not given immediately. A boy lying next to my sister died of the disease, but Mirka overcame it and recovered. I admired Mother's courage. Her action had repercussions among the people in the camp.

The Great Deception

We have already been here three months. The group of pioneers lives as a commune. People are starting to recover a little; their mood is improving. Day by day they wait for news of the impending journey, to be exchanged for Germans living in enemy countries, maybe to go to the Vitele camp in France, from where positive letters have come from the transport that had left Warsaw a few months before. Everyone is daydreaming.

In November 1944 the news came, but we heard that only those with permits to Latin America were going to Honduras, Paraguay, and Costa Rica; the wealthy Jews had bought them for a thousand dollars each. They were sold by middlemen such as Lulek Skosowsky and Adam Zuravin—Jews collaborating with the Gestapo.

Our group of three hundred fifty people going to Palestine is staying in the camp, with another group of a few dozen people who have genuine personal documents to countries abroad. The Germans explained that those with documents are going to a winter camp called Bergau and they need not worry. They will be exchanged at the end of winter. There is no need to take a lot of belongings; it will be brought to them in a special railway carriage. What is better? To go or to stay?

I hope they do not send us to our deaths, *na giemze* [the skin-leather industry, a cynical expression invented in the ghetto]. Yesterday the pioneer group got together. Eliezer Geler, the "Gordonia" leader and ours here, said that they intend to swap Hela Schipper with another girl, and Hela would stay with the Palestinian group.

"We have no idea what is going to happen. It's better if we separate as much as possible," he said. "If we see that the train is going to the east, in the direction of Poland, we must jump off the train. We'll try to escape individually and get to the partisans."

We felt the fatal importance of that moment and the sorrow of parting. Hela and I remain and they are leaving—maybe to a better future. And who will survive? Those going to another camp, with the *promisas*, or the small group whose names are written on the certificates no one has seen?

The atmosphere among the remnants of the fighters is heavy. They have plenty of experience and don't believe a word the Germans say. I hug the girls, shake their hands, and we part with the Movement's greeting, "Fear not! Be strong!" We find it hard to look into each other's eyes, lest the dread in our hearts be revealed. Pnina wept quietly.

"Don't cry. In the end we'll all meet in Eretz Israel."

"We've been lucky so far, so why should our luck leave us now?" Ktana tried to comfort us. She had become hardened after losing all her family.

"At least we are together," said Dina, as though reading her thoughts.

"We'll manage somehow," added Erella.

Quiet and withdrawn into themselves they climb into the trucks.

Toward the end of the war, we heard from Auschwitz survivors what had happened to those who went by train: It arrived in Auschwitz in the middle of November 1943, and without *selektzia* they were all sent into the gas chambers. No one survived. My cousin Lazar was also among them. He had escaped from the burning ghetto and from the informers on the Aryan side. Miracle followed miracle, but in the end he too was defeated, the great survivor.

That was the end of the last of the fighters who had saved themselves by getting out of the ghetto through the sewage canals, the five young girls who had hidden in the monastery (where I was supposed to join them), two thousand five hundred Jews, extracted from safe hiding places on the Aryan side, also those with genuine documents who were supposed to leave for freedom.

This was the way of the Germans—deception, deception, deception.

Love across the Barbed Wire

After the group had been reduced, we were moved to Block 10. They added about a hundred Czech Jews to us, mixed couples, meaning only one of the couple was a Jew. Next to us was the camp of privileged Jews from Saloniki in Greece.

I found girl friends my age—Rina Altbeker and Gavriela, who has a younger brother and her mother with her. Her mother is an impressive-looking woman. Her hair and her eyes are black and beautiful, her nose is straight. She is a heavy smoker and constantly tries to get ahold of cigarettes. In exchange for cigarettes, she gives bread—her own and her daughter's.

Gavriela's six-year-old brother is a lovely little boy, but he is sad. He doesn't play with other children, he sits on the *prycza* wrapped in a rug, and rarely gets down. Gavriela is a lively girl, fire and brimstone. She is furious with her mother and tells us, her voice shaking with anger and tears, "Mother is selling the little we have for her cigarettes!" We understood her resentment.

But when the darkness fell on the world and each one was lying in bed, shivering with cold and fighting hunger, suddenly a wonderful alto voice was heard—that of Gavriela's mother. Her deep voice penetrated the heart, raised our spirits, and took us back to the good old days of operas and operettas by Strauss and Kalman.

I did not like the handsome Jurek Orlovski, who later became the well-known author Uri Orlev. He gave the impression of being arrogant and despising everyone. He was there with his aunt Stella and his little brother Kazik. Stella saved them from the ghetto and brought the two children to the camp. They quarreled with her all the time, and it was quite interesting and amusing.

Our girls started to flirt with boys in the Greek camp, particularly Tosia Levin, who fell in love with one of them, a good-looking fellow. They started sending notes to each other and making various signs. I considered it totally wrong. I told her repeatedly that there was no room for love in an awful place like this, but she refused to listen. The Greek boy used to send her notes in English, and we all helped with the translation and with her answer, as though the boy belonged a little to all of us.

One day they came to a decision. The boy managed to get through the barbed wire and met Tosia. We didn't know about it. But on the next day, during the *Appell*, we suddenly saw the Greek boy being led by the Germans who gave him a terrible beating in front of all the people in the camp. They didn't catch Tosia, who stood there motionless. That was the end of our longing for love.

The Way to the Showers

Once a fortnight they led us along the main road to the building with showers. It was near the housing of the officers and of Commander Haas. Through the gate we could see their well-tended gardens. Every fortnight we were afraid that gas might come out of the showers instead of water. Who could assure us that they wouldn't want to get rid of us someday?

We marched to the showers. The prisoners of the concentration camp passing us stared in wonder at people wearing their own clothes, at children holding their mothers by the hand, and also at our faces that didn't look as haggard as theirs.

Who are you, where do you come from, what are you doing here? There was whispering in the lines of the miserable-looking figures, dressed in thin striped clothing throughout the winter, wearing wooden clogs on their bare feet. They could barely drag themselves and the wheelbarrows they had to push. Others, looking hideous, were standing by the barbed wire fence. They called them *Muselmann* [the starving]. They were extremely thin, almost skeletal—only their eyes had a feverish glow.

In 1944 walking to the showers became extremely painful. Our legs also refused to obey us, as there was less and less food. But the worst, the most horrendous part, were the piles of human skeletons, arranged in a crisscross pattern in front of their huts, mounds reaching right up to the roof. How can they murder people in this way and line them up like piles of wood ready for the winter? And beside them sat the *kapo* [guards].

They were fat. They cooked on small gas burners, they talked and laughed. Collaborators, carrying out murders for their masters—the scum of the earth, many of them German criminals. There were women among them, most of them fat, with curly hair, wearing high leather boots. The day would come when they would be paid back. If I believed in God, I would curse Him now because how could He have created such creatures?

My fury was replaced by utter emptiness. I dragged my feet. I must hold out—survive, *überleben*!

Hunger

I am hungry. Hunger and boredom, these are the two leeches gripping my heart and creating a dark scene before my eyes. No star shines here. Emptiness ahead, and behind me pain and suffering. There is no hope. I am surrounded by black night. There is no way out.

I would lie on the bunk and daydream: I saw a huge bowl of pasta with butter, cheese, and sugar on it, a long sausage and lots of bread. Nothing but food, although I have only just finished supper: a thin piece of bread and coffee-like water.

In our special little camp we had self-government. We elected engineer Solovieczyk to be our leader: He was a proud, wise man, and we trusted him.

The distribution of food in the huts was carried out fairly and meticulously. We all would stand around the only table in the passage between the bunks and watch how the person handing out the food measured the bread with a string. One day the Germans put in the yard barrels full of creatures from the sea. We called them crabs—a type of snail in their shells, mixed with sand.

Mother went up to them, smelled them, and went on. The other people in the camp did the same. Sometime later, someone, "a man of the world," said that one can eat them, and that in these disgusting snails there is a lot of iodine and minerals that could help us. At once people appeared with their red food bowls, and since then we ate those crabs several times.

The Murder

I can still hear their screams. "Mother—God save me!" They screamed in all languages: French, Yiddish, Polish, Dutch, German. Their voices came through the brick wall separating their hut from ours.

We sat on our bunks, wrapped up in rugs, trembling with fear. None of us slept. We hugged each other. I held my little sister. There was horror in her eyes. It was clear: On the other side of the wall, they were killing people by beating them. Suddenly a low noise was heard in our hut. From my high bunk I looked in the direction of the noise. I saw a thin young man, covered in blood, his eyes wide open in terror, pleading, "Hide me, good people, they are murdering us!"

The women began to get down from their beds. One gave him water, another wiped his bloodied face. They went back to bed. I trembled and asked Mother, "What's going to happen, where can we hide him?"

"Be quiet, Liza. They may come in here to look for him. They'll punish us too."

She hugged Mirka, who was crying quietly. I looked around. I refused to accept the situation. My neighbors were silent. Their silence said it all, and I understood. There was no choice. The man understood too.

The pale light of a new dawn penetrated the hut. I never saw the young man again. In the morning I looked out through the slits in the door. From the neighboring hut, the *kapo* were cursing and dragging human skeletons, naked and covered in blood. They threw them on piles in wheelbarrows. Other prisoners pushed them to the crematoria. The massacre went on for several days.

Behind our block were huts, and a fence separated them from our block. We were able to get close to the fence. At the end of 1944 they brought to those huts thin, wretched men in striped clothing. They had come on death marches from Auschwitz, Mauthausen, and other camps, as the Russian front approached.

I stood by the fence and saw how they were given food. They brought a cauldron of soup, and the Polish *kapo* gave it out. They all pushed and shoved. The first ones got a ladleful of soup. Suddenly the *kapo* turned the cauldron over. They all lay down on the ground at once to lick the remnants. The *kapo* stood by, impassive, looking on. After a few days of this way of feeding them, they sent the weak ones to the hut next to us, where they murdered them.

We were in shock. Maybe there are relatives or friends of ours among these men. When will our turn come? A few days later we were told that we would be transferred to an adjacent camp.

The Sad News

We stood on *Appell* for four hours. Why? Because during the lineup in the hut not all the rugs had been folded in the right way. There was a drizzle, the cold penetrated to the bone, and the emaciated bodies shivered out of control. During the winter of 1944, in northern Germany, we were wearing only remnants of the clothes we had brought from Warsaw.

The children next to me couldn't remain standing. They swayed from side to side. Little Juzio nearly collapsed. He sat down on the muddy ground. Other children looked around in fear. In the end they also sat down. For some reason, the German guarding us looked away. He looked older. Maybe he was just a soldier of the *Wehrmacht* [German army], an ordinary person with a family. The commander of the camp pretended not to see it.

My shoes were completely torn, and my only sock peeped out through the sole of the shoe that had come apart.

"Mother, maybe we could get wooden shoes, like those of the *katzetniks* in the camp? I'll give someone my bread in exchange, after I collect it for several days," I whispered to Mother. [*Katzetnik* was a person in a concentration camp, from the German KZ *Konzentrationslager.*]

"All right," she answered. "We'll ask in the Dutch camp opposite, maybe someone will sell us a pair."

My eyes wandered beyond the barbed wire, to the belt of forest. The gray sky spread over us like a rug. Salvation would not come from there either. At last they let us leave the *Appell*.

On the other side of the barbed wire I saw haggard women file past. When the guards moved away, I went up to the fence and asked, "Where do you come from?"

"From Warsaw," she answered, looking at me hopefully. "I was in the uprising."

"But how did you survive?"

We quickly exchanged information. Suddenly I heard the name "Poniatow."

"You were in the Poniatow Camp? What happened there? Maybe you got to know Shimon Melamed?"

She looked at me for a moment and answered, "They were all shot dead."

"When? Where?" Time was short and I pleaded.

"On the third of November 1943."

I didn't ask anymore questions. She went on and her eyes were blank.

I didn't tell my mother and my sister. Maybe one percent of hope still remained. Miracles do happen, like to this woman. But I knew for certain: Father was no longer alive. Nor was Aunt Biela.

Yet There Is Still Strength

With all my strength I tried to preserve my human dignity and keep to the principles I believe in. Mira Fuchrer's words at the last meeting of the troop in the Warsaw cellar were ingrained in my heart: "Your real test will come when you remain alone. When you are surrounded by friends, it is easy for you to remain loyal to the Movement and to preserve your moral strength, but when you face the enemy alone, it will be a real test of your fortitude. Be strong, for you will face the enemy and death—alone."

Maybe it was these words that made me feel out of place among the girls my age. I felt I had a secret. I mustn't reveal that I was in the Warsaw underground. Not yet. Anyway, I felt different. Sometimes their chatter annoyed me. I felt that, as a member of the Hashomer Hatzair, I had a mission to fulfill—if I survive.

I felt I had been given a great responsibility. I wasn't quite sure what kind. I knew I mustn't lose my human dignity, and that meant that I must behave morally.

I tried to get close to Hela Schipper whom I considered grown up and very high-minded. I wondered how I, just an ordinary member of the Movement, could gain the attention of the heroic liaison who went on missions to Polish towns on behalf of the Z.O.B.

To keep myself going, I taught little Helenka Hebrew in exchange for a piece of bread, while I learned Hebrew from Hana, paying her with that same piece of bread. I also learned French on my own, from a book about the history of the French Revolution that someone had brought to the camp. I repeatedly practiced the words of the language I loved so much. In the ghetto I had studied French in the complet and acquired a basic knowledge, so now I could sit for hours and learn. This gave me great pleasure, and I promised myself to seek every possible means to acquire an education after the liberation.

But my sorrow was overwhelming. When they put out the lights in the hut, a profound sadness engulfed me. Scenes from the ghetto passed before my eyes. A surge of tremendous longing for Father and for my friends from our group overwhelmed me. I lay as though paralyzed, covered by my only dirty rug, and felt how miserable my life was.

I looked down to assure myself that there was someone else in the world: Mother and Mirka. I comforted myself by thinking that I had an aim in life, something to live for: to tell about the heroism of the members of the pioneer movements, about young people with a lust for life who gave up their young lives of their own free will, owing to a sense of responsibility for the Jewish people. It was self-evident that we, the youth, must be in the vanguard of our people, defend the masses devoid of their rights, to fight and sacrifice our lives willingly with unfailing determination. Yes, that feeling saved me from falling into the abyss of depression and despair. Only that deep sorrow, rising from within, accompanied me throughout life.

The Washroom

In the large camp there were many Jews from Holland. They were no longer strict about separate housing. Men and women lived together in the long huts. Some strange people arrived lately. Hundreds—maybe thousands—of Hungarian Jews in army uniform, forced laborers who had served in the Hungarian army. They were tired and thin, and what's worse, they brought with them the plague of lice.

Until then we had been careful about this plague. At the end of our block was a washroom with basins and cold water taps. The windows of the washroom were broken, but this did not stop many of us from washing there.

I found a way of having a wash naked: I wrapped my head, including my face, in a towel, so that I wouldn't see anything and wouldn't be ashamed that others could see me. Even in the northern winter cold, I used to undress and wash, like many others, for this ritual went far beyond the need for cleanliness of the body. It made my life meaningful, making me feel that I was a civilized person, in control of my body and soul. Interestingly, I never caught a cold.

Apart from measles, which spread as an epidemic among the children in the camp, we were rarely sick. Measles left us extremely weak, but still alive.

March in Single File

I slept on a bunk on the third level. I climb up on a ladder. At the end of the bunk there was a bowl for urine. Everyone had such a bowl. Who from among those sleeping on the top had the strength to climb down in the night? My legs were swollen, I was too weak to go down and all the way to the end of the passage to the latrine, used by dozens of people.

Unintentionally, my legs touched my urine bowl, followed immediately by Mrs. Lubetzky's frightened shouting. I looked down in despair: a thin yellow stream leaked onto my bed and her rugs on the second level.

"Urin, Urin!" shouted the highly respected lady of German origin. Mother and Mirka, sleeping at the bottom, could hardly restrain their laughter. In a feeble voice I begged her to forgive me.

On the bunk next to mine slept an unknown man, and I didn't speak to him. Just another thin man, introverted and silent. Most of the time he sat and hunted lice on his clothes.

In the morning, before we went out to the *Appell*, I tried to get rid of the lice, crawling in single file along the seams of my clothes. From where do they pop out all the time? I crush one line and at once another line crawled out of the sleeve. Disgusting! I managed to crush them. Quick, quick! They were getting the better of me! And then they suddenly appeared in another seam and marched along, proud that they deceived me. God! I drop back helplessly. Should I laugh or cry?

The Human Bonfires

It is spring. The news we get from the older German soldiers who treat us humanely is that the end is approaching. Beyond the fence of the Dutch camp is an open field. The wind brings in a horrible smell from there. In the distance we can see circles of smoke rising, and dark figures busy around the fire. What are they carrying? They are corpses for which there is no room in the crematorium. They are burning them on the ground one by one. Their ashes mingle with the soil, the rain creates human mud.

"All are of the dust, and all turn to dust again," said the Lord. Maybe that is God's will if He exists at all.

Human beings: beautiful, with black eyes, blue eyes; writers, teachers, students, disappointed lovers, proud, cowardly, selling fish on the market, fathers and mothers and those who had not yet tasted love. "The Chosen Jewish People" burned like dung in the field.

The winter of 1945 was hard. What may have saved us from starvation and death were the Red Cross parcels that arrived in March.

A few months before, a train came to Bergen-Belsen full of Jews from Budapest. They were supposed to go to Switzerland and from there to Palestine. When they left, they took with them to the free world lists of the people in our camp. After all, we were also supposed to have been exchanged.

When we suddenly received food parcels with such treasures as cubes of sugar, peas, chocolate, and hard cheese, we realized that it had been arranged by the people on the Hungarian train and proved that they had reached safety and freedom. [It was the famous Kastner train. Dr. Kastner made "a deal" with the Nazis, and they enabled him to send a train from Budapest to Switzerland with over sixteen hundred Jews, who were to be sent to Auschwitz.]

At the beginning of spring 1945, the guns thundered. We felt that the end for the Germans was near, and there were many indications that it was so. The main one was that they stopped giving us food. Every day we stood at the fence along the main road, waiting for the soup that came late, often only in the evening.

Evacuation from Bergen-Belsen

Allied planes flew above us making a dull drone, and there was nothing to stop them. A few days ago there was an air battle between English and German planes, right above the camp. I hid with the others under the bunks, not that I was afraid, but a shrewd thought was on my mind: Now, just before liberation and the end of the war, I could be killed by an Allied bullet or bomb.

I am sure there is no God, only chance rules my life. There is no one to pray to, no one to beg. Maybe my lucky star that has protected me until now will continue to do so. Will I manage to survive? A sweet feeling of revenge filled me as I realized that our murderers were also suffering and being killed. My strength waned, my feet were swollen from hunger, I became apathetic to my surroundings.

On the eighth of April, an unexpected order came to prepare for evacuation. We heard the thunder of artillery in the distance. They said that the city of Hanover was in the hands of the Allied armies. And they were approaching the little town of Celle. Evacuation? Where? To the gas chambers?

A terrible smell filled the air. I was hardened, cynical, no longer capable of feeling anything. After the terrible murders in Block 10, adjacent to us, nothing could move me. I remembered I had to survive to tell the world about my friends. I hugged my mother and sister. They mustn't separate us.

Mother consulted Uncle Leon Melamed. Aunt Irena, practical as usual, was already packing the most important things.

"There is nothing we can do," she said with typical decisiveness. "We have no choice. There is no point in staying in a camp that is no longer getting supplies of food. We'll starve before they come to liberate us."

We agree with her. We got into a long line, men, women and the children who were with us, hundreds of Jews from various blocks.

The people's faces mainly expressed uncertainty and acceptance of the situation. We again passed by the piles of skeletons, new ones every day. In the huge concentration camp on the other side of the road, we saw shadowy figures moving.

Mother and I took the few remaining clothes, the notes I had written in the camp and on the Aryan side, and a passport photo of Father. We had no personal documents, nothing reminiscent of our previous life. Mother had only a silver fruit knife that she took with us when we went to the *selektzia* in Warsaw. My legs wouldn't carry me. We had to go eight kilometers to the railway station in Celle. The road seemed endless; my body was weak and not used to moving. Every step called for super-human effort. We crawled along slowly.

Gavriela was carrying her five-year-old brother on her back. Her face was red with the effort. The child had no strength left, he was apathetic. Their mother walked beside them and slapped him gently on his face. Her legs were also swollen from hunger. I walked on. I couldn't help them, I had no strength left.

Suddenly a man walked up to me. I recognized him: It was my neighbor, from the next bunk. Without a word he put his arms under my armpits and dragged me along. I leaned on him with all the weight of my body. I didn't get to know him, although we "lived next door," and now he was helping me!

Who can understand the depths of good and evil in the hearts of men? This small deed, the hand held out in support at a critical moment, imbued me with hope and strength to continue on my own.

People began to drop their belongings. We also stopped every fifteen minutes and sadly threw down a few things. At the end of the march, my backpack held only a little food and two or three items of underclothes.

This experience has affected my lifelong attitude to things. Losing things or parting with them means nothing to me, causes me no sorrow. They certainly have no value in themselves, only if they are connected to some precious memory.

My legs were swollen and painful. I couldn't feel them any longer. I longed to sit down, to rest, to close my eyes and disappear. I struggled constantly against this urge. Mother was dragging herself along, but walked erect, as always. Mirka walked along well. Suddenly we saw railway carriages. Surprisingly, they were normal "pullmans," regular cars, not freight cars. The exhausted people lay down on the platform. At the station we were given a little food and water. Our journey had begun.

The Most Precious Turnips

We traveled by train for eight days. The train moved little; it remained standing a great deal. The front line was everywhere and chaos all around us. German families fled with their belongings in all directions in carts and on foot. Have they been encircled? What a cheerful thought! Our leaders and various oracles, experts in solving riddles and interpreting rumors, said that the Germans wanted to use us as hostages.

Besides our group, hundreds of Dutch, Greek, and Hungarian Jews were with us on the train, all supposed to be exchanged, from the special camps in Bergen-Belsen. In the meantime the most important thing was to get food.

During one of the stops, I saw people jumping from the train and rolling down. I also wanted to do so, but my sister was quicker and out already. I joined her. We rolled down the high embankment to a wonderful pile of animal feed, yellow turnips. I filled up my dress feverishly, grabbing as much as I could carry, and climbed back.

But at the moment when all the children began climbing up the hill, guards on the roof of the train opened fire on us. The Germans were apparently surprised and reacted late. I ran and lost my sister. I didn't see a thing, but I was determined to get the turnips into the carriage. The bullets whistled around us, but I didn't drop the turnips. I didn't even look back to see who fell and who survived. Only on reaching the top, under cover, did I look back in great fear, in search of Mirka. She stood up next to me, trembling but smiling. We had food for the rest of the journey.

The Danger Was Not Over Yet

After a six-day journey, we approached the front line. We realized that we were apparently traveling southeast. The experts said that we were approaching a large city in central Germany, Magdeburg, on the banks of the Elbe.

One day the officer commanding the military escort called our representatives. He was well-mannered and received them politely. Hela Schipper wrote in her book, *Parting–Mila 18*: "The commander took off his military cap and turned to the Jews in fear: 'Ladies and gentlemen, the end of the war is near. What shall we do?' Engineer Solovieczyk advised him to surrender to the Allies and put up a white flag on the roof of the train."

Our representatives came back and described the amazing meeting excitedly: The German asked the Jews for advice! Maybe he'll also ask them for help. That's a good sign.

In the night the whole escort team fled, using the locomotive. What would happen to us now? We were alone. Slowly, people started leaving the carriages. The train was standing in the middle of a field. I also got off, with my faithful friend Tusia (Rina Altbecker). We saw a small pond not far away, and "our people" were catching little fish there. Those among them with initiative found a tin, made a fire, and cooked the fish. We joined in, glad to share the job.

We breathe fresh air, the sky is clear, it is spring. Although we were weak, exhausted by hunger, hope was reflected in all the faces. Of course, there were also some "ravens," prophesying that the Germans would not give up as long as they can harm us, but who listened to them? Mother was also pessimistic.

Visiting a Village

Mirka and I joined the stream of people going to the nearby village of Ferstleben. The village houses were pretty, clean, surrounded by gardens with fruit trees. We entered a garden in full bloom. I knocked on the door of the house. A woman wearing a big apron came out. Her face expressed amazement at the two figures facing her. Evidently we looked like ghosts.

"*Kartofel, Kartofel, bitte,*" [potatoes, potatoes, please], I whispered. At that moment the woman started to scream. I didn't understand a word. She pushed us out. I ran to the trees and began to shake them, so the blossoms fell off the branches. A large stone flew at me. We ran away.

That was the first and last time I asked for food. I felt ashamed. Mirka and I decided not to tell Mother about it.

The Fate of the Certificates

That night we were right in the front line. We spent the night lying under the carriages. We did not dare flee from there because there was nowhere to go. To hide in the German village? They'll chase us away like dogs and hand us over to the authorities. We had no choice but to remain in the carriages and underneath them. Whatever happens to the others would also happen to us. Artillery shells flew above us with a terrifying noise. They may have aimed at the train. It was a miracle that we survived till the next morning.

Before dawn the locomotive returned with our escort. People who got out of the carriages in the morning were amazed to see lots of pieces of paper floating on the small pond. They looked strange, and they had not been there the previous day. When they went to look at them, they were devastated: these were our certificates and other papers protecting us! So we did have such papers. It wasn't just a deception by the Germans.

After the war the mystery was solved: as I wrote, at the end of 1944 a group of two thousand Hungarian Jews from Budapest came to Bergen-Belsen, on their way to Switzerland. Our leaders gave them a list of our names, and they passed it on to the Swiss and Jewish institutions in Palestine, trying to save Jews. Apparently it was only then that they sent us the certificates; now at the end of the war, the Germans found them useless.

But the Germans escorting us had a different plan for getting rid of us. They didn't want to let the birds in their hands escape, even though the Allies had already encircled them on all sides.

Liberation

Suddenly someone ran from carriage to carriage, screaming in terror, "The Germans want to drown the train in the river Elbe. Save yourselves!"

At the height of the panic, when we heard shots in the distance, we ran outside. People burst out of the carriages. Suddenly someone shouted, "The Americans are coming!"

To our great surprise, a tank came slowly down the hill opposite, followed by another one. I ran toward the tank, laughing hysterically. It stopped. I embraced the wheels, kissed the iron plates.

The amazed soldier who came out called his friends, and they immediately started throwing chocolate to us. They smiled in embarrassment and didn't know what to do. We had won the war. It was the thirteenth of April 1945.

Part III : Return to Life

8 : STARTING AGAIN

We were tired and ill. I went to the village and stood in front of the dairy, in a long line of our people waiting there. Others went to look for food in the stores. Someone gave me a cup of milk. I drank it at once and filled the tin container I had taken with me. I returned to the carriage to bring milk to Mother, but she poured it out on the ground immediately.

"No, no, we mustn't drink milk, it would kill us."

I didn't understand. "Why, Mother, even babies drink milk."

"Don't be angry, darling, but after such a long time, our stomach cannot digest milk," she said. In the meantime Mirka came with some other foods.

Soon American officers also arrived, leading the German soldiers, our escorts, now prisoners of war. The Americans had arrested them at once and did not let our people get close to them and inflict vengeance on them. Among the survivors there was confusion and chaos. They ran all over the place and didn't know what to do.

Our happiness was too great for us to grasp fully. Many people wept and hugged each other repeatedly.

Paper or Food

The American army transferred our whole transport to a beautiful town called Hillersleben. The people living in its small family homes, surrounded by gardens, were evidently privileged. Apparently they belonged to the SS.

Our people immediately occupied the houses, evacuated by their German inhabitants at two hours' notice. They did not have time to take their property with them, and the houses were lavishly stocked. The shelves in the cellars were full of cans of food and jars of jam and other essential foodstuffs. Even after five years of war, they lacked nothing.

I left Mother and Mirka and ran to a large office building. There would be a lot of paper there. Yes, paper, pens, pencils— real treasures! I took some paper and I was happy. While in the camp, I had longed for paper to write or draw on, and I wrote my diary in the one and only little notebook I had brought from Warsaw, in tiny, crammed handwriting to save paper. And here I found piles of precious paper! Ever since then I love smooth white paper and treat it with great respect.

While I went in search of paper, the people from the camp collected abundant supplies of food, but we were left empty-handed, because Mother would not participate in the general pillage. She said it was beneath her dignity.

In the end we were allotted an apartment with two rooms. Unbelievably, it contained bed linen and quilts. I treated having a bath as an act of worship. The water lovingly caressed my thin body. Addicted to the pleasure, I closed my eyes, and all that had happened until then seemed just a bad dream. Surely I would wake up in our Warsaw home and Mother would come and wrap me in a towel. That night I slept, for the first time in two years, on a white sheet. I had again become a human being, living in a civilized world.

The First Cigarette

On the eighth of May 1945, the radio announced Germany's total surrender and the official end of the war in Europe. I stood at the window of our apartment in Hillersleben. It was getting dark. Mother came up to me. She looked troubled. My heart was also heavy. The dark snake that would afflict me often throughout my life began to gnaw at me inwardly, penetrating my body, gripping me tighter and tighter, and striking, pouring in the venom of despair and depression. All the while, joyful sounds filled the air. Dance music issued from the improvised tent where people held parties every evening.

Dreadful rumors reach us from liberated Poland: Jews murdered by anti-Semitic Poles, forces of the "Armia Krajova" attacked Jews coming out of hiding places. Should we go back there? Maybe Father is alive? Maybe what the woman I met in Bergen-Belsen told me about the murder of Jews of Poniatow and Traviniki in Majdanek was not true. Maybe he managed to escape. After all, miracles do happen. People tell fantastic stories. A rational person can hardly believe them, but they are all true.

We put our names on all kinds of lists, published by the Allies and by Jewish organizations. Maybe Uncle Sima, Mother's brother, who left Warsaw at the beginning of the war and got to central Russia, is alive and searching for us?

I wanted to get to Eretz Israel. Mother wasn't keen on it. She never felt any affinity with Zionism, and the hard life in Palestine certainly had no attraction for her. She was racked by doubt and so was I.

I took out a Camel cigarette I was given by an American soldier. I had never smoked, but now I lit a cigarette. I looked in Mother's eyes and our eyes met. She understood me and said nothing. That was my first cigarette.

Where Shall We Go?

At last I had a real diary. I found it in our new apartment with the inscription "To Lenny with love from N., 1941." Lenny may have been a member of the Hitler Jugend. What do I care!

The nice American soldiers were very happy and running wild. Why not! They would go home; every one of them had a home with parents, a wife, and children waiting for them. A normal life. And what about us? We had to start our lives from the beginning. I was not happy. I was afraid.

In fact, I was really born during the war, for it was the war that had molded my personality. I was used to constant change; there was no stability in my life. The situations were generally unusual; they cropped up suddenly and changed my way of life drastically. There was no need to plan anything, as we did not have any control over what happened, and everything was constantly turned upside down.

And now, to return to a life when one has to think about food for tomorrow, and one has to decide and organize everything, it was all up to us. The thought was really frightening.

When the war broke out, I was eleven, and until the moment when I lost my home and began trudging from place to place, I was not aware of a normal type of existence.

I was now seventeen, almost grown up, and yet totally unprepared for a "normal" life. I got to know people in Bergen-Belsen and hated them. Egoists, trampling on corpses to obtain what they needed. Mean and cunning products of war. My ideal of a moral person, creative and sharing with others, vanished in that harsh reality. I knew people from the youth movement. They were different. Maybe that is why they did not survive.

I think that a person can behave humanely only up to a certain point, but under conditions of extreme hunger and humiliation, one loses one's humanity and turns into a beast. One may not change completely; maybe the change is only superficial and temporary, and then the person becomes his true self again.

I had lost my belief in people. I had become suspicious. I scrutinized the people I met. Maybe this one handed people over to the Germans. Maybe that one is just putting on a show and actually he was a *kapo*.

I lost too much without being able to part properly: my family, my father, my friends from my troop "In Flames," school studies, three years of intellectual and physical development during adolescence. That's too much! I was weary, so weary. I had no strength left to fight on. I felt like an adult, an old woman with too much experience to live with.

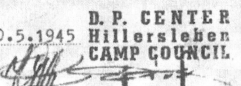

CAMP COUNCIL
CONSEILLE DE CAMP
Hillersleben

1691 ℁

Certificate / Certificat

Name
Nom.   M a l a m e d   Liza

born
né   19.7.1928   in
à Warszawa

was since
était dépuis   15.7.1943   till
jusqu'au   7.4.1945

in the german camp   Bergen-Belsen
dans le camp allem. und.

as
comme   designated for exchange to Pale-
imprisoned . —   stine
emprisonné . —

          Got off: April 13th 1945.
          Libéré: le 13. April 1945.

The liberation was in the train (exported the 7.th April 1945
from concentration camp in Bergen-Belsen) near the station
Farsleben 16 klm. from Magdeburg by the 9th US. Army.

La libération eut lieu du train (exporté le 7. April 1945
du camp de concentration à Bergen-Belsen) près de la station
Farsleben 16 klm de Magdeburg par la 9me Armée Ameri-
caine.

Remarks
Remarques

                    D. P. CENTER
Hillersleben   10.5.1945   **Hillersleben**
                    CAMP COUNCIL

A document given us at liberation by the American army.

Excerpts from My Diary

Hillersleben, 12th May 1945

It's very hot. I am sitting in my room that belonged to someone else, sleeping in the bed of a German boy or girl, driven from home, and I am dreaming about revenge. But what kind?

Opposite is the housing of forced laborers from Italy, Poland, and Ukraine—not Jews. There is a fence between them and us, but one can walk through freely. They sit outside all day, sing, play ball, and in the evening they dance. They are not worried. "Ordinary" people, whom the poet Tuvim describes so well in his poem "Crazy Zosia." When they return home, they'll work hard all week. On Sunday they'll put on nice clothes and go out to look for a girl and to have a drink. They don't rack their brains where to go, where to live.

While we, where are we to begin? In the meantime, a large number of the liberated people from our train are ill with typhus and dysentery. Many of them are dying. They bolted down the food and fell ill immediately. Our mother went on foot to the villages, exchanged clothes for chickens, and made bouillon for us. I am sure it was thanks to her practical sense and initiative that we didn't fall ill.

18th May

Once more I recall the wonderful songs we sang in the Movement. Songs from that happy period, gone forever. They open a wound bleeding in my heart. I shall never, never forget my friends from the troop, from the Hashomer Hatzair Movement, and their supreme sacrifice. You remained among the ruins of the Warsaw Ghetto of your own free will. You did not flee, even when it was possible; you were burned, your bodies riddled with bullets are lying on the roofs of the houses, from which you shot at the Germans. You have no grave—no one to weep over you.

I am the one who has survived. I shall weep over you all my life. Maybe someone else has also survived to the bitter end, like me?

Maybe I should not have obeyed Rut when she told me to go out to the Aryan side and save myself. Why did I survive? I am such a nobody. Why me? There were five more girls with me, those in the monastery. Why did it have to be me? How shall I bear the burden of your death?

19th May

In the evening I went to the tent where they are dancing. I stood on the side and watched. Most of the survivors are young men, there are few girls. They wanted me to join them in ballroom dances. I don't know them. They were forbidden in the Movement.

A group of Jews, liberated from the camp next to Magdeburg, started singing songs in Hebrew and dancing the hora. They didn't know how to dance it, they just shouted and walked jauntily around in a circle. I felt a stab of pain in my chest and left. What's the hora to them? It's the dance of the pioneers! Their hora is just walking around in a circle and shouting. What does it mean to them, apart from a dark period in a concentration camp?

The memory of dancing the hora in the Movement was that of a painful loss. A frosty evening, an hour before the curfew, a small square in Mylna Street in the Warsaw Ghetto. The ground covered with frost, and above us the splendor of the star-studded sky. We dance the hora. Faster, faster! All thoughts and feelings gyrate with the exhilarating sense of being together, a wonderful rhythm of beating hearts and feet, drunk with youth and happiness. You feel that you love the boys and girls around you. It is a bond of friendship and loyalty, you share the same goal. Yes, happiness, a fleeting moment.

12th June

We have decided to return to Poland and search for Father. I am not convinced it is the right decision, but maybe it is a good way to begin our lives once again.

The Gitel family and two sisters we know, Minia and Frania Perelman, went to the Russian camp and found out that one can get to Prague and from there to Poland. But they tricked us. The two girls joined a group of Slovaks and left without letting us know, and Gitel, known as a clever *macher*, managed to get in as well, with his family.

Mother was very angry. Maybe it's better that way. What would we do in Prague? Besides, we have no money, nor friends, how would we manage in Poland with the ruins screaming at us on all sides, and the Poles now even more anti-Semitic? It's better to stay with the other people from the camp, to trust the American army that they will take us somewhere, and we'll look for a way to get to Eretz Israel.

One evening I was sitting on a bench in the square. It was dark and the youngsters were dancing as usual. Ryshek, a boy of about nineteen, who had been with us in Bergen-Belsen, sat down next to me. When we were there, I paid no attention to him, but here, all of a sudden we began talking, and I felt engulfed by a pleasant gentleness. He has lovely blue eyes and fair, curly hair. We talked late into the night and parted as close friends.

Maybe? Since then I have been thinking about him and looking for him. I so much want to love and feel life running in my veins once more. I felt close to him, and I think that he is also seeking my company. Am I wrong?

Going West, to Freedom

3rd July

We left a week ago, some two thousand Jews, parting from the town where we had recuperated. We traveled in a long train in the direction of Belgium. On our way west from Magdeburg, we saw German refugees, dragging their legs and pulling carts with their miserable belongings. During the night we passed Hanover, a city destroyed even more thoroughly than Magdeburg.

In the morning we passed the cities of Westphalia, the German industrial region. They were totally destroyed by Allied bombing. The refugees are fleeing from the Russians, they travel in freight cars among military supplies and equipment.

We are glad to see Russian prisoners of war, returning to their homeland; we wave to them, we love them. In one of the trains passing us at high speed, they thought mistakenly that we were Germans, and someone shot at us, badly wounding a Dutch Jew. In the night there was an interesting incident: Two Germans, disguised as French soldiers, stopped us and tried to get on the train. They caught one of them, and the other one managed to escape to other carriages, but they also caught him. They are suspected of belonging to the SS. It caused great excitement.

On the sides of the train they have written in Hebrew: "We are going to Eretz Israel." My friends, Rina and Tusia, are also with us. We've shared our food with other families. There is a wonderful atmosphere in the carriage. We are starting a new life.

I looked for Ryshek. During one of the stops we sat outside in the warm sun. I think he is interested in me and seeks my company. He is also looking with joy into the future. Life seems to me very interesting and full of possibilities. The spring, the scented air also contributes to my happy mood. Am I in love? I love being in love.

They have brought us to an improvised camp in Belgium. Once again tiered bunks, communal showers, and soup given out from a cauldron. But the camp is totally different from that other one. We have plenty of food and plenty of room. We can go into town and anywhere we like. In Hillersleben, after the liberation, we asked Mother to make us soup out of brown bread. We remembered how marvelous it tasted when we got it in Bergen-Belsen as an extra for children. Mother cooked the soup, but it tasted awful. There we were hungry, and even bland food tasted wonderful. But now our normal sense of taste had returned.

We've already seen two movies. I was completely confused and almost drunk with that experience. I hadn't seen a movie for five years, and I realized what I had missed. Then a group of us youngsters went to a dance club. And what did I see?

My mother was dancing with a man from our camp. We both danced and I was happy. What a beautiful mother I have! She is only thirty-six and she looked completely in love. How delightful life can be!

Shall I Go to a Boarding School?

They have transferred us to another camp by the town of Mons. I dare to speak French and it's going quite well. Mother says that I have a talent for languages. I only learned French for a year and a half in the ghetto and I speak it fluently.

The food in the camp is poor: meals of soup and a roll. Mother worries what will happen to us, and so do I. A few days ago some people from the refugee organizations came and persuaded us to send Mirka with the other children to a boarding school where she'll be able to study and get good food.

Mirka is twelve and a half, she has fair hair and a pleasant, lovely face, but she is thin and small like a ten-year-old. At first she was against it, but in the end she agreed. Mother will be able to visit her, and it's important for her to develop and catch up with girls her age.

They also suggested that I go to a boarding school for youth my age. I am in a dilemma: On the one hand, I want to exploit every opportunity to 'study; on the other hand, they say that one should seize every moment of happiness, and I've only just begun, I've only experienced one kiss. I am still not sure about Ryshek's feelings for me. Should I really give it up before it has started?

"The freedom train"—Jews liberated from Bergen-Belsen are leaving Germany on their way to Belgium, summer 1945.

With the Soldiers of the Jewish Brigade

25th July

I've been in Brussels for four days and am staying with Mother in a rented room. Mirka is still at the boarding school. I was there for a week and I ran away. Everything irritated me. It turned out that there were no studies. On the contrary, we, the older ones, had to work and look after the young children all day. I am not a sucker!

Boys from our camp came to see us, and they brought cakes, cigarettes, and candy. When they heard that we had to work the whole day, they suggested that we run away. They got our belongings out in secret, and we jumped out of the window. I even have a scratch on my hand from broken glass. Now I am free again. I don't want to be confined by any framework.

Brussels is a fascinating city, and we have a free ticket for the trams and free entry to cinemas. The city is full of soldiers from all over the world, and Belgian girls, all dressed up and made up, are hanging on their arms. Yesterday I walked in the street with Rina. Suddenly two soldiers with a Star of David on their sleeve came up to us. We were so amazed and confused that we almost fainted. They both belong to the Jewish Brigade and are looking for company. I am so proud of them! They invited us to a restaurant.

The boys are nice. We are speaking in two languages. I know a little Hebrew and Rina some English. They ordered the food. We were served some meat with a strange name. God! How embarrassing! I try to cut it and eat it politely, using my knife. And the meat is stone-hard and I can't cut it. I look at Rina and she looks at me. She can't swallow it. What should we do? What will they think of these two refugees, so provincial, with no table manners? I am sure they smiled in secret, but they didn't show it. We parted, excited by the experience and happy that Jews from Eretz Israel participated in the war effort—although too late.

I saw films with Jeanette MacDonald and Nelson Eddy. I want to catch up after years spent in darkness.

But yearning for my friend Miriam, for Father, for everyone. How can I live with all the mourning within me, that dreadful snake? I keep on recalling the poem by Mickiewicz, the Polish national poet:

> Lithuania, my homeland
> Like the elixir of love
> Only he who has lost thee
> Knows thy worth.

I am sure that Miriam—Tzelina Hammerstein—my friend since the age of seven, is no longer alive. We parted when I went out to the Aryan side. Maybe she and her family also got out. Thin and tall, her face pale but her skin dark, black curly unruly hair, a gentle, sensitive expression on her face, very intelligent, shrewd and maybe even oversensitive. She is my soul mate, I love her. There is no friendship without love, and maybe there is no love without friendship—a spiritual bond between two kindred souls. And yet we are so different.

Brussels, 8th August

We've heard that the Eretz Israel office has received certificates. We've registered for them, together with many people from our transport. We are all tense and full of expectation. We don't know yet if we are on the list of passengers. Mother and I go there every day, and there is no answer.

After the liberation, in Belgium: My sister Mirka (on the right),
mother Raya (in the middle), and I (on the left)

Brussels, 10th August

I've just returned from the Eretz Israel office. Tears overwhelm me! How outrageous! We are not going. All the others are: the leader of our group from Bergen-Belsen, engineer Solovieczyk, the Landau family, Hela Schipper, my Uncle Leon with his family, my friend Moshe Dudkiewicz, fifty Belgian pioneers.

I am not going. Maybe I began to concern myself with the journey too late, because of my preoccupation with my love for Ryshek (he is leaving, but immigrating to South America). Hela crossed me off the list of pioneers. She thought I would only go together with my family. She shouldn't have done it. I was ready to go on my own, ahead of Mother and Mirka.

And what's happening now: All of them are going, pioneers, and also people who have never been interested in Zionism,

With the aliyah emissaries in Belgium: Hela Schipper (on right), Ed Lingweil (second from right), the author, and a soldier of the Brigade, in summer 1945.

while I—a member of the Hashomer Movement from Warsaw, I who always intended to fulfill my aspirations to become a pioneer and a member of a kibbutz in Eretz Israel—I am not going. Maybe I am not sufficiently smart. I don't seek out the right connections and don't exploit opportunities. To put it simply, I am still naïve.

I weep. I feel angry and insulted.

Immigration to Israel—My Aliyah

4th September [written on the journey, the only and the last entry in my diary]

I am sitting on the deck of the ship *Matroa*. The unbelievable has happened. It is a reality intertwined with miracles, amazing events, and almost imaginary coincidences. This is the first ship with immigrants sailing to Eretz Israel legally after the war, bringing, in addition to hundreds of lucky people with certificates, also hundreds of *Ma'apilim*, illegal immigrants or pioneers without permits from the British Mandatory Government. The atmosphere is wonderful, and in spite of the overcrowding and the hard conditions, no one complains.

It's incredible how I got here. The story is like a fantastic movie. It all happened thanks to my adventurous spirit and fearlessness, sometimes excessive. Mother would say, as usual, "Liza, you are not realistic. You think you can get whatever you want. You endanger yourself."

And I don't listen, I just smile and go my way. But this time I had terrible pangs of conscience. This time I overdid it. I went off without telling her; one night I simply left. It was a sleepless night, a night of soul-searching, hesitations, and finally a crucial decision.

This is what happened: In my disappointment and despair that I did not get a certificate, one night I went with Rina to enjoy myself to a villa outside Brussels, in the Château de Ratandelle, where former concentration camp inmates were living together with dozens of pioneers. We immediately sensed the mysterious atmosphere and the whispering that stopped as we approached.

"What's happening here? Don't you think they are being unfriendly toward us?" I asked.

Rina, whose attitude to life is more straightforward, declared, "Something is happening here. They are hiding something from us."

That evening there was going to be a dance as usual. But some people were running about among the rooms. We went up to one of the girls whom we knew from previous visits. After several attempts at persuading her to tell us the secret, she did.

"Tonight a group of illegal immigrants is leaving; they have no documents or certificates. It's Aliyah Bet." [Aliyah Bet was illegal immigration to Israel in ships attempting to break the British blockade around Eretz Israel, until the establishment of the state.]

She also disclosed the name of the leader of the group, Pasko. At that moment I became terribly excited. Rina wasn't impressed at all, as she was supposed to get a certificate together with her mother, Mrs. Altbecker. I was thrown into a state of feverish excitement: "Should I try to get accepted?"

"It doesn't seem to me the thing to do, but do what you think is right for you."

And what do I think? I brought up arguments for and against: It's the quickest way to get there. Mother will arrive with Mirka in a few months' time, in one of the waves of legal immigration, as we were promised at the Eretz Israel office. I shall fulfill my commitment to the Movement, my promise to Rut, my leader in the ghetto.

Having survived—and I may be the only one—I must tell the story of the struggle of the pioneers and the Hashomer Hatzair in the Warsaw Ghetto. It's my duty, that's why I went out to the Aryan side and left the ghetto two days before the uprising broke out.

But, on the other hand, it isn't fair to Mother. I have no clothes with me, no money, nothing. That's not the way to travel to another country and to determine one's fate. I must get Mother's permission, at least to say goodbye. I may also be able to meet Ryshek and tell him how he had disappointed me, or maybe the break between us is just the result of a misunderstanding and our unexpected journeys, changes of address. Maybe I am important to him after all.

We went to the leader of the group. An older man, maybe forty. It was already two-thirty in the morning. He explained to me that it is a group of twenty youths, there is only room for twenty, and there isn't a single girl among them. I can join, in principle. But I may have to switch to another group in Holland, where they are going to collect additional groups of pioneers. It's a chance and a risk. It's up to me. He seemed very doubtful.

Another round of decisions. Half an hour later I decided to join the group leaving. I wrote a letter to Mother, asking her to send me money, documents, and personal belongings with Moshe Dudkiewicz, a close friend who is about to leave legally. I asked her to forgive me. I had to do it. My duty to the Movement is stronger than I am. I wrote that I love her and Mirka, and we are sure to meet within two or three months. Goodbye, Mother!

I had to hurry. We were leaving at seven. I got to know the boys I was joining. I already knew some of them quite well. One of them gave me a vest, two underpants, and I also found a bag. A hurried parting from my friend Rina and a promise of eternal friendship. In the morning she would go to Mother, would tell her everything, and give her my letter.

We traveled in silence across the Dutch border where we were given uniforms of British soldiers, belonging to the Jewish Brigade. I hid my hair under my cap; I had to pretend to be a man. Soon we were traveling in a line of three army cars covered by tarpaulin, accompanied by a soldier from the Brigade and people belonging to the Aliyah Bet operation.

Among them was Ed Lingweil, an impressive young man of German origin, one of the people responsible for our aliyah. I got to know him in Belgium, but I didn't know he was one of the aliyah leaders. His personality already impressed me at the time. He was like the people of the Warsaw underground, with the same spirit, the same boundless devotion to our ideals.

An overnight stay in Paris. The house was full of boys and girls running about, getting ready for aliyah like us. At last a shower and a bed.

A day later we reached the surroundings of Marseilles, the Vieille Chapelle chateau. I was worn out by the journey and from sitting at the back of the truck with very little air, and still excited by what I had done. In that chateau I opened my eyes to the beauty of nature. It was the end of August, and the russet leaves of the end of summer covered the paths of the garden. I remembered the fall five years ago, when the war broke out. I was still so naïve then. During those last days before the outbreak of the calamity, I was full of plans, getting ready for the sixth grade.

Now I am a free person again, and I may be able to continue from where I was interrupted to go to school and to a course in painting, as Mother had promised, to play at "ladies" with Miriam, to gather chestnuts in Saski Park on my way to school and come home for lunch, prepared by Stefa, our devoted maid.

The author (in the center) together with the Aliyah Bet group that left Belgium, wearing the uniforms of the Jewish Brigade, autumn 1945.

There is no point in yearning for the past. I must turn my eyes to the blurred, unknown future. If I get to a kibbutz, it will turn out all right. From now on that will be my family, and my conscience will be clear. I shall fulfill my commitment to the Movement, what it has taught me.

From Vieille Chapelle we were transferred to a big camp, and a week later the large transport from Belgium arrived, including my friends and my Uncle Melamed's family. I was there with my group, for we were supposed to board the ship, using certificates belonging to people who had disappeared in the Holocaust. The Haganah [defense forces] and Mossad leaders told us that the names we were to adopt would be given to us together with the documents before we got to the port of Toulon, where more groups, similar to ours, would be coming.

The anticipated great day arrived. We again went by trucks covered with tarpaulin to our "freedom ship," *Matroa*. The excitement was tremendous and the tension great; we were silent. I trusted the leader of our group. So far he had organized everything well. Especially in looking after me, protecting me from the lust of the boys in my group, who repeatedly vied for my attention. We reached the port and we kept on asking where are our certificates? Where are the people from the Haganah? Where is Ed Lingweil, the one responsible for us?

People began to get into line in front of the checkpoint. I left the group for a moment and ran to look how it worked. I was alone and I had a feeling that there was no one to depend on. At the checkpoint were two British officers and someone from Eretz Israel, and they were checking the names on the list. Suddenly someone from the Haganah arrived and told us,

"Guys, you don't have certificates, I am sorry. Try to get on the ship on your own!" That's all he said, and went off. My feelings and apprehensions were justified.

Within a second all the boys disappeared and I remained alone. Most of them were survivors of the Buchenwald camp, and they knew all about survival. They didn't rely on anyone, only on their own presence of mind. I was like that too.

Immediately a plan came to my mind. "I'll use the name Melamed, my own and that of my uncle's family. Their name is on the list presented to the immigration institutions." Trembling with excitement, I walked on in the line. Momentarily, the line at the *selektzia* flashed before my eyes, but I dispelled the nightmare. And here I was facing the two British officers, scowling at me. I gave my name and they began to search for it on their list.

Here it is. Melamed. Yes. And before they could check my first name, I was already well past them, walking fast inside the port. I understood that the man from Eretz Israel was already making sure that the matter was closed. On the ship's gangway, I met two more boys from the group. All those in our group managed to board the ship, each in his own way.

In the last large camp, I got together with a boy from Warsaw, Sewek, who had been in the Movement before the war. He was also alone, and we decided to handle things together. We met again on the ship and stayed together. There was nothing emotional or romantic between us. It was a functional friendship, born of the need not to be alone.

Of course, my uncle and aunt and their two sons, Adash and Meir, had boarded the ship. Although I had complicated matters for them, they did have proper certificates. We were glad to meet, but I remained with Sewek.

Adash, my age, scoffed, "Who is that mug you've got hold of?"

"He isn't a mug, and it's none of your business!"

I cut him short, but he went on, "I'll tell my parents that you've joined up with a stranger and not with us. They won't like it."

"As if they cared about me. I didn't see that they tried to help me when I was in Belgium, and we didn't succeed in getting a certificate."

"You have a mother who looks after you, but you've run away from her too," he said.

"You wouldn't be able to understand why I did it. You've never been a Zionist!"

"Now I am also a Zionist," Adash answered seriously. I believed him.

Who would have thought at the time that he would sacrifice his young life for the state in the making; that after surviving the *selektzia*, life on the Aryan side, and the *aktzien*, he would die in Israel, by the little bridge, facing the Egyptian army descending on Tel Aviv during the War of Independence? That's how my aunt and uncle lost two of their children: Hanale in the ghetto and Adash, already free in his homeland.

On the *Matroa* there were more than two thousand people. A child was born on the ship. It was very crowded, but we were in high spirits, and we sang and danced.

No one checked us when we disembarked. We arrived at the Haifa port and were immediately transferred to a train. It was so hot, the dry air hit us in the face. We waited and traveled slowly until it grew dark.

We were told that we were going to the Atlit camp, where we would only remain a few days to get sorted out. When the train arrived at the station, they led us on foot, in complete darkness, accompanied by people from the Haganah, in charge of Aliyah Bet. They ran about in the rows and with the help of flashlights looked for the *Ma'apilim*. I kept a tight hold on Sewek's hand, so as not to get lost in the crowd. The people around us walked fast and in silence. I didn't know where they were leading us.

Suddenly we heard whispers, "*Schwarze links!*" [The illegal ones, without certificates, to the left!] I saw people leaving the crowd and going in the direction of the voices. Sewek pulled me after them. We started to run. My feet repeatedly bumped into stones, my dress got caught up in thorns, but I ran breathlessly until the outline of a truck appeared in front of me. They pushed us from behind, and we climbed up quickly. The truck was covered by tarpaulin and started off immediately, driving fast. It climbed up the mountain. It turned out that we had come to Kibbutz Mayan Tzvi, on the Carmel.

It was the feast of Rosh Hashanah [the Jewish New Year], September 9, 1945. The kibbutz members surrounded us, welcoming us with smiles. They tried to talk to us, and for the first time I was able to use my knowledge of Hebrew, the little I had learned in Bergen-Belsen, and I even managed to tell them where I had come from and how.

I was terribly excited. I looked at Sewek and saw that he was also excited and trying to talk to the people. Suddenly I felt that tears were streaming from my eyes. Was this really the homeland I yearned for throughout those dreadful years, I prayed for, in my longing? Have the words of our songs come true?

Someone wearing shorts led us to a table. Through the veil of tears I saw a table, laid for us with sandwiches, fruit, jugs with drink, cakes. I remembered that I had not eaten all day, and even before that, on the ship, where the food was meager and tasteless. Excitement had made me forget that I was hungry.

Sewek pushed me with his elbow. "Go on, eat! Why are you crying?"

I stood there helplessly, as though all my strength had left me. He filled a plate for me and pushed me toward it. "That's enough, calm down. Look how nice these people are to us." Sewek was a good friend; I thanked him for his understanding.

"Sewek, do you think that our war is really over? That we'll be able to live like ordinary people? That we'll be like these people here in this kibbutz?"

Sewek wanted very much to calm me down, but not to overdo it. "I don't know, Liza. I don't even know what will happen tomorrow. Do you know what? In the meantime let's get some sleep."

That night I slept in a wooden hut, with only sheets on the bed. It was hot. I woke up in the blinding sunshine. Birds were chirping outside the window.

Two days later, the people who had come with us that night began to disperse. Someone from the kibbutz asked Sewek and me where we wanted to go, if we have relatives or acquaintances in the country. We didn't know anybody, but we had a definite destination. We said we wanted to get to a branch of the Hashomer Hatzair Movement, or the Kibbutz Artzi. They suggested we go to Haifa to look for the Movement's branch there.

It seemed quite natural to us to say goodbye to the kibbutz people and go down the mountain on foot, to the Haifa road. The fact that we didn't have any money to buy a bus ticket didn't trouble us. I was holding a little suitcase that Mother had sent to Marseilles, and I was confident and believed that everything would work out all right. We are in our own country, after all!

And the driver really was nice. He asked the passengers if anyone was willing to pay for the two new immigrants. Of course people offered to do so. We traveled to Haifa, the workers' city I had heard so much about. I still couldn't believe it. I pinched Sewek to see if it was all really true.

"That's enough! Stop behaving like a little girl," he reacted, but he was also in high spirits.

First we went to Hehalutz Street, to the Histadrut [Workers' Union] office. There they explained to us that the Hashomer Hatzair branch was elsewhere, that we had to go up on Mount Carmel. We walked up on foot, as we had no money for the bus. We walked on and on, and suddenly I was overwhelmed by terrible anxiety. I felt as though I was walking in unfamiliar Warsaw streets, and I didn't know how to reach my destination. And maybe there is no destination for me anywhere in the world, and I'll wander again, homeless and defenseless. I dispelled the nightmarish experience by force.

After a long search, we reached a square where the members of the Movement used to meet. Sewek had also been a member of the Movement before the war and was expecting an emotional meeting. We were surrounded by younger boys and girls in blue shirts. God, what shall I say to them? What do these youngsters, apparently all of them from good families, have to do with those Movement members, who had suffered so much? A thousand years separate us. Will they understand what planet I come from, bursting into their life of fun and games?

I turned to some of them and they immediately formed a circle around us. In my poor Hebrew, I explained to them simply, "I've come with Aliyah Bet. We are members of Hashomer Hatzair in Warsaw. I know no one in this country."

There was a little commotion and the youngsters began to whisper among themselves. Suddenly their leader appeared from somewhere. I explained our situation to him in detail. He looked excited and at a loss, and called his friend. They told us to wait. They came back to us with an older boy and girl.

"What are your names?"

"I am Lilit and this is Sewek."

"We suggest that you go to sleep at the youngsters' families, and tomorrow we'll take you to Kibbutz Merhavia. The leader of the Movement, Meir Ya'ari, lives there."

I had heard a great deal about Meir Ya'ari. He and Ya'akov Hazan were the founders of the Movement and their authority was undisputed. It was to them that Mordechai Anielewicz sent the few letters from the ghetto, asking for assistance, concrete and moral support. And now I'll meet him and tell him about the glorious Movement that had surpassed their expectations, and about its members who sacrificed their lives in avenging the horrors perpetrated against the Jewish people in the ghettos. I shall present my testimony to him. This is the moment I have been waiting for.

Meir Ya'ari welcomed us warmly. He listened to my story with great interest. Of course, I spoke in Polish. He knew the story of the uprising and the fate of the fighters in Warsaw, but was interested in the details about the young members and about the escape from the ghetto. My report about Hotel Polski made a great impression on him, as did the account about the way the members escaped from the Warsaw Ghetto through the sewage canals, and how the murderers later caught up with them.

Meir Ya'ari told me that Tzyvia Lubetkin and Yitzhak Zuckerman, the leaders of the fighters, members of the "Dror" Movement, had survived. He knew about a few more fighters, but mentioned sadly that all the leaders of our Movement had been killed. Meir asked me many questions about Mordechai and Mira. He hardly knew anything about Mira Fuchrer, and now he heard that she was one of the leading figures among the older members and in the Z.O.B. I was sorry not to be able to answer his questions about Yosef Kaplan and Shmuel Breslav.

Meir asked us what we wanted to do, where we intended to go.

"What do you suggest?" I asked. "I want to study. That's my primary aim. And also to become a kibbutz member."

"How old are you?"

"I am seventeen and Sewek is nineteen."

"I think it's best for you to enter the framework of Aliyat Hanoar [Youth Aliyah]. It will enable you to study Hebrew and various other subjects, and work half the day. We'll look for a suitable group for Sewek, unless…do you want to stay together?"

[Youth Aliyah was a project established in 1934 and in operation throughout the following period, also after the establishment of the State of Israel. It brought youth from abroad to live and be educated in Israel. Later it also dealt with groups from poor neighborhoods in Israel.]

Sewek and I exchanged glances. "Not necessarily," I said.

"Fine. Tonight stay in the kibbutz and we'll look after you tomorrow."

9 : In Beit Alfa

Is this really home? It all seems fine. We study and that's wonderful! I am making great progress in Hebrew, and I am also eager to learn the other subjects. I am seventeen and I am allowed to fool around—that's what I tell myself.

Our guides, Shlomo Gancewich and Yechiel Kadmi, are excellent teachers, patient and devoted. They asked me to tell my story to the kibbutz members. The dining room was full to overflowing. They all know Polish. Most of them lost their families in the Holocaust, and many did not see their parents since they parted from them. They did not know it was forever.

My cheeks were burning, I was excited. It was the first time I was giving a full report about my past in the Warsaw Ghetto. I also told them about myself. They listened in painful silence, and I forgot to come to an end. We sat there into the night. They were stunned, even though they had known about the Holocaust for a long time, and the newspapers had also published stories by survivors.

I found two more girls from Poland here, Naomi Altman and Julka-Yael Appel. They had survived Auschwitz on their own; their parents died there. Rina Altbecker, my friend from the camp, also joined me. We felt we are different from the others in the group, which was composed mainly of youth from Hungary and Romania who lost their parents or left them in those countries. The boys from Romania had experienced great suffering, the others less so. None of them had been in the war for six years, as we were. Most of them immigrated in 1944, by means of dangerous rescue operations. We tried to bridge the language gaps and cultural and behavior differences.

The boys and girls found it hard to adapt to physical work and to the strict kibbutz rules, and to tolerate the lack of understanding of the *sabras* [people born in the country] in the neighboring educational institution, who were unfriendly and arrogant toward us. From the few talks we had with them, it appears that they saw us as miserable Holocaust refugees, and silent accusing questions hung in the air: Why didn't you defend yourselves? Why did you follow German orders and let them murder you?

And sometimes it seems to me that this life was not real, all a façade. The real life was there, during the war, and I return to it repeatedly, whenever I have a free moment.

Rina said, "Next year I'll go and study in the city, my grandparents live there. I'll be like one of the *sabras*. I'll try as hard as I can to shake off my past and to live a happy life." That was her way.

Can I discard—like unwanted clothing—all my past, all that was significant and dear to me, all that has shaped my life? To fold it up and throw it away or conceal it in the depths of the unconscious? No! No! I shall try to confront it, as I have confronted all that has happened to me so far. It may cause me suffering. And I shall continue to tell my story and pass on the memory. Will I succeed? Time will tell. It is my duty.

In the fall of 1945 in Beit Alfa, the sun beat down harshly. Opposite our huts, in the soaring heat, the Gilboa Mountains rose in their rocky bareness. Our sore fingers dug into the cracked soil, trying to uproot the weeds in the vegetable garden in the Beit Shean Valley, an extension of the Jezreel Valley. That is the homeland, the valley we praised in our songs, hugging each other on the mattresses in Mila Street 61, when despair overwhelmed us: "Sleep our valley, our splendid land, we are guarding you… Rest comes to the weary…" Is this the longed-for rest?

I worked bent over, struggling against the soil of my homeland.

"Aliza, come along, time for breakfast," Naomi called me. I must go through with it. I must hold out, they mustn't see how hard the work is for me. They've added the letter A to my name and now I am Aliza. No one asked me if I agreed. I suppose that's how it is here. I didn't want them to call me by my name in the Movement, Lilit.

At last the promised excursion. We climbed to the top of the mountain. Mount Gilboa was covered with colorful flowers, anemones everywhere. It was wonderful! I was so happy, I pressed Rina's hand. For some time we climbed the steep slope together. I was starting to fall behind. I looked at the ground and pushed the stones under my feet. Rina ran ahead with the others. She was already far above me, and the mountain rose higher and higher. The others have been in the country a whole year, and they are healthy and strong.

The youth leaders didn't notice that I was left behind. I took a breath and another. I had no strength left. I accused myself of defeatism. Or maybe I still hadn't recovered sufficiently after the camp. Who would understand it?

Many years have passed and I am still ashamed that I gave in to my body's weakness.

During the early days on the kibbutz, I suffered from unidentified stomach pains after meals and at night. I had several examinations, but they didn't find anything. Mother was far away, in Belgium, and I had no one to talk to. The member in charge of us, Tziporka, was suspicious and considered everyone a shirker, putting on a show.

Yesterday I had a visitor. I was lying in bed sick and the guide, Shlomo Gancewich, came to see me.

"They told me that you haven't been feeling well lately. You didn't work for several days." (*What does he understand? Does he intend to interrogate me?*)

"Yes, I am suffering from stomach pains."

"Have you been to the clinic?" I feel he was trying to be nice, but his intention was clear.

"Of course, but they can't find what's the matter with me."

"Maybe you find it difficult socially? Maybe the work is hard for you?" he tried again.

"Maybe. I am only five months out of the war. It hasn't occurred to you? Maybe I haven't yet got used to proper food? Maybe all those years of hunger caused some damage? You haven't thought of that?"

He blushed, moving uneasily. He didn't expect me to attack him. He wanted to help, get me into the routine of work. He left.

After a few months of adjustment and with the help of medicines, the problem was solved. I didn't pretend to be sick, as my guides thought, but to this day I don't leave home without something to munch in my purse. Some food—just to be on the safe side. My children smile knowingly.

Naomi (Zosia) Altman was an only child. Her parents were doctors. She came from Zaglembie in Poland. She was taken to Auschwitz with her parents and was the only one to survive. She was a lovely girl, gentle and sensitive. She also felt different from all the others in the group. She also yielded to phantoms from the past and was plagued by painful nightmares.

One day she came, smiling happily: "I have an uncle in Australia, he has found me. I am the only one left of his family and he has sent me a telegram. He'll soon come to visit me."

And he did arrive. We all looked at them, happy for them and also envious. Zosia radiated with happiness and went arm in arm with her uncle to the dining room. On the next day he took her to town by special permission. On her return she brought with her packets of clothes that the uncle had bought for her: dresses (lovely ones), vests, shoes. We didn't possess any private clothes, only those provided by Aliyat Noar, shirts and pants.

Tziporka made a face. "You know you won't be able to wear them here in the kibbutz," she said in Polish, in order to emphasize the importance of the issue. "We don't have our own clothes here."

"But Tziporka, these are *mine*. My uncle bought them for a lot of money, just for me. They are my first clothes since the war!"

"Naomi, you must adapt to our way of life here. How will your friends feel when you dress up and they don't have such clothes? What did you think? You just didn't think. We are sharing our clothes."

Naomi ran to us, weeping, offended. We, who have lost everything in the Holocaust and have no real souvenir from "there," understood her very well, and we were angry with Tziporka. But she had no choice. The clothes were put into our store and waited for an opportunity. And that opportunity came.

One night a fire broke out in the wooden storeroom, apparently due to an iron that had been left on. The store burned down, in spite of all the kibbutz members' efforts to save it. And Naomi's lovely clothes were burned together with all the others.

After that accident Zosia withdrew, she became quiet and introverted. After a year in the youth group, she decided to leave and go to Jerusalem to study. We were worried about her, even though the uncle supported her. She was so fragile and sensitive, so anxious.

Four years later, Naomi-Zosia was hospitalized in the Talbie psychiatric hospital in Jerusalem. The attempts to rehabilitate her failed. The last time I saw her she was living alone in Bat-Yam during one of the attempts to release her from hospital. She never recovered. I can't help thinking that it may have been the lack of understanding by the local Jewish community toward us that also contributed to Naomi's breakdown. Did her loss of those clothes take her back to that much greater loss during the Holocaust?

The day when I will have to make a decision is approaching. The period of Youth Aliyah will soon be over—the intensive study combined with work, a lively social life, excursions, as well as the first loves and also the preparations for a possible war between us and the Arabs, practicing the use of arms and doing physical fitness exercises, and much more. In Europe, the refugees, streaming south to the coast of Italy and France, exert great pressure on the British to enable them to enter the country. A ship carrying *Ma'apilim* got caught almost every day, and the Jewish community in Eretz Israel was in upheaval. A short time ago it was the "Black Saturday": British soldiers looked for weapons well hidden in kibbutzim, arrested Haganah activists. The country was in turmoil. A storm brewing.

I have to admit that I was not as agitated as the others. What kind of war was this? Raids by gangs, here and there someone gets killed. What do they know about war? The real war was over there, in the Diaspora; here it's just child's play. War was aerial bombing, the loss of one's home, famine, mass murder, people who have been expelled trudging along the roads. I belong there, I can't help it.

I didn't quite understand what was happening in this country.

One day they called me to the telephone, the only one, in the kibbutz office. I immediately thought it might be my Uncle Melamed's family. But it wasn't. An unknown voice said in Polish: "Hello, Liza?"

My heart fluttered with crazy hope. "Who is it?"

"I am your cousin, the son of your father's sister, Sala Weissberg. Do you remember me? I am Henryk Weissberg."

I calmed down, although I was surprised.

"Yes, I remember you. I was at your wedding before the war." I also remembered that, at the beginning of the war, he set out east from Warsaw, in the direction of the territories occupied by the Soviets.

"How did you find me? Where do you live? Do you know anything about other members of our family?" I had not yet lost hope completely.

"Oh no! I left Russia in the middle of the war with the army of General Anders, the Polish army that was supposed to fight Germany on the southern front, in support of the Soviets. I fled from there and now I am in Tel Aviv. I want to see you."

We made an appointment. My cousin had been living in this country for several years. His wife was born here, and he had two small daughters. I was glad that someone else had survived from the large Melamed family, numbering almost sixty people before the war—my father's eight brothers and sisters and their many children.

Tzelina (Miriam) Hammerstein (right) and the author while with a group training for settlement in Kibbutz Mishmar Heamek, in the milk shed, 1947.

Henryk came and wanted to take me for a few days to a small hotel on the Carmel, but our guides did not let me go.

"She must study and work," they told him. "She belongs to a certain framework and she can't go off just like that."

"But I have only just found her. I want her to get to know my wife and children, it's very important for us," he pleaded. I was silent, I knew the rules. I so much wanted to go away with Henryk, to have a good time, to get to know the Carmel, his family, to live, to enjoy life.

My cousin left with the promise that I would get leave at the appropriate time, together with the others. I rebelled. If living on kibbutz means lack of personal freedom, a rigid framework, I don't want it. I've had enough of barbed wire fences, of rules that trample on the freedom of the individual. I was liberated, wasn't I? I want to go to live in the city to continue my studies, to acquire a proper education as I promised myself in Bergen-Belsen. Only a free individual can develop and create.

But this was countered by a weighty argument that won the day: personal responsibility for my commitment to the ideals that the Movement had instilled in me. How could I betray all that? Shall I abandon my beliefs and prefer an easy life to a creative life of toil within a communal society?

I had long had my doubts about the socialist justice of the U.S.S.R. On my way I had met people who had fled from there, from severe punishments in Siberia, from unjust expulsion from home. I believed we were different.

And thus, throughout my life, two angels have stood by my bedside, and it is the more conscientious one that has had the upper hand. I am still living on kibbutz, even though at least twice I was about to decide to leave it.

10 : AS TIME PASSED

I began writing down my memories at the age of seventeen, and I am concluding them, having passed the age of seventy and the millennium. My sister and I have been fortunate in having been able to enter the new millennium, leaving behind the twentieth century, engulfed by wars, hatred, and genocide but also marked by feats of heroism, soaring technological development, and progress toward an easier life. Will life also become happier? I doubt it.

My mother, Raya, died at the age of ninety, on the threshold of the new millennium. She and my sister immigrated two years after me, not just a few months later, as we were promised in Belgium. After all the vicissitudes of the war, they were not spared the unnecessary suffering at the hands of the British. They sailed on a ship of the *Ma'apilim*, *Theodor Herzl*, were arrested by the British and forced to remain in a camp in Cyprus until their liberation in the fall of 1947, a short time before the United Nations decision about the establishment of the State of Israel.

Mother married in this country and lived a comfortable life in Tel Aviv. She was never again the strong and cheerful person

I knew during my childhood. Her nerves were wrecked. She built around herself a protective bubble of routine and rarely enjoyed the pleasures of life that miraculously came her way. For many years she was pursued by memories and had to take medicines to enable her to function in her daily life. Her struggle for our survival during the Holocaust may be considered the manifestation of her supreme heroism and that of many Jewish mothers.

Mirka-Miriam has lived all her life on kibbutz. She married and has a large family. She is active in her profession and in the kibbutz. Like me, she strove to adapt to the *sabra* society, to fit in. She participated in the War of Independence and tried as hard as she could to shake off the past. Did she succeed? Is it at all possible? She also carries on her back the burden of her past.

My friend Miriam (Tzelina Stashefsky) parted from me when I left the ghetto. She and her family hid at the home of Polish people and survived, after being at the mercy of informers and suffering greatly. They immigrated to Israel and our paths crossed again in both our professional and our kibbutz life. Our two families are bound by deep friendship. Together we studied psychology and education at the university. Tzelina studied in the United States with Professor Salvador Menuchin and in Israel focuses her practice with Holocaust survivors. Both of us made a career for ourselves in these spheres.

Tzelina's inability to forgive some of the Polish people who were anti-Semitic and cooperated with the Germans is great, and she cannot forgive them for their treatment of the Jews, particularly in Poland immediately after the war, when the survivors began to come out of hiding. Nazi anti-

Semitism reinforced their own, and many of them were disappointed that not all the Jews had been exterminated.

My private life took many twists and turns and suffered several blows. Soon after the war, while I was still with the youth group in Beit Alfa, I got to know a young man who had emigrated from Budapest, and our love was stormy and painful. We were both cut off from our parents who had remained abroad, and we suffered from longing for our loved ones and from nightmares about the war.

It was a fateful meeting of two young, immature people, who had lost their youth in the Holocaust and who tried to cling to each other as a substitute for the warmth of a home. We were unable to create a healthy and lasting relationship. Chanan, my eldest son, was born of this marriage. We both know well that he bears the burden of his parents' lack of stability and of firm roots.

Fate had it that he was born on the same day of the year when—as far as I know—my father was killed, the grandfather he never knew. Did the birth of a beautiful, healthy baby symbolize my father's legacy for me? Was his separation from me when he grew up symbolically related to my parting from my father under such tragic circumstances? Who knows the meaning of such coincidences.

I separated from my husband and went with my tiny son to another kibbutz, to start from scratch. During those years I suffered from nightmares. That same person, who a few years before would take great risks to work for the underground without any sense of fear, now suffered, in times of peace and security, from inexplicable anxiety. I have often asked myself, if I haven't unintentionally passed on some of my anxiety to my son. Yet at the same time, he inherited from me the strength to survive, the stubbornness to overcome the difficulties life has placed in his way.

When he was already grown up, he told me, "When I was small, you used to sing me a lovely lullaby, I can remember it. Do you know that it was the song about Ponar, about the murder of the Vilna Jews?" I recalled that I had loved the song very much: "Hush, hush, my son, let's be quiet, graves are growing here…"

"Chanan," I answered. "It was the most beautiful song I knew at the time. Its melody resounded within me."

Since then many new and more beautiful melodies have become mine.

In my new kibbutz, Ein Hamifratz, I got married again, to Yoshua. He was involved in the theater as a producer and actor. He also translated classical drama and loved books. He was a self-taught intellectual and an art lover. He was originally from Russia.

He also carried the burden of a deprived childhood in his country. As a youth he joined the Hashomer Hatzair Movement, participated in a training camp, and with his friends founded a kibbutz in this country. During those years I also discovered I had a talent for acting. He set up a drama group in the kibbutz, and we performed together in many plays.

We had two children, a boy and a girl. My second son, Asa, excelled in sports and we were proud of him. My daughter, Iris, was born when we were older. She brought a great deal of joy into our home.

At that time I traveled a great deal. Lecturing in schools, to soldiers and in kibbutzim, telling the story of my life during the

Holocaust as a testimony. On Holocaust Remembrance Day, I organized memorial evenings in my kibbutz and participated in all the activities of the *Moreshet* [Legacy] group.

Asa did not like it that I was so preoccupied with preserving the memory of the Holocaust. One day, when he was seventeen, he told us that his group, the Israeli junior volleyball team, had been invited to play in Germany. I remember how he could not look straight into my eyes when he said, "Of course I think I'll go along with my team, but…" He knew well that I objected to visits to Germany and that I shall never tread on its soil. I sensed his dilemma.

"Mother, you must understand that I belong to another generation. I can't feel what you feel toward them. I have to live my life my own way, not yours." He asked me to understand him, in spite of my opposition.

"I am trying to understand you, but it's hard for me," I mumbled.

"Mother, don't make it hard for me!"

"Of course you have to go," I said, looking straight at him. I didn't feel angry, only sad that normal relations with Germany were being established so soon.

Our children grew up with humanistic values of respect for the other, and demanded that their views be also respected. They were a generation free of the "prejudices" of their parents, and they had the ability to choose their own way in life. And they did so. All three of them left the kibbutz and two of them even left Israel. It was hard for me to accept it. My elder son, Chanan, left the kibbutz together with his wife, Kalia, and his two children, Royi and Tal. Today they both study at the university. Their being far from me is hard.

A few years later Asa also left. He went to study at the university and married Dovrat. They have two lovely children, Adar and Petal. A short time ago they moved to Canada.

My daughter, Iris, also chose not to live on kibbutz, and together with her husband, Per, is bringing up Yonatan and Amalia in Denmark.

Many kibbutz-born young people left the kibbutz, for lack of affinity with its way of life and its inability to adapt to the changes occurring in the world surrounding it. Together with all these partings, another, the hardest parting of all, awaited me.

My husband, Yoshua, got cancer and died within a year. My world grew dark. I was afraid. How shall I survive? I was aware that parting was traumatic for me ever since the Holocaust, and as it happened, so many partings awaited me later in life: from my children, and now—far worse—from my dear husband. But my survival instinct protected me.

Gradually I recovered. I devoted myself to my work as a special education teacher and teacher guide. I also served as an educational advisor and worked with youth. I have been working in the sphere of education dozens of years: first in the nursery, then with toddlers, later as a kindergarten teacher, and going on to remedial teaching, including many years of study. Among children I feel fulfilled, confident and radiating empathy and love. Children return my love and give me the strength to cope with the transitions in my life.

My life and that of my children changed for the better when I got to know Tzvi. He had also become a widower not long before and, like me, felt very lonely after the death of his wife. We have a great deal in common: he is also a Holocaust survivor, a kibbutz member since his youth, a teacher and educator—and suddenly we fell in love. A late love, mature, profound and all-embracing. I found in him a sensitive and understanding friend, a gifted person with broad horizons.

Tzvi has three daughters, all of them beautiful, married, and mothers of children. They received me into their family, and together we have built a new home, in Tzvi's kibbutz.

My children helped me a great deal during that time. They supported this relationship and they love Tzvi, thus making it easier for me to make a difficult decision—to leave my kibbutz where I had lived for thirty-two years and where Yoshua is buried.

Again I had to confront a new society. The mentality of the members of Kibbutz Givat Oz is different from the one I was used to. There is a different landscape around me, no beloved seashore. I have taken up new work. It was all so different, hard for me at my age, already a grandmother. I have followed most of Tzvi's grandchildren since they were born, and I am their grandmother, in quite a natural way. In the course of time, his daughters also left the kibbutz, each one going her own way, and we meet frequently.

Several years ago, the Jewish agency suggested to Tzvi and me to go as Zionist emissaries to Budapest, the capital of Hungary. We considered it a one-time opportunity to exploit our educational and professional knowledge and experience, since our task was to teach Hebrew and Bible studies in a Jewish high school and a rabbinical and teachers' college. Hungarian Jews became assimilated during communist rule, changed their names and forgot their Jewishness, even becoming alienated from it. Many of the older generation did not tell their children that they are Jews, and of course avoided telling them how they had survived the Holocaust.

Within that reality, the emissaries of the Zionist Federation had to try to bring their assimilated society back to Judaism and to foster Zionism. We considered teaching the subject of the Holocaust and its implications an important task. We organized lectures and prepared curricula. I spoke to students of all ages and to synagogue audiences as I told them my story and that of Polish Jewry. I found tremendous ignorance about the subject, nor was it important to them, as though the memory had faded.

I asked the grandparents of the students, those who had survived Auschwitz and the ghettos, "Why didn't you tell them about it?"

"We wanted to spare them the sorrow and anguish. We wanted them to be just Hungarians like all the other people, no longer to suffer by being Jewish," was frequently the answer.

That erroneous attitude of assimilated Jewry, of converts, which reappeared at various times and in various places, was of no use. They were compelled to deal with the issue of their Judaism once again.

Those were two happy years. I enjoyed the cultural life in Budapest, the walks in the beautiful city, and our independence. We saw many operas and listened to concerts. We replenished our energy and derived great pleasure from life.

And finally I was able to finish writing this book.

On a visit to Warsaw in 1992, standing in front of the monument in memory of the heroes of the ghetto. From the right, childhood friend Tzelina (Miriam) Stashewski (Hammerstein); Gil Migdan, her sister's son; the author; Tzvi, her husband; Ruti Margalit, Tzelina's daughter; and Israel, Tzelina's husband.

The author (left) with a youth group from Israel on a visit to the concentration camp at Majdanek, Poland, 1996.

On the Jewish Agency mission to Hungary. The author presents her testimony about the Holocaust in a Budapest synagogue, 1993.

11 : To Touch the Past

Life, I cry out to you! I, a weak human being, a tiny crumb, so easy to squash under foot, I cry out to you... What awaits me? What will my tomorrow be like? Will it be bright and shining, or gray and hopeless, like my present?

This was written by Tamar, a girl of fourteen, during the troubled times in the ghetto, and it has remained in my mind, reminding me of "The Scream," a painting by Edvard Munch, the famous painter.

"Why have they robbed me of my future?" Tamar protests. I bear Tamar's cry within me.

[Tamar's article was published in 1942 in the underground newspaper *El-Al*. The original manuscript is in the Jewish History Institute in Warsaw. There is a copy in the "Moreshet" archives in Givat Haviva.]

All my life I bear the burden of the past, and from time to time I encounter it face to face. And then I feel I do not belong, I am a stranger to the here and now, distant, incomprehensible to my surroundings. It has always happened to me suddenly—something someone said, a familiar smell from the distant past, a sight reminding me of another—awaken these feelings within me.

HORRA.

Ramiona splecione mocno, reka przy rece, glowa przy glowie, pre ku srodkowi w wirze szalonego, symbolicznego tanca. Dudni podloga pod mlodymi nogami, lwci daleko mloda piesn, piesn wzwlonej horry. Tetni dzika krew, z hukiem przelewa sie w zylach, i parzy... parzy... Serce wali, dudni... Dusza, serce, wszystkie mysli przelaly sie w te horre, te jedna...

Ile mysli, ile wrzen i oddania i tego niewypowiedzianego szczescia ma w sobie szeroma horra. Rozwiewaja sie krawaty, te drogie, niebieskie krawaty, bluza wydyma sie na wietrze, oczy blyszcza i smieje sie tak, jak usta rozwarte w usmiechu, wlos rozwiany tworzy aureole. Razem, naprzod, hej,dziewczeta, chlopcy, oddajcie sie cali wirowi tego tanca!

Tu, w tej horze, przewija sie cale szomrowe zycie. Na poczatku byla slaba, niesmiala, nierowna. A teraz? — horra i szomer to jedno. Im one mocniejsza, tym zdrowszy tworzy sie szomer. I po tym poznaje sie rozwoj.

Ta horra, ze wspolnie splecionymi ramionami, ze wspolnymi uczuciami i myslami, to obraz wspolnoty i rownosci. Tu czlowiek i horra to jedna calosc. To horra doroslych szomrim. I my dazymy do tej horry. I my powoli dojdziemy do tego, ze bedziemy mogli tak tanczyc.

Horra to najbogatszy taniec swiata. To cos, czego nie mozna wytlumaczyc slowami.

Lilit "Basjaz"

Article entitled Horra, written by the author, published in the underground newspaper *El-Al*. It was found after the war in the Ringelblum Archives, hidden in buried milk cans in the ruins of the ghetto.

Once I was sitting with my daughter on a swing and I felt I was sinking deep into myself. She told me something and I didn't hear her. She bent down facing me, looked into my eyes, and began to pinch me. "Mummy, mummy, don't you hear me? Where are you?"

I heard her, but I did not feel her presence. I sat there like a stone. I did not belong.

To get close to the past but to remain here and now, that is the task I have undertaken, consciously or unconsciously. I have often asked myself why I don't leave everything and just dedicate my time to travel with the youth delegations from Israel to Poland. Where? To the cold, the gray streets whose names are correct, but they are in a different place, with new houses and gardens built along them, on top of the ruins of the Jewish ghetto, razed to the ground.

Why do I travel about in buses to commemorative gatherings, wishing to speak to young people, to soldiers? Why do I return again and again, as if through a compulsion, to the same places, like a horse returning to the empty stable, still hoping to find something there?

Because of Tamar's cry.

It also happened to me that I slipped, I didn't take care, I didn't safeguard myself from her cry, and it pierced me. Years ago I saw the film *Miracle in Milan* with some friends. I didn't suspect anything. After all, it was about another country, Italy. There was a scene showing the Nazis kidnapping the parents and piling them onto a cart, and their little child running on behind it. He remained alone on the road, weeping, looking after the disappearing cart.

I broke down. I did not try to pretend that I was able to overcome it. I couldn't. Since then I have been very careful. I have built fences. Not impenetrable walls, but purposeful partitions, in order to remain in control. However, the feeling that the "real" life was "there," and here and now it is just make-believe, comes upon me again and again.

Many of the people who experienced the Holocaust perceive as their personal victory over Hitler and his regime the very fact that they have survived and succeeded in becoming integrated in society, in building a family and having children—those fine *sabras*—in their economic and professional achievements and in their great contribution to the establishment of the State of Israel. This is true to a certain extent. Their life is proof of the failure of the Nazis to carry out their plan—the extermination of the Jewish people.

Man has within him the urge to live on, in spite of everything. To go on, to grow into the future and to fulfill his life's purpose. So do those who came from there. Only as they grow old, their wounds open again, their strength to hold on is sapped, the memories surge, and past traumas that were never dealt with, now resurface. All these now weaken them and drive them toward ill health.

The exciting experience of the resumption of their life, as though it had been granted them as a gift, fades in the face of the undercurrent of sorrow that had not succeeded in disappearing, though covered up by such declarations as "life goes on as usual and all is well." Even those who did not want to remember and swept everything under the rug of building a family or a career, however successful, evoke their childhood and the significant people in their past, even more painfully and intensively. On the threshold of old age, feelings from the past are intensified: disappointed loves, unkept promises, guilt for having survived.

The dilemma of the survivors was whether to continue to live with the past, or to stretch out their hands to the new reality and push their previous experiences deep down inside. In later years, each one reflects upon his life. The desire to stand firm on one's feet, when facing an environment preferring to deny the past while admiring the future and the "man of the future—the pioneer, the victorious fighter" exacts its price today.

Suffering cannot be stored away. It resurges in various ways, and ends up by weakening the person. I have learned this from experience. Although I always found new funds of inner strength, in the long run deep cracks have appeared. After many years of becoming integrated within Israeli and kibbutz society, in the effort to cope with the repeated wars, the raids and the partings, I feel exhausted.

In my diary I expressed blind hatred toward the German people and a tremendous desire for revenge, eye for an eye, tooth for a tooth. Today I do not want to turn blind hatred on another people, nor on any ethnic or religious group. Not because of the many years that have passed, nor my old age. He who has seen hell must not create hell for others. This is particularly cogent for us Jews. We are, after all, a nation like any other. There are mean sadists among us too. We must fight them like any evil in any nation, and even more so, for they have forgotten. Maybe they never knew the Holocaust and did not learn its lessons. They act in an arbitrary way according to their own interests, or obeying wicked orders, without consideration for moral values.

I learned from experience that evil exists side by side with beauty and decency. It is intensified under contributing conditions, when the end justifies the means. Even in the ghetto there were informers, handing Jews over to the Germans for money, Jewish policemen leading Jews to cattle cars. Under unbearable conditions, people lose their morality and become cynical. It is hard to judge a frightened, threatened, hungry, helpless person. Today it is hard to condemn the head of the community who collaborated with the Germans to save himself, his family, or members of his own community.

Let us beware of judging others, while we live in a free world and have the precious right to choose and decide of our own free will how to act.

I sometimes ask myself, where is the fine line between the message "remember and do not forget what the enemies of humanity perpetrated against us," and the emotional burden we impose on the youth of the second and third generations after the Holocaust, in demanding that they confront those harsh experiences, strange to them.

When I travel to Poland, to accompany youth groups and bear witness, I put on my armor. Once I broke down completely. It was in Majdanek. We stood in front of a huge mass grave with a signpost: *Eighteen thousand Jews were shot dead here on November 3, 1943*. I went aside and sat down, I felt I was about to collapse. Tears I had held back broke out. The boys and girls sensed that something unusual was happening to me and stood in silence. I went back and told them only after regaining my self-control.

One of the girls, Naama, from the "Arava" group at the kibbutz school "Mevoot Hanegev," wrote about it later in her diary about the journey to Poland: "Aliza, our Holocaust witness, told us that exactly on that date her father was murdered. In fact, it was only now that she connected the two and came to the conclusion that her father was murdered here, in Majdanek, on that dark damned day. On the same date, seven years later, her eldest son was born.

"Aliza wept, we all wept with her. When I stepped down to place a flag into the ditch where the victims lay, I felt as though I was treading on dead people. As though I myself had died. They are still there, deep down, piled up. How ghastly! To feel, to see, to remember!"

On their way back, the boys and girls sang for me the wonderful lines by Ya'akov Gilad from his poem "Dust and Ashes," well known as sung by Yehuda Policker:

> And if you go, where do you go
> Eternity is only dust and ashes
> Where do you go, where do you go

It's years and nothing is erased…
There was your childhood
It is no more, little woman,
People now no one knows
Not even a house, a reminder.

Afterward they wrote me many letters. I'll quote just one passage:

"We'll never forget what we experienced with you, both the beautiful and the hard moments. We thank you with all our hearts that you have taught us to connect with the past. You helped us to grasp and understand the incomprehensible and you gave the whole journey a concrete dimension."

The incomprehensible becomes concrete. Absorbing with the senses, concretely, that is the only way to turn history into a personal experience, with personal implications for the visitor. When the eyes see the hair and the shoes in the camps, when the feet tread on the floor of the crematorium, the ears hear the howling of the wind in the wood clearing in Treblinka and the fingers feel those cold stones—all this together creates a one-time experience of the majesty of eternity, engulfing the visitor in this earthly hell.

During the visit of one of the Israeli groups I accompanied on that journey, we walked, without any symbols or flags, in the streets of one of the Polish towns. Two thugs blocked our way. The two girls walking in front retreated in alarm.

"Jews, go back to your country, get out of here!" they shouted. I saw confusion and even fear in our group. I felt furious. I grabbed two of our boys under their armpits and walked with them toward the thugs, motioning to the group to follow me. I poured out Warsaw slang at the thugs: "How dare you open your mouth! Times have changed, there are no *jids* anymore! Anyone can go where they please. Scram or I'll call the police!"

They went off. Their faces were like those of the men who caught me when I came out of the ghetto and demanded my money, or threatened to hand me over to the Germans. I knew at the time that my fate was in their hands, but pretended I had self-confidence and was not afraid. Today I don't have to pretend, I have the backing of the State of Israel, a source of strength and security. I shall never again be afraid of them.

We talked a great deal after the incident. I do not want Israeli boys and girls, or any Jews, to cave in when facing crude anti-Semitism. "Never let them feel they are at an advantage. Be proud of your people and of your forefathers who built the state," I pleaded. "We haven't come here to pick a quarrel, but when such a thing happens, we respond."

A new generation is growing up, and I would like our youth to meet with Polish youth, in order to talk about that painful topic. On the tours of our youth, there are sometimes insulting incidents, but this does not mean that anti-Semitism is rampant in Poland. The Israeli groups are overprotected all the way, like a fortress, and this creates a sense of danger, siege, and isolation among the children. That is how people behave who are always afraid and search for enemies everywhere. It is a shameful attitude, typical of the Diaspora. When we were dependent on other people and lived among them, we were always compelled to be careful. Today there is no need. "The whole world is against us" is the attitude of people with paranoia. It is a pity that it is being transmitted to our youth.

I can also understand and respect the young visitors' need to amuse themselves and enjoy their visit to a strange country. After the horrendous sights in the Majdanek and Auschwitz camps, they wish to shake off the anguish, and to feel they do not belong there. Their present is totally different and their future is secure in their own country. They do not suffer from existential dread. They are stunned at the sight of the graves of the victims, but it usually brings them closer to their Jewishness and their own people.

When my generation has passed on, will only the collective memory remain in the form of "and thou shalt show thy son," or will they know how to distinguish between the various people whose lives were so brutally cut short? Those daring young people, high-minded, imbued with their mission, those killed in battle, in the sewage canals, in the extermination camps, the bunkers, with the groups of partisans, and those who survived, like burned out embers—will future generations remember them as individuals with names? All the people slaughtered in the thousands. Shall we remember their names?

Their memory is engraved within me like a commandment. In the ghetto I joined the Hashomer Hatzair Movement and this became for me a fateful step and the pivotal point of my life. I have sometimes despaired of kibbutz life and considered leaving, following my son. But my loyalty to this way of life since my early youth had the upper hand.

I tried not to become immersed in the past, nor to deny it. I may have tried to reconcile myself with my past in order to dispel the hatred, at least to be reconciled with the landscape of my former homeland, which I yearn for as I do for my childhood, which had been happy and good to me until the outbreak of the war.

Now the beautiful and the evil dwell within me.

I touch the past and make sure I do not come too close to the suffering, as it may bring me to the mouth of the abyss. The abyss of despair is always lurking, and only my love of life is stronger. I have not been robbed of the ability to love nature, music, art, all the joys life can offer, uplifting the spirit and pleasing the senses. Juicy watermelon and red strawberries, the whispering of the woods, the sun reflected on the sea, the music of Sibelius, good wine, and in recent years, the love of grandchildren.

The hope that eventually there will be some kind of peace between the two nations living in this land strengthens my belief that my grandchildren will live a happier life than my generation's and that of my children.

May they live a peaceful life in the promised land.

> After all those years
> The memory lingers
> Of a branch of purple lilac
> Against the sky in flames
> And collapsing walls of houses.
>
> After all those years
> I've planted lilac in my garden
> Maybe this time
> The sky will remain blue...

ABOUT THE AUTHOR

Aliza Vitis-Shomron was born in Warsaw as Liza Melamed into a wealthy merchant family, where Jewish tradition mixed with Polish culture. In September 1939 when the Nazis began their reign of terror in Europe and invaded Poland, Liza was eleven years old.

In her diaries—furtively written on scraps of precious paper, which she kept throughout the war—she described the history of her family, struggling to survive in the occupied Warsaw Ghetto, and those diaries and later writings formed the basis for this memoir. Becoming a member of Hashomer Hatzair, the noted youth movement in the Warsaw Ghetto, gave Liza hope and encouraged her to fight for survival. Liza also took part in the Jewish Fighting Organization (Żydowska Organizacja Bojowa, the Z.O.B.).

The 1943 Warsaw Ghetto uprising was the first large-scale rebellion against the Nazis in Europe and the single greatest act of Jewish resistance during the Holocaust. It is portrayed valiantly in Leon Uris's renowned book *Mila 18*.

On April 17, 1943, two days before the eruption of the uprising, as requested by her organization, Liza slipped out of the ghetto and moved to shelter from the Nazi invasion and the ultimate burning of the ghetto. "You are too young to fight and someone has to stay alive to tell our story," was the message passed by Rut Heiman, the liaison to the commander of the uprising, Mordechai Anielewicz.

As a result of an extraordinary series of "miracles," Liza managed to survive after being sent to the Bergen-Belsen concentration camp. She was among those liberated by American troops and ever since, she has continued to tell the story.

On September 1945, at seventeen, she arrived in Israel, became a member of a Hashomer Hatzair kibbutz and studied psychology and education. She married and had three children. Her family has grown to include seven grandchildren and five great-grandchildren.

Aliza is among the last of the Warsaw Ghetto survivors to tell the story. She has been passionately lecturing around the world about the revolt and its legendary leader, and she has escorted numerous youth groups on their visits to Poland. "I want every teenager to remember that despite the unspeakable horrors around them, individuals fought for their freedom and did not lose compassion for each other."

Recently—seventy years after the Warsaw Ghetto uprising—Liza spoke on behalf of Holocaust survivors in the official ceremony marking Israel's annual Holocaust memorial day.

In 2002, Liza published her memoir in Hebrew about life in the ghetto. This is the expanded English publication, with both images of crime, as well as portrayals of individuals' compassion in cruel and inhumane conditions. She said,

"I had promised myself to perpetuate the memory of those wonderful young people from the pioneer movements, and to preserve the story of their extraordinary efforts and determination under impossible conditions, their struggle against the enemy who destroyed our people, and the sacrifice of their young lives in order to save its honor."

Now eighty-nine, Aliza lives in Kibbutz Givat Oz, Israel, and continues to tell the story.

ACKNOWLEDGMENTS

A few days before the outbreak of the Warsaw Ghetto Uprising of 19th April 1943, Mordechai Anielewicz called our Hashomer Hatzair group of youth, ages 15, for a last meeting at *Mila 18*. His last words to us were these: "There are not enough weapons for you to participate in the upcoming fight. We may not survive. Your mission is to find a way out of the Ghetto as soon as you can, to live, and to tell our story."

This is what I have attempted to do all my life and with this book as well.

I wish to express my thanks to Dr. Ruti Margalit, daughter of my best friend Tzelina Stashefsky of Kibbutz Sasa. Tzelina is Miriam in the book, and she shared with me most of the experiences of that time. Miraculously we both survived and met again in Israel. Our very close friendship continues to this day and forever. Ruti made it possible for English readers to learn our story.

I wish to thank Sandra Wendel, our editor, and Lisa Pelto and her publishing team for their interest, enthusiasm, support, generosity, and dedication in working with Ruti and preparing this English version for publication.

I wish to express my love and gratitude to my husband, Tzvi Shomron, who supported me through the years and did not live to see the English version of the book. I dedicate this book to him.

For more diary excerpts and photos, see our gallery at www.WarsawGhettoBook.com

Made in the USA
San Bernardino, CA
08 July 2016